306.8743 Bet

Between interruptions.

PRICE: $32.95 (3559/ex   )

Between Interruptions

Between Interruptions

30 WOMEN TELL THE TRUTH ABOUT MOTHERHOOD

EDITED BY
CORI HOWARD

KEY PORTER BOOKS

Library and Archives Canada Cataloguing in Publication

Between interruptions : thirty women tell the truth about motherhood / Cori Howard, general editor.

ISBN-13: 978-1-55263-911-5, ISBN-10: 1-55263-911-8

1. Motherhood. 2. Parenting. 3. Mothers—Family relationships.
4. Mothers—Biography. I. Howard, Cori

HQ759.B528 2007   306.874'3   C2007-901839-4

THE CANADA COUNCIL | LE CONSEIL DES ARTS
FOR THE ARTS | DU CANADA
SINCE 1957 | DEPUIS 1957

ONTARIO ARTS COUNCIL
CONSEIL DES ARTS DE L'ONTARIO

The publisher gratefully acknowledges the support of the Canada Council for the Arts and the Ontario Arts Council for its publishing program. We acknowledge the support of the Government of Ontario through the Ontario Media Development Corporation's Ontario Book Initiative.

We acknowledge the financial support of the Government of Canada through the Book Publishing Industry Development Program (BPIDP) for our publishing activities.

Key Porter Books Limited
Six Adelaide Street East, Tenth Floor
Toronto, Ontario
Canada M5C 1H6

www.keyporter.com

Text design: Marijke Friesen
Electronic formatting: Jean Lightfoot Peters

Printed and bound in Canada

07 08 09 10 11 5 4 3 2 1

TO HTU HTU, TY AND JAZA:
MY ROCKS, MY ISLAND, MY HOME

Jonah Did

Take me for a ride
I'll stay inside your belly

and learn to play love songs
on your rib
cage

We'll dive for quarter
moons

and let the sea fold arms
around our secret

Revolution

—DEBORAH VANSICKLE

After that the baby is carried in, solid, substantial, packed together like
an apple. Jeanie examines her, she is complete, and in the days that follow
Jeanie herself becomes drifted over with new words, her hair slowly darkens,
she ceases to be what she was and is replaced, gradually, by someone else.
    —MARGARET ATWOOD, "GIVING BIRTH," FROM
    DANCING GIRLS AND OTHER STORIES

Contents

PART THREE: GUILT

PART FOUR: DEVOTION

PART FIVE: REDEMPTION

Between Interruptions

INTRODUCTION:
THE WHOLE
MOTHERHOOD THING
CORI HOWARD

A million years ago, I was sitting in a bar with an old friend discussing my future. I was pregnant, thirty years old and totally freaking out. As I sat there nursing a cranberry juice, she asked if I always knew I wanted kids. She wasn't remotely interested in having any and is still, at thirty-five, voted by our friends as least likely to succumb to motherhood. Yet her question threw me. I'd never really thought about it. Motherhood, for me, was always an assumption, a given.

For as long as I can remember, I wanted babies and bottles and the whole motherhood thing. Never mind that "the whole motherhood thing" came with no visual image. It was like a grey Polaroid—underexposed and murky. I wanted babies the way I wanted a new sweater—something to hug and snuggle and keep me warm. The desire was deep, passionate and desperately naive.

When I had my first child on May 3, 2001, I was still desperately naive. I really believed my life was not going to be any different. I'm not sure why it was so important that my life remain the same. I'm not sure why I was so resistant to "the whole motherhood thing," when that was what I wanted all along. I expected I would give birth, figure out how to feed, clothe and bathe the baby, give it a few hugs and get back to work. Really.

My work, at the time, involved a lot of travel. One day I would be on a plane to Los Angeles to cover the Academy Awards, the next I was heading to Mexico to write about a women's conference. When I look back on it now, it seems more than a little odd that I didn't for one second think it might be difficult to continue doing all that with a tiny infant in tow. It also didn't sink in, although I was warned, that there would be far fewer dinners out, movies, and drinks with friends. I didn't realize I would become a totally different person. For a journalist, my lack of research into the mothering experience was appalling.

A few people waved the red flag. An editor at the *National Post* told me it would be hard for me to go right back to work, that I might not *want* to. The thought had never, not once, crossed my mind. People told me I would be tired, overwhelmed, uninterested in my husband and in sex. I laughed at them. In my Zen-ed out, pregnant state, I let all their negative thoughts wash right over me. I believed with all my heart I would be different.

So when my son came along, I was as ill-prepared for the massive transition to motherhood as you can get. And I had absolutely no clue that I would become the kind of mother I am today. Today, I am the mother of two children under five. I sleep with them. I rarely go out at night. I go insane when I'm away from them at work and feel cheated of the time I miss with them. When I'm not working, I inhale them. Poor kids. I kiss them non-stop. I am insatiable. My friends have abandoned me. I'm obsessed. I'm a walking advertisement for the overattached mother. I know it. And I can't help it.

I have became one of those crazy moms I used to roll my eyes at—wearing their babies in slings, breastfeeding until toddlerhood, bringing their kids everywhere. I was radicalized by becoming a mother. This was my revolution. Poof. There I was. Reincarnated as a Totally Different Person.

Of course, it wasn't really as sudden as "poof." My transition to motherhood took a few months. In that time, those blissful first few summer months, I walked all over Vancouver with my baby in his stroller, breastfeeding on park benches or lying under big trees, marking my territory. Within weeks, I felt my ambition ebbing away. I was lulled and besotted with my new life: walking around the city, napping in the afternoon, sitting in cafés staring at my beautiful child. It was with some horror that I realized one day that I didn't want to go back to work. That was my first clue to the new person emerging inside me.

Then, when my son was eighteen months, I left him. It was, not counting labour, my first real rite of passage into motherhood. A good friend was having a book launch in New York and my pre-baby self was dying to go. I told her I'd be there and booked my ticket. A few days before I was to go, I called to cancel the ticket. I was torn up inside. It was as though I was deciding on the fate of a nation: I was consumed, tormented.

I wanted to go, but I didn't want to go. It was the war of my pre-baby self with my mother self, and it was horrible. I called my friend to apologize, and she persuaded me to come anyway. So I called and rebooked another ticket, and the anxiety about leaving my baby began creeping back. A few days later, the anxiety was killing me. I cancelled the ticket again. My friend was sympathetic, to a point. Okay, she said. Trust your instincts. If you don't think you can handle being away from him, stay home. I went. It was a disaster.

I spent the whole weekend miserable and hormonal, crying and trying to relieve the pain of my swollen, leaking breasts in the shower. The battle being waged in my heart had been decided, and I was sad. I was mourning the loss of my old self and my old life. Perhaps, as so many people said later, I had to go through my New

York disaster to know how strongly I felt about being with my son. The trip provided a good lesson: I had to trust myself, my new self. Before New York, I couldn't do that. I didn't know who I was. Struggling with self-doubt, I let other people decide what I should do—not just about New York but about co-sleeping, choosing a day-care, feeding my child the right foods. Until I accepted and trusted the person I'd become, I was bullied and pressured by other people who felt they knew everything about motherhood.

In making the decision to go to New York, I encountered many mothers who felt I needed to get away. I needed "a break." That was my favourite line. I never understood why I might need a break from my beautiful child. They said it was good for me. Like wheat germ. They said it would be good for him, too. They said, at eighteen months, he needed to learn to be "independent."

In retrospect, it seems so ridiculous. I don't know where people get these ideas. I don't know why people think they can tell other mothers what to do. It's such an individual thing, how you mother your children. That much will quickly become evident as you read the essays in this book. Mostly, we just do the best we can. And mostly, that's enough. But if I had been encouraged to "do what I felt was right" rather than doing "what I thought was expected," maybe my identity crisis would have been a little easier. Or maybe it's all just part of the rite of passage.

I don't want to be too hard on myself. There's enough judging of mothers and mothering by friends, family and perfect strangers. I'll leave the criticism to them. I'm more interested in figuring out how this happened. How a woman like me, raised with more opportunities and choices than any previous generation of women, could be so unprepared for motherhood. Just like women in the 1960s, mothers today are discovering that the ways we are brought up and the goals we set for ourselves are strangely, and often painfully, contradictory. Liberation, autonomy and equality are all good principles for women to aspire to, in theory. But they don't fit so well with mothering. How can you put yourself and your kids first at the same time? And then, where does your partner, assuming you have one, fit into the picture? You get the idea.

But it's not just women from the sixties who will find parallels in today's mothering experience. As any reading on the history of motherhood will reveal, cycles repeat themselves and mothers today are struggling with many of the same issues as mothers of previous generations. Perhaps the one mark of distinction for today's mothers is our widespread sense of dissatisfaction with the way things are: with our "motherload" (the career, the kids, the house, the husband), with gender roles, with society's expectations. It's hard to be satisfied when you are brought up to believe you will have a fabulous career, a fabulous family, a fabulous social life and a fabulous house, and when you suddenly find yourself with all those things, you realize it's not at all fabulous; that having all those things means losing yourself; that motherhood has much more inherent value and joy than we were ever taught to believe; that having a job and kids and an "equal" relationship or marriage is highly stressful, and not always possible.

Maybe I wanted to write this book to write myself out of madness. That is what it feels like every time I write something about motherhood—a big exhale. Except I didn't want to do all the writing myself. So much of what I've found interesting about the struggles of motherhood has been hearing other women's stories, sharing their experiences. It can be vindicating, depressing, surprising or just a plain relief to know I'm not the only one having trouble, say, weaning my two-year-old or swearing in front of, and sometimes at, my kids. (Those are the printable confessions.)

I've had many life-altering moments in my five years of motherhood. But to give room to the other voices in this collection, I'll tell you about just one more. My second turning point as a mother happened in my car. My son was two, and I had just dropped him off at daycare. I was starting a new job four days a week, and I'd found this wonderful woman who ran a daycare out of her home with just a handful of other children. She was a Greek goddess with three grown boys, a huge house, a lovely garden and a firm but loving understanding of children. I knew I should feel comfortable and stress-free leaving my son in such a great place all day. But instead I felt sick, physically and emotionally sick. I would spend the first five minutes of my ride to work downtown crying and slamming my hand on the steering wheel in anger, while my husband sat beside me aghast and deeply frightened. Then I would have five minutes to make the transition from sobbing mess to professional journalist. I was like Clark Kent, only the car was my phone booth and my disguise always felt transparent and fraudulent. Then one day, driving away from the 120th tearful goodbye, I realized that this was just not the life I wanted. It was suddenly so clear.

I hadn't thought through "the whole motherhood thing." I hadn't thought ahead to what would happen when my babies were toddlers and then in school and then teenagers. I hadn't thought about how, or if, I could change my job to accommodate them. I hadn't thought of anything, really, other than swaddling and snuggling them. So when I realized I didn't want to have this corporate, mainstream life of working and daycare, I had to think hard and fast of a way to end the commute and seal the gap that opened in my heart every time I left my son at the door.

So I had another child. It was an irrational response to the crisis, of course. But I'd wanted another child anyway, and the sooner the better. That's the saying, right? Well, that got me a year at home with my two children. And when I had to go back to work, I went back three days a week. Now, my husband and mother alternate taking the kids and my husband works at home starting up his own business the other days. It's not perfect. We are financially stressed, to put it mildly. And my relationship with my husband has weathered some serious storms as we negotiate this new tag-team approach to parenting.

Just now, as my daughter turns two, I feel myself slowly staggering out of the haze of early motherhood. But I still crave the conversations I have with my mom friends, conversations about how we manage with the career, the house, the husband, the kids. Why do we want to have it all? Do we have to? What are the alternatives? Mostly, these conversations take place in the park, in the grocery store, at the community centre, and sometimes, although very rarely, at the bar.

I wish I'd been privy to these conversations before I had kids, but they only really happen between moms. And even if I'd had a chance to listen, I expect I was too self-indulgent and arrogant to have heard what they were saying. That these conversations are still hidden behind the door of motherhood is a sure sign of society's response to birth and motherhood: we don't really want to hear about it; we don't want to celebrate it. We just want mothers to do it quietly and leave the rest of us alone.

Until I was thirty-one, my only hands-on experience with a baby was helping take care of my sister who is ten years younger and, while travelling in Guatemala, helping some women in a village take care of their children. Here in Canada, unlike Guatemala or any number of Third World countries, we like to keep babies and children separate from the adult world. We don't integrate them into the fabric of our lives. Strangers aren't likely to come up to you on the street cooing and wanting to hold your baby and talk to you about your life. They might smile politely, or say something like "Oh, what a cute baby. How old is he?" As if his age matters. After that, the conversation usually dies.

Into that conversational void with society at large has come conversation among mothers. It's our modern-day ritual of celebration and connection. It is that conversation, a conversation constantly interrupted by kids, husbands and work that started this book. Since I've become a mom, I've been having the most intense, emotionally raw conversations of my life. They are the conversations I expected and never found at university. We talk about all the mundane day-to-day details, of course: diapers, poo, how to make macaroni and cheese. But we also talk about our jobs and how they work or don't work to make a family life possible and sane. We talk about our marriages, our friends, our quest for community, the meaning of life—ours and our children's.

I wanted to bring women together in this book to continue this long, constantly interrupted conversation. I wanted to provide a space where mothers could talk about the huge transformation involved in becoming mothers. I wanted them to explore the difficulties they've had in the process of becoming mothers; the choices and decisions they've faced and how they've handled them; how they've managed the identity crisis, the career crisis, the relationship crisis.

This book is my ritual. My offering to mothers everywhere.

PART ONE

Ambition

MOMMY, I WANT YOUR FLAK JACKET

MARINA JIMÉNEZ

It was somewhere along the desert highway, just before the Jordan–Iraq border crossing, that I began to seriously question my sanity. The mother of an eleven-month-old boy, I had just signed a waiver saying I would not hold the Hashemite Kingdom of Jordan responsible if I was hurt on the "very dangerous" road into Baghdad. Vultures flew overhead. Not a good omen.

I was crammed into the back seat of a van, the only woman in a group of six, which included a driver, translator, cameraman and two other journalists. My son, Alvaro, was thousands of miles away, being cared for by my husband and nanny. I missed him desperately, his soft skin and sweet smell, his almond-shaped blue eyes, his tiny, perfect hands. I should have been home rocking him to sleep, not rocketing toward Baghdad. Instead, I had exchanged my baby carrier and diaper bag for a flak jacket and a laptop. I was surrounded by grizzled war correspondents. Torn between two worlds. Heartsick and homesick.

I HAD RETURNED from my maternity leave only three months earlier, and my assignment at the time of the American invasion of

Iraq in March 2003 was supposed to be covering the "safe, easy" story in Jordan, where hundreds of Iraqi refugees were expected to arrive. But after I'd spent two weeks waiting by the hotel pool for word of the refugees' arrival, they had failed to materialize, and trying to capture the mood of the "Arab street" had grown old. With the Americans marching toward Baghdad, and the fall of the Iraqi capital imminent, the four-hundred-odd journalists camped out in Amman grew impatient. We scrambled out of the Jordanian capital to drive the notoriously dangerous nine-hundred-kilometre highway into Baghdad.

That day, April 8, we made it only as far as the abandoned border post. It was too dangerous to travel at night, so we camped overnight in no-man's land in the freezing desert and waited for sunrise. We hadn't eaten in hours. Unlike some of the crews from CNN and BBC, who carried portable showers, camping stoves, tins of food and gasoline, our rations consisted in their entirety of a Thuraya satellite phone, water, a box of chocolates and some biscuits pilfered from the mini-bar of Amman's Hotel InterContinental. Like countless other journalists, I had been unable to get a visa to cover the conflict in Iraq. Now, it didn't matter.

I looked around at the other journalists tumbling out of their vans and pitching tents in the dusk and realized I didn't fit any of the foreign-correspondent archetypes. There were the "Papa corros"— older, perennially single men, loudly sharing anecdotes about the last Gulf War, in 1991, accustomed to living out of a suitcase and eating at hotel restaurants. Then there were the "cowboys," young men hungry for adventure, growing beards to look convincing in their field portraits. Next came the "war babes," gorgeous young women just starting their careers, still single or hooked up with hunky photographers, not always wearing sensible shoes, and, in fact, not always sensible period. Finally there were a few grizzled war broads, women who had never had children or had long ago bade them adieu.

Apart from cnn's Christiane Amanpour, mother of a three-year-old boy and an archetype unto herself, there appeared to be few if any others in my demographic: a thirty-eight-year-old new mother in need of a haircut, with a knot in her stomach and a lump in her throat. I asked myself for the umpteenth time why I had schemed so desperately to cover this dangerous story. It went against the very essence of motherhood, which was all about nurturing, protection, selflessness and love.

I told myself that Alvaro would one day understand, and promised myself that this would be my very last foreign assignment, that I would quit my job if I came out of this unharmed. Alvaro was a dream child, who rarely cried and slept through the night at six weeks, his head always in the same position, as if he was looking off to the left. He had a sunny disposition and an adorable dimple in his right cheek. He crawled at seven months and loved banana puree and blueberry yogurt. What kind of a mother would leave such a beautiful baby and sign up to join the convoy into Iraq? What kind of a journalist wouldn't want to cover biggest story of our times?

EVERY WOMAN STRUGGLES with the work-life balance, and none more so than careerists who have a first child later in life. The scales always feel tipped in the wrong direction. Too much time at the office, not enough bonding with the baby. Too much time on email, not enough time with building blocks. Too many mommy groups, not enough foreign assignments. Not any, in fact. I had imagined I would somehow tote my baby everywhere I went, that he would experience every new adventure with me, getting an up-close view of world.

In a speech she gave in 2000, Christiane Amanpour put it this way: "Before my son was born, I used to joke about looking for bulletproof Snuglis and Kevlar diapers. I was planning, I told everybody, to take him on the road with me. At the very least, I fully expected to keep up my hectic pace and my passion as a war correspondent. But now, like every working mother, when I think of my son, and having to leave him, I imagine him fixing those large innocent eyes on me and asking me, Mommy, why are you going to those terrible places? What if they kill you?" I wince.

AT THIRTY-SEVEN, I felt blessed to be able to get pregnant. It had taken my husband and me a year to conceive, in part because of constantly being on the move. A foreign writer for the *National Post*, I travelled on assignment to places like Haiti and Colombia, the world's kidnapping capital. It was exciting, but it meant I was never in town on the "right" day. I was also lucky to have such an easy pregnancy, my job for the most part unaffected, except for an assignment to Guantánamo Bay, Cuba, which was abruptly cancelled by the U.S. military once they realized I was with child.

But mostly, I carried on, working right up until my due date. During my first trimester, I travelled to Pakistan and Lebanon in the weeks following the 9/11 terrorist attacks. I was in Peshawar—in Pakistan's volatile Northwest Frontier province, close to the Afghan border—the night the U.S. bombs started to drop on the Taliban next door. Covering demonstrations there, I was forced to take refuge in taxis and alleyways to avoid inhaling the tear gas that was inevitably sprayed at protesters during the daily demonstrations. I hid my swollen belly under a shalwar-kameez, and no one ever suspected.

At thirty-three weeks, I was due to fly to Moldova and Turkey to do an investigative story on the organ trade, tracking down Israeli patients who came to Istanbul to receive kidneys from women from Moldova who had been operated on by an infamous Turkish surgeon. My husband nixed the Moldova portion of the trip after discovering the medical facilities in the country were so poor that foreigners had to be med-evacuated to Germany. An officious *National Post* human resources manager cancelled the second part of the trip to Turkey, arguing there was no insurance to cover employees who gave birth outside Canada. (Luckily, then–Deputy Editor Martin Newland—a father of four—reinstated it.)

In Istanbul, my Turkish translator, a woman a few years my junior, was also pregnant and didn't mind the hourly pee breaks and constant food stops. When we dropped into the Istanbul clinic of the notorious surgeon Dr. Yusef Somnez, the receptionist thought we had both arrived for our ultrasound appointments and ushered us in, only to unceremoniously kick us out the moment she realized we were journalists on the trail of Dr. Somnez and his legally and morally questionable procedures.

At thirty-seven weeks, I took my final trip—to Ottawa, by train, carrying my special "birthing bag" in case the baby came early. But Alvaro came on time, on May 5, 2002, at 11:38 p.m. at Toronto's Mount Sinai Hospital after several hours of labour. I was helped along by such generous doses of medication via an epidural that I could barely push, and the baby had to be suctioned out.

The next morning, strung out on morphine to help me get over the pain of a tear, I was euphoric, unable to grasp that my new and very different job had just begun. The reality of round-the-clock feedings hadn't yet sunk in. In the hospital, I soon became the "project" of an overbearing Cuban nurse who informed me that I wasn't breastfeeding properly and ordered me to supplement with formula. "¡Hay que suplementar!" she barked. The hospital's lactation consultant immediately issued contradictory advice. And from the haze of my sleep-deprived state, I became trapped between these two warring camps and quickly discovered that the politics of breastfeeding were every bit as complex as Iraq's Sunni–Shia conflict.

Discharged from the hospital after four days—the breastfeeding war finally over, as I elected not to use formula—Alvaro and I adjusted to each other at home. He was a beautiful baby, with a big head, a high forehead, a sweep of dark hair and a long, thin body.

Seven pounds, ten ounces and twenty-one inches long. I never tired of looking down at his sweet face and smothering him in kisses.

What I hadn't expected was the solitude of motherhood. Hours spent breastfeeding in front of the television. The highlight of my day was a trip to the drugstore to buy diaper cream and wipes, or an outing to the pediatrician's. Suddenly, my world had shrunk to the four walls of my midtown Toronto bungalow.

To keep my sanity, I began madly planning adventures: how many trips could I cram into my eight-month maternity leave? How many outings could I organize in a day? How many new classes could I join? I told myself that Alvaro, an oblivious newborn, needed the stimulation. It was really his mommy who needed to get out of the house.

Hungry for the company of other mothers, I signed up for two mothering classes, a lap-rhymes and lullaby class at a local bookstore and an exercise class at Gymboree, complete with a giant, coloured parachute and a grating clown named Gymbo. My mother was incredulous. "Pay to sing nursery rhymes and bounce your baby on your lap?" she said. "In my day, we plopped the baby in a pram and let him watch the traffic go by."

But I was happy to share tedious stories of diaper rash, stool texture and teething rings with other new mothers. Though I felt a bit like an elderly imposter in this world, I was ready to embrace it—and indulge in the glorious consumer side of motherhood. Robeez leather slippers, Jacadi cotton outfits that cost more than my Gap jeans and Lululemon yoga pants for my slowly shrinking belly.

My husband, John, and I took Alvaro to Fishers Island, N.Y., when he was two months old, and to Alberta to see his two sets of grandparents and aunties and cousins. I lugged him along to Florida on my annual girls' holiday. He even accompanied John and me on an eleven-day cruise to the Arctic and Greenland, where he became what my husband dubbed a "coddle-seeking missile." He was passed around like a football and admired by all, even celebrity guest Margaret Atwood, who looked knowing, and addressed him as "one of the little people."

By the time my maternity leave drew to an end in January 2003, I was just starting to get the hang of motherhood. Life at home could be fun, even if I lacked the requisite glam factor, club memberships and designer home improvement flair to join the yummy mummies. The prospect of leaving Alvaro to go back to work was torture. I cried as he and the wonderful nanny I was sharing with another mother waved from the living-room window, wondering how I would survive without him.

But once back in the newsroom, I was tortured again—by what I perceived as my loss of status. With the U.S. expected to invade Iraq, I was the only foreign writer not assigned to the "war team." It may well have been an honest oversight, but to me it felt as if I was being downgraded now that I was on the "mommy track." My editor probably didn't imagine I wanted to be away from my baby. And I didn't. Except part of me wanted to prove to my bosses—and my conflicted self—that I could do both.

Though my husband was wholly supportive, my employer didn't initially plan to send me to cover the war. I was relegated to doing rewrites and television hits for Global, describing a war thousands of miles away. I was only dispatched to Amman after a colleague there requested a break. I was supposed to stay put and cover the Iraqi refugees—the refugees that never came.

AS WE ENTERED IRAQ, our translator told us to zip up our flak jackets. The road ahead was perilous, filled with bandits and Fedayeen, fighters loyal to Saddam. I fought off tears as we made our last telephone calls on our Jordanian cellphones. I called the newsdesk and then my husband, who told me to buck up. This was, after all, the assignment I had lobbied for. Alvaro was just fine, he reassured me. He would never even remember Mommy being away. Still, I was consumed by guilt about the dangers that lay ahead.

By the morning of April 10, U.S. Special Forces had taken over the Jordan–Iraq border crossing. We were among the first journalists to come through. Looters had stripped the post of everything—from the air conditioner and rugs to the safe-deposit boxes. Food was left half-eaten on a grubby kitchen table, and border files with lists of visitors were strewn near the waiting room. We knew that driving past the towns of Ramadi and Fallujah—hotbeds of support for Saddam Hussein—would be tense. As we passed Ramadi, a Sunni stronghold and support base of Saddam Hussein a hundred kilometres west of Baghdad, we were shot at. A cameraman from another vehicle was injured by the gunfire.

As we neared Baghdad, we began to pass dead bodies lying in the streets—evidence of the battle between U.S. troops and those loyal to Saddam. Shots rang out. There were looters everywhere, wheeling office chairs and carrying furniture down the street. We were forced to stop on the city outskirts and wait for an armed U.S. military escort to get safely to the Palestine Hotel, a seventeen-storey monolith in the city's east end, near the Tigris River.

The city had quickly fallen to the Americans, but Baghdad was by no means secure. Fighting continued, and the streets were tense as the air filled with rounds of gunfire. Tanks and a razor-wire fence surrounded the hotel, and the marines, who had installed themselves in the once-grand salons on the ground floor, made everyone submit to full body checks. The hotel itself was in a state of chaos, with rumours that guerrilla fighters had infiltrated. The employees had all but lost control of the facility. American bombs and missiles had wiped out Baghdad's phone lines, electricity and water stations, which meant no functioning elevator, no clean sheets or towels, and hard crusts of bread and hard-boiled eggs for breakfast.

The only room left was a dingy office on the sixteenth floor. I spent the first night there, hunkered down on the floor beside my four male colleagues, one of whom proved to be an exhibitionist. Instead of waking up to the sound of my beautiful baby boy's gurgles and his sweet scent, my Baghdad morning featured the sight of my colleague's large, hairy posterior as he wandered around the room. I dashed away in horror and brushed my teeth in the filthy bathroom in the lobby. "Please," I implored the clerk at the front desk, "it is not right, making a married woman sleep with four men." "Yes, I see your point," he said, grabbing the crisp US$100 bill I thrust at him. Being in a Muslim country was not without its advantages. He gave me the sheets from an extra bed in his own room, ripped a towel in half and found me another room.

Just in time, as it turned out. The next morning, U.S. Marines stormed into my colleagues' room, shoving M-16 rifles in their faces, demanding to know if they had weapons. They were searching for Fedayeen fighters, who had infiltrated the hotel and were rumoured to have stockpiled munitions. Baghdad was a security nightmare, with pockets of fighting breaking out on the streets and the sense that at any moment the war could all be over. I spent my days driving around with my translator, touring the bombed-out buildings, the looted National Museum, the empty prisons. I spoke to Iraqis who swore they could hear the voices of their relatives inside the jails, begging to be let out—though we never found anyone inside. We interviewed many Shiites, a persecuted majority under Saddam, who had come out of the woodwork to demand a role in the new government. I visited the victims of war inside the few hospitals that were still functioning. I could scarcely bear to look at the faces of injured children, an all too painful reminder of my own tiny son, so far away. At the same time, I felt guilty crying for my baby when he was healthy and happy. Back at the hotel, desperate Iraqis pushed up against the security perimeter, shoving scraps of paper into my hand with the telephone numbers of overseas relatives. They begged me to call them on my satellite phone and let them know they were still alive.

A severe bout of food poisoning a week later sent me back to Amman with the cameraman, who was also ill. I lay in the back seat of the minivan, sick as a dog, moaning and hallucinating processions of little men in bowler hats clutching umbrellas. Roadside stops were just that. The InterContinental had never looked so good. I later joked that the only upside of the "Baghdad diet" was that I lost the last of my pregnancy weight. I had had enough of Iraq. And as it turned out, enough of being a war correspondent.

ALVARO'S BABY BOOK reminds me, as if I needed reminding, that he first said "Dada" and "bye-bye" at six months. For his first Halloween he wore a white-and-pink bunny suit knitted by his grandmother, for his first Christmas Eve a Santa suit and cap. His favourite book was about a polar bear. But between eleven and twelve months, there is a gap in his baby book. I can never get back those four crazy weeks I spent in Iraq and Jordan, proving that I still had what it takes to be a foreign correspondent. Adjusting to motherhood has been, for me, a long and somewhat mysterious process. My life has changed irrevocably. I cannot simply pick up my childless life where I left off. Hard as it is to admit, I can never be the roving correspondent I once was.

On May 5, 2003, I threw a party in a room at my parents' condo building for Alvaro's first birthday, inviting a handful of other babies and their parents. I set out fish crackers, cake and apple juice for the babies and wine and cheese for the parents. The children crawled around, blissfully oblivious to the occasion we were celebrating. The following Monday, I joined *The Globe and Mail* as a national correspondent. No more month-long sojourns in war zones. From then on, I was sticking close to home.

And yet, while I knew I couldn't stomach another Iraq, I soon realized that I wasn't altogether ready to give up foreign reporting. A few months into my new job, I was already lobbying my editors to send me somewhere: Pakistan, Vietnam, Cuba, Mexico. I have somehow juggled these assignments, and various others, around Alvaro's swim classes, birthday parties and school holidays. Each time I leave, I cry, saying goodbye to my darling boy, his eyelashes fluttering against my cheek, his soft breath warming me as I struggle to explain where I am going and for how long. Being away from him is still torture, but I know I couldn't survive if I could never go anywhere again.

It's a balancing act that seems impossible to get right. And there are so many unanswered questions: would Alvaro be better off if I were at home full-time, or would I just be a crabby parent, channelling my excess energy into too many after-school activities, and scheduling my child to death? I know I can't be the roving foreign correspondent I once was. It's a career that just doesn't work with being a mother. It's taken me a long time to accept that and figure out how to carry on.

Now four, Alvaro knows the names of many of the places Mommy has visited. He coloured in a map of Venezuela when I was there recently. He is curious about the flak jacket that sat in our hallway the night before I flew to Haiti to cover the February 2006 election. "It's a special jacket for journalists," I explained. He didn't press the point. The truth is, being away is hard on both of us, especially now that he is older. While infants have no sense of time, four-year-olds really don't understand why they can't come with you. The best part of every foreign trip is walking back through my own front door. Alvaro usually regards me with some suspicion until I haul out the presents and win back his affection.

And yet, according to my husband, my son gets on very well without me. He claims Alvaro cries for Mommy only when he is being disciplined—although when I went on a recent assignment to London, he didn't understand why he wasn't allowed to travel with Mommy to see the Tower of London, the bobbies, the double-decker buses and the London Eye. My husband never complains about the time apart. On the contrary, Superdad loves his role. He gleefully overlooks the food I have prepared and instead takes Alvaro out for as many hamburgers and fish and chips as he can stuff down, stopping on the way home for the latest Playmobil pirate ship at the local toy store. You just can't micro-manage when you're thousands of miles away.

Sometimes I wonder: should I chuck in this career and do something else? With each passing year, my career seems harder and harder to justify. But for now, I have decided that for as long as I can, I will try to be both: a doting mother and a journalist, willing to go, if not anywhere, at least to most places. I just can't kill the traveller inside me. And it seems I may have passed along the bug. Already Alvaro loves to point out the continents on a laminated map of the world that hangs on the blue wall of his room. At his Montessori school, his favourite table is the one with the flags of the world. He knows all the names. "Mommy, I want to go to the Antarctic to see the penguins," he said recently. A child after my own heart.

MOTHERHOOD
UNPLUGGED
AMI MCKAY

I don't wear a watch. In fact, I haven't worn one in more than seven years. These days it's more of an act of wilful defiance, my bitchy little way of getting back at all the anal-retentive timekeepers of the world. My turn of indifference to the clock is much like my cat—she yowls and paws at the door to my studio (she's doing it right this minute), and then pads off with an aloof flick of her tail when I finally break down and open the door. Time. Bah. You don't own me.

This dismissal of time didn't start as a conscious decision. It wasn't born of New Age philosophy or Zen meditation. Like most things that have become important in my life, it was an accident. When the worn leather band on my beat-up old water-resistant, glow-in-the-dark, been-on-every-hiking-biking-and-camping-adventure-since-1982 watch broke, I did a quick fix with a rubber band and forgot about it. When the rubber band snapped—just as I was packing the last of many boxes of books into a moving van—I shoved the timepiece in my pocket and forgot about it again.

A few days later, after I'd made my way from Chicago to Nova Scotia with my husband, my son, two cats, three goldfish and everything we owned, I found the watch. I pulled it out as I was picking

35

through pockets to do a load of laundry. I stared at it, wondering why I had found it so essential. Somewhere along the highway, between my old apartment in the middle of one of the world's largest cities and the farmhouse I was now calling home, everything was supposed to have changed. I was supposed to be letting go of all the "shoulds" in my life. I was supposed to be following my bliss, forgetting about time. At least that was the plan.

A FEW MONTHS BEFORE, I had been living a different life, living every second by the clock. I was a single mom, teaching full-time, and struggling to make rent. In the handful of hours I had for sleep each night, dreams rarely, if ever, made an appearance. My sporadic attempts to keep a journal all read the same: *"Maybe next week—no that won't work—maybe next month, I'll take a day off just for myself. Maybe this autumn, I'll visit the Art Institute. Someday, I'll have time to dance. Someday, I'll have time to cry. Someday, I'll have time to write."*

My "someday" arrived at 7:45 a.m., October 13, 1998, at the corner of Sheridan Road and Cuyler Street in Chicago, Illinois. As I was driving to work, a car came out from a side street, its driver ignoring the stop sign, and plowed into the front of my car. A head injury and trauma to the eye, plus too many scrapes and bruises to count, added up to a month off work and plenty of somedays. During the weeks that followed, I fell in love with an old friend, fell in love with Nova Scotia, fell in love with an old farmhouse on the Bay of Fundy and gave my notice. A few months later, I'd married my best friend, my son had a new father and we were on our way to a new life, a life where I was determined to follow my bliss. Of course, making the decision to forget about time and follow one's dreams is a fine start, but it's also terrifying. I needed a place to start. I'd always had "something more important to do." What next?

A BABY.

While I was keeping busy learning (pushing myself) to do all the things I never had the time (or in some cases, the need) to do— how to bake cookies without burning them, how to keep jam jars from bursting, how to stack wood so it will dry before winter, how to keep slugs out of the garden, how to hang clothes on the line so they won't be blown away on the Fundy breeze, how to make a proper pot of tea for a neighbour—I became pregnant. Along with the excitement in the house that came with my pregnancy (my husband and I were both thrilled, my son was giddy at the thought of having a brother), I began to dream. I'd no sooner shut my eyes than visions would appear. Most often they were about the baby: he would come out of the womb with the ability to speak, or he was falling from the sky and I was running to catch him.

It's difficult to forget about time when you're pregnant. Nine months and counting. Everything, for you and everyone close to you, is set against the backdrop of expectancy. How long since your last period? How far along are you? Let's see how much weight you've gained this month. You mark the due date on the calendar with a heart or a smiley face or a big red X. As the "day of arrival" gets closer, matters of time intensify: *how many minutes between contractions?* I had set aside my watch months before, only to replace it—happily—with a forty-week pregnancy plan. I felt as if I'd swallowed a clock.

Ideally, mother and child are synchronized during the first few months after a birth. The midwife who assisted in our home birth was always gentle but firm in reminding me of this. "Give yourself time to adjust. Let someone else do the laundry. Sleep when the baby sleeps. Accept your neighbour's offer to cook your meals." There I was, my inner drive for "getting things done" still in place, and there was no other choice but to give in and follow my baby. This sometimes colicky, always diaper-soiling creature had my attention and the key to the clock.

He nursed—a lot—and while he was at the breast, my mind would wander to ideas and places I hadn't thought about in years. I had always kept a few dusty notebooks under the bed but had never allowed myself the time to fully explore my thoughts in writing. Each afternoon, I'd go upstairs and lie in my bed, the baby snuggled on one side, a notebook and pen in my hands. I scribbled. I day-dreamed. I wrote page after page and I realized what I'd always wanted most was to be a writer.

AS MOTHERS, WE are our own worst critics. We feel guilty and selfish if we take the time to follow dreams that exclude our chil-dren, that are ours alone. Yet ironically, and maddeningly, if we devote ourselves entirely to our babies we feel guilty about that too: we feel less than perfect if we are just "mother," and nothing else. I'll raise my hand right now and tell you, I'm no exception to either of those rules. For years, I had an identity. I had labels—sin-gle mother, teacher; ambitious, punctual. Then, on my first social outing with my new son, I sat down with a large group of people I hadn't seen in months. There was baby spit-up down my front. My hair was falling out of a scrunchy. There were dark circles under my eyes, and I felt as if I had little to offer and no way to describe myself.

I was sitting, breastfeeding the baby, and one of my husband's female colleagues walked over and started a conversation. "So, Ian tells me you're not planning on going back to teaching?"

I shook my head. "I've got my hands full with the baby."

She nodded and smiled. "Certainly. That's smart."

I adjusted the baby, switching sides.

Reaching out to touch the baby's head, she rubbed his fuzzy newborn hair as if she wanted to see if it was real. She was a first-year teacher at the local high school where Ian was teaching, and her tentativeness around me made it obvious she wasn't ready to settle down and have children. "What about when he's older? Do you think you'll go back to work?"

I stared at her, not wanting to admit to being *just* a mother.

She nervously backpedalled, thinking she'd offended me. "I mean, a lot of moms are just moms. Well, not *just* moms. You know what I mean. I guess I can't imagine what it's like. I don't think I could do the stay-at-home thing. It's not my thing, and from what Ian's told me about you, you seem like someone who's used to having a lot going on, having lived in Chicago and all."

A lot going on. I sat there wondering what to say. Which would be worse, to start lecturing her, explaining how being a mother *is* to have a lot going on, or to tell her that much as I loved being a mom, I also wanted to write? I was tired. The baby had kept me awake all night. So I blurted out, "I'm a writer."

"Hmm? I thought Ian told me you were a music teacher."

"I was. But now I'm a writer."

"Oh, cool. What have you written? Maybe I've heard of it."

Oh God, oh God, oh God. Did I just tell this woman that I'm a writer? I had no watch to check. No appointment to run off to. I improvised and sniffed the baby's bum. "Oops, I think someone needs changing. Excuse me, won't you?"

Ego battered, I went home thinking, Who are you kidding? A writer?

Still, I couldn't shake the urge to get things down on paper. I continued to write every day, eventually showing bits and pieces to my husband. "This is good. Keep at it." Even when I protested, he insisted, "I'll take the baby for an hour or two. You go write."

A few weeks later, at another gathering, a different woman approached me. As usual, I was nursing the baby. The first thing she said was, "I hope you don't mind me coming over, but you look like a painting."

"A painting?"

"Yes. I'm a painter. Sometimes I see people or things and they look like something I know I'll end up painting."

A little blond toddler came over and held on to the woman's pant leg. She patted the little boy's head. "I'm a mom, too. Watching you reminded me of when I was still nursing." She took his hand when he reached for her. "He nursed so often that I used to paint and nurse at the same time."

Laughing, I said, "Wow. And I thought I was doing something special by writing and nursing at the same time."

"It's amazing what comes out, isn't it? It was such a creative time for me, and I knew that if I could paint with a baby in one arm, I could do anything." Her voice fell quiet and serious. "So, you're a writer." She wasn't asking. She was declaring it.

Nervous about the last time I'd admitted to the "w" word, I sighed. "Well, sort of. I haven't had anything published."

She smiled. "When you're ready, you will."

Until that moment, I'd felt like a fraud. Even though my husband was being supportive of my desire to write, I couldn't help feeling that it would lead to nothing, that I was wasting my time. Yet here was this woman, another mother, but also an artist, holding out her friendship to me like a lantern in the window, telling me there was nothing to fear. I looked at her wrists and noted the conspicuous absence of a watch. I bounced the baby over my shoulder to burp him. "That's what my husband says, too. I hope you're both right."

In the months and years that followed, she became not only an inspiration but also a friend. She welcomed me into her tea circle— along with a playwright, a textile artist, an unschooling activist, an osteopath-midwife, a puppeteer–organic cook, and an amazing nurse—all of us mothers, all of us gathering for long hikes and conversation, leaving our watches behind as we chased our dreams by the light of the moon.

THERE ARE CLOCKS everywhere in this world. Time flashes alternately with the temperature and date outside banks. Computer screen toolbars and cellphones keep us honest to the minute, and we've all learned to compensate for the incorrect digital display on the car's dash—mine is one hour and twenty-five minutes behind, due to daylight saving time plus the additional minutes the mechanic spent with the battery unhooked during the car's last tune-up. If I need to, I can always find the time. What's more important is that I can just as easily let it go.

FALLING INTO GRACE
LEANNE DELAP

Simone was two weeks overdue when I got the call from John Macfarlane, my old boss at *Toronto Life* magazine. We'd had a fiery relationship when I was an associate editor there years before. I had been a mouthy Young Turk who had outgrown the position, but had no plan for what was next. So I was thrown by his offer: "Do you want to edit your own magazine?"

My strapping toddler son with rock-star white-blond hair was sitting beside me mashing cars into his peas. I told John all I wanted was to lie on the sofa and drool. After years of rushing headlong into my life, I had a fantasy of just *stopping*. I would spend long hours pushing a Silver Cross pram, meet friends for organic scrambled egg wraps and smilingly refinish furniture in the backyard.

My marriage, my second marriage, rather, was great then. We had two babies, pop-pop, seventeen months apart. We'd bought our first house, a Victorian semi on Queen Street West in Toronto. We had a nanny keeping the house together and doing shifts at the drop-in (I really can't stand drop-ins). Or the park, actually. My husband, Jake, had just been hired at the *National Post* reviewing restaurants and luxury cars. I was looking forward to a long maternity leave from a job I still loved, fashion reporter at *The Globe and Mail*, where I got to jet off to Europe for the ludicrous and delicious rounds of shows. We were in a giddy, golden zone where we tossed clever dinner parties, floated to other people's soirees and raced home to talk through the evening with each other.

Our daughter's birth was elegant. Really. After being induced, I spent six pleasant anaesthetized hours reading the paper in pleasurable silence. I felt totally competent swinging her home that Halloween night after a glass of champagne, my body not even sore. Four days later, I slipped on a ballgown and headed out for a brief appearance at the Giller Awards cocktail party. I am not boasting. It was just such a contrast to the stunned, lumpen mess I was in the aftermath of my first-born.

When my brain returned a few weeks after my daughter's birth, I looked around and wondered how the hell we were going to afford a nanny and the mortgage. What had I been smoking to think I could just lie around playing socialite mommy? So, despite my couch fantasies, when the call came from the publisher I let the seduction begin.

Looking back now, I see that the big money and the glamour of editing a fashion magazine tickled my pride. Plus, I was scared of losing myself again the way I had with my first baby. I went to the interview totally unprepared and whacked from sleeplessness. I presented an off-the-cuff strategy to reposition the magazine as younger, more urban, smart, irreverent. I pushed the media trends of the day, slung around the lingo, worked the room. I threw in lots of celebrity-glossed story ideas and a few earnest but genuine thoughts about strong, female voices writing between the shoe ads.

I had 'em, and I knew it. I loved the rush of pulling off a challenge I wasn't even sure I wanted with two babes under two at home, one still on the breast. I was reckless, a macho mom feeding off all the people who wondered, sensibly, "How does she do it?" I had the wanton arrogance of a young and overly blessed woman, refusing to believe consequences existed. But my run at having it all was delusional, and when the streak ended, I was left holding a big mess I spent years ignoring.

There is no way I could have dreamed of relaunching that magazine had I not been in a baby daze. I did not know that the existing staff would resist my every move, and that I would have to blast the place clean and install my own team. I charged into the breach, making things up as I went along, running home to breastfeed my baby girl. Often, I would jump into a cab, stranding the car at work. I just gave up on details.

From the minute I stepped in the door, Simone would be in my arms until I left again the next morning. She took what she needed, cuddling flush against my side through the night. We called her pithead, for she would burrow into my armpit, her hot little baby head making my tired body sweat. Her long toes would tickle her dad all night, the three of us in a double bed, Mommy and Daddy already long of limb and short of space. I had no hippie romance about a family bed. This was survival. I had said yes to the damn job, and I was already careening on empty. I needed all the sleep I could get.

I'm glad I didn't know how hard it would be. I wasn't wise enough to manage my energy, and I was susceptible to getting emotionally involved, in everything. In addition to leaving my car at work, I went through half a dozen wallets and cellphones. I got into the wrong cars when I was expecting my husband to collect me in the evenings. More than once, I unloaded my day on completely innocent people who just happened to be parked near where I thought Jake might be. Really. I was so tired that I could get into a white Neon and think it was his green Jaguar.

Then, I had to fire an editor in Vancouver. That was a real low point. I had to fly out there, do the deed and find someone new. But that meant I had to stop breastfeeding. I put it off for six months, but things got worse. I was tortured. I didn't want to leave my kids.

This was supposed to be the year I had alone with them, and here I was, not home and far away. Sitting in the bathtub of my Vancouver hotel, sobbing as my breasts ached, I expressed a soured final meal into the water gone cold around me. I felt pretty damn sorry for myself, and remembered, too late, the tsunami of depression that comes, for me, with taking a baby off the boob.

I went home to juggle evening events, speaking engagements, launch parties and client schmoozes while still keeping up with bedtime stories. I wondered how my young kids saw the woman in the gown, who floated through the house at dinner, plucking broccoli or cheesy noodles off their plates and then clopping off to another gala. I suspect they will remember those years as the golden time. I suspect they would rather have Mommy and Daddy and Nanny together in one house instead of what they have now: shuttling back and forth between parents and houses as divorced kids.

One vacation, in Jamaica, just before things started to slide downhill, Simone clung to me happily for ten days straight, simply saying, "Mommy back." I could have learned from that. My body, my energy, my grip were all starting to give. I was bone-tired and drinking too much; it seemed the only answer. My lifelong method of dealing with stress had been to crank up the volume and spin. I'm soothed by the tornado I create, and it's the perfect camouflage for avoidance.

Mostly, I was bored with my job. I just couldn't write "Perfect Skin" and "Sexy Hair!" cover lines any more. I balked at encroaching corporate constraints: I couldn't do another peppy management retreat where building Lego is an insight into leadership skills. The truth is, I became more enamoured of the perks—Dolce and Gabbana suits and Prada shoes—and I lost the plot. I got fired. I got a payout. I got out.

There is a piece of artwork my son, Max, did while I was working full tilt. I keep it now in the box of keepsakes under my bed. He cut out pictures of me from all different issues of *Fashion* magazine, glued them to a piece of construction paper and overlaid them with clippings of house plants. Brilliant boy.

Once I had lost the vision for the magazine, I also lost my grip on my identity. I lost the vision for the rest my life, my marriage, my place in the world, my role as a mother. I refuse to sugarcoat it any more: the years that followed sucked. I had no experience being unsuccessful. It was a drag not to have an assistant with a posh French accent sorting your days and dealing with your drycleaning. (She was awesome. Even my mother, calling me at work, would be told it "wasn't possible" to speak to me.)

The first time I heard my kids talking about my being fired, I was horrified. Like every parent, I was shocked by how much they saw, heard and tried to normalize. Our lives had never been normal. That was the one thing I could see clearly, the thing I wanted to change. When my husband left, I finally had the year alone with my kids. We began forming our own rituals, to replace the happy-family stuff we used to do. The rituals are still in place. Every Friday is Movie Night in Canada. Once a week or so we go to the Drake, where we sit in the sun on the roof in summer and by the fire in winter, playing hangman. We walk up and down Queen Street and stop in to see friends in galleries and second-hand clothing stores. They get to play Bedamon on the cement floor of 69 Vintage while Mommy tries on clothes with her friend Kealan. Who said rituals can't be self-indulgent?

I'm now struggling to live on a budget, even to pay the most basic bills. My marriage, which was once magic, is gone. In hindsight, I wish we had dealt with it better, but great love ends in great anguish. We ate each other alive. We waited until the kids were in bed, but I know they saw the safe unit splinter. I will live out the rest of my life with the guilt I felt on hearing my son say, "At least Daddy won't slam the door on your foot, Mommy."

I'm a soccer mom now, even though I'm the only one on the field doing interviews on a cellphone, wearing Chanel. My kids will always have a wacky mom, and I don't think they'd trade that. I make cupcakes. I bribe soccer coaches to appear at birthday parties. The end of this story is unfolding. I ache having them with me only half the time. I swallow my bile when they talk about the woman their father is dating. But I meant to have kids with him, and for better and worse, I want them to have both a father and a mother equally, even if they can't have us at the same time.

I have started to date again, a comic array of men: a multimillionaire mathematician turned vanity philanthropist who whisked me to Mexico on the second date; a male dancer (classically trained modern, not the naughty thing you are thinking); a painter. The other half of my life I spend joyously locked down with the kids.

I look at what I do now to make ends meet, freelancing as a writer. I have no career trajectory. I just want to be able to pick up my kids each afternoon and go home. Maybe I'm lucky to have worn out the glamour. There is no better day for me than a perfectly ordinary day. I pinch myself standing in the kitchen, whacking schnitzel and steaming green beans, working on birthday party invites for Simone and a pioneer project with Max. There's a fire log burning. We read Harry Potter and talk about who has the fastest ship in the galaxy.

Han Solo, of course.

THIN WHITE LINE

CAROL SHABEN

I came to motherhood at knifepoint. I didn't feel the scalpel's razor edge as it sliced through flesh and sinew and muscle. I didn't see blood, the slow seep of crimson across my belly. All this was hidden by a disposable blue drape.

The anaesthetist had inserted a needle in the base of my spine—a sharp, painful prick. I felt the slow advance of numbness, then the cool, wet touch of an ice cube on my abdomen.

"Can you feel this?" she asked.

"No."

She traced the ice cube up an imaginary centre line over the mound of belly. I could sense more than feel its movement, the trickles of water that beaded down the taut arc of my skin onto the soft mattress below.

"This?" She moved the cube up farther toward my breastbone, but its icy touch did not register.

"No."

"You're ready," she said, nodding to the surgeon.

I didn't think of the sharp blade of steel that would open me, splaying the flesh of my body so my baby could be born. I didn't think of how that baby would change the landscape of my life. Nor did I understand that as this new life was handed to me from behind the blue drape, part of an old one was being taken away.

I wasn't ready.

HOW IS IT, I wonder, that I could have been so unprepared for motherhood? When my husband, Riyad, and I first met, we spoke of many things—our dreams, our desires. I told him that I expected, one day, to be a mother. This wasn't mysterious or unusual. In a vague, confident way, I was certain that motherhood would be another checkmark added to my plus column of experiences— travel, work, friendships—a heady, self-indulgent collection of adventures. The thought that I might have to give something up just didn't occur to me. After all, as a teenager and young adult, I had largely gotten what I'd wanted. This was the tenor of life for women of my generation. Sure, there were jobs we didn't get, loves we lost, opportunities we missed. But mostly, our lives had been about having more, not less.

Sacrifice? What did I know about sacrifice? I am part of the catch-and-release generation. We sink our hooks into experiences just to try them on. When things aren't to our liking, we often let go, moving blithely on to the next big fish. We remember little of the time when women were expected to make few demands and to have even fewer aspirations—when we were judged to be at our best, our most praiseworthy, when devoting ourselves to others.

My twenties and a good part of my thirties passed before I even considered motherhood. I lived in a realm where not only did I not have to *think* about children, I rarely had to encounter them. I had single, career-minded friends whom I dined with in trendy, adult-oriented restaurants. If anyone under five feet tall toting a pack of crayons was seated anywhere near me, I asked to be moved. On the long flights I often took for work, I seethed in annoyance if I was within ten rows of a screaming child, and glared at its mother with an expression that said, *Why can't you shut that brat up?* Basically, I was tuned out of kiddyland—so tuned out that joining the mom club was a complete revelation.

I was thirty-seven when I got pregnant, and I felt as if I had it all—a great relationship, a successful business and the time and money to do what I wanted. Riyad and I worked hard and played harder. We had a funky townhouse near Jericho Beach in Vancouver and a garageful of gear—climbing equipment, tents, skis, windsurfers, bikes—you name it. We were into scaling rock walls and grinding up local peaks with eighteen-kilo packs on our backs. We indulged our whims, and becoming a mother wasn't going to change the equation.

I was seven weeks pregnant when the bubble burst. It was a Saturday morning. Valentine's Day. Riyad and I were curled up in bed reading the newspaper and drinking coffee, just as we had done for six besotted years. Our cherished weekend ritual was to read the paper front to back, passionately discuss the events of the day, eat breakfast at noon, then head out on some adventure. The two of us against the world.

On this particular morning, Riyad folded the newspaper and turned toward me. "Let's ski up the backcountry trail to the top of Mount Seymour," he said.

Normally, I was game for anything, but this morning my entire body screamed *bad idea.* I'd felt like puking since my eyes opened. A knot of bile had taken up permanent residence in the pit of my stomach since I'd conceived, and my body felt as if it had been slammed by a truck. But, hey, it was a beautiful day and I wasn't going to give up on adventure for a half-ounce embryo without a fully developed backbone.

An hour later, we were halfway up a crusted mountain trail. Riyad was several metres ahead, manoeuvring nimbly, while I felt

like a walrus on ice. My skis slipped constantly. Tentatively, I slid one
forward, willing it to grip the slick incline. It didn't. Suddenly I was
sliding backward, my skis shooting out on either side. I grappled to
dig in my poles, to stop myself flying down the mountain.

"Riyad, help!" I cried as the ends of my skis splayed apart
behind me and I fell forward with a whoomph—my stomach hitting
the hard-packed snow.

I heard him laughing. "You look like a giraffe."

I knew I probably looked hilarious, my skis flattened under me,
arms flailing, chest and chin on ice. But at that moment, I could
think of nothing less funny.

"That's it!" I screamed. I was getting off this mountain. I had
only to turn my skis around, point them back in the direction I'd
come and glide smoothly home. But I didn't. Instead, I took a deep
breath, heaved myself up and pushed on, miserably, to the top.
When we finally reached the summit, the vista was awe-inspiring,
but a cloud hung over me. I knew that I wouldn't get back to this
remote, carefree place for a long time. I had taken the first slippery
step away from a life I loved.

The only road map I had for the journey into motherhood was
one I knew I couldn't follow. My mother had five children, each a
year apart. I imagined that we popped out like gum balls, round and
perfect and protected by a colourful sugar coating. Pictures of our
family show us lined up, eldest to youngest, neatly dressed, the girls
in matching green velvet smocks my mother had sewn, our wild
dark hair carefully combed. She baked cookies and bread and volunteered for the hospital auxiliary to care for the ill and elderly. She
dropped us off at the skating rink at six in the morning and was
there with hot chocolate and warm cinnamon toast wrapped in tinfoil when we got off the ice at eight. Her world now seems to me
long gone, as strange and distant as those frosty mornings at the
rink—a world of wholesome meals turned out three times a day, of

dainty canapés for once-weekly bridge games with other moms, of clothes mended, washed, and pressed like new.

Growing up, I was only vaguely aware of what she might have sacrificed, of what she gave up or perhaps never even considered so I could have more. Was she content to stand on the front stoop and send me off to a bigger life? To university in the city? To India to float lazily down the Ganges and watch the funeral pyres consuming the flesh of those who had died of hardship?

A year after my birth, Betty Friedan published *The Feminine Mystique*. Had my mother had the time to read it, would she have agreed with Friedan that domestic life was a "comfortable concentration camp" that denied women their identities?

By the time I was old enough to read *The Feminine Mystique*, it seemed to me that the ideal mother—all-giving, self-sacrificing—no longer existed. My friends and I embraced the feminist movement's disdain for caring for the home and kids. We wholeheartedly rejected the ideal of female altruism. Forget the service ethos, we said. There was more to women than caring for the old and sick and educating our children.

In my second trimester, the nausea was a dim memory, and that "Oh, she's put on weight" puffiness had morphed into the obvious bulge of pregnancy. Riyad and I headed out to our favourite local café. We hadn't walked two blocks when I saw a woman pushing a stroller. I smiled congenially. Another block passed. Another stroller. Then another. As we neared the café, I was startled by the number of young mothers I saw. "Wow," I said to Riyad, "do you see that?"

"What?"

"It's Stroller City out here. Our neighbourhood is *totally* changing."

He laughed, shaking his head. "It's no different than it always was. You're just seeing it for the first time."

Perhaps my powers of perception were a bit dim, but at least my organizational skills were intact. I'd started arranging my consulting contracts to wrap up a couple of weeks before my fall due date. I told my clients I'd be taking a few months off but that I'd be back in the saddle in six months. I ignored anyone who tried to tell me otherwise. I was prepared, capable and in complete control of my future. I was setting up my life to return to normal after my child was born.

No one told me there'd be no normal to return to.

In my third trimester, I registered for a prenatal class. I diligently took notes. Riyad and I learned birthing positions and practised them. I drew tiny stick figures on chairs, kneeling on all fours, squatting, lying on beds. I had a list of what I'd need to pack for the hospital. I picked out the music that would play softly in the background.

On the last day of our class, I decided to walk the hallways instead of watching a video on C-section deliveries.

"It might upset you," Riyad had said, knowing how squeamish I get around the sight of blood.

"Then I don't need to watch it." Why should I, I thought? I was strong, fit and healthy. There'd been nothing out of the ordinary during my pregnancy. No excessive weight gain. No high blood pressure. Besides, my mother had five vaginal births without a hitch. No, a C-section was definitely not part of the plan.

I settled back into my chair just as the instructor introduced a lighthearted closing exercise. She held up a sheet of paper divided into two columns of twelve squares. "These squares represent the hours of the day," she said, handing a sheet to every couple. She then offered a stack of labelled Post-it notes to go with each sheet. "These are the tasks you'll need to do after your baby is born," she explained. "Fit them into the empty spaces of the day."

We spread the Post-it notes out on the carpet in front of us and took stock:

Breastfeeding baby	8
Diaper change	5
Meals	3
Laundry	1
Dishes/Cleaning	1
Groceries/Shopping	1
Visits from/with friends and family	1

As the page filled up, I felt a slow panic rising.

"What about sleep," someone asked. Everyone laughed. But inside me, something was exploding—my idealized view of how life with a child would be.

Where *were* the spaces in the day for sleep, career, sex, back-country skiing with my husband, reading, writing, freedom, procrastination, independence, spontaneity? How was it that in twelve hours of my baby prep class—in thirty-seven years of living—a mere ten minutes was devoted to telling me what life would be like *after* my child was born? How could it be that I'd spent almost half a lifetime being female, educated, and competent and didn't understand this fundamental fact of motherhood?

I pushed these thoughts from my mind. Instead, I focused on the upcoming delivery. I had typed and printed out a birth plan:

1. Spend as much time as possible labouring at home.
2. Use the shower during labour or, if available, request the delivery room with the big tub.
3. Avoid the use of drugs or medical interventions unless absolutely necessary.

AT THIRTY-SEVEN WEEKS, I visited my doctor for what had now become a once-weekly checkup. Everything was going as planned. Everything, that is, except I was three weeks from my due date, and the doctor couldn't find the baby's head. She moved her hands over the mound of my lower abdomen, pressing here and there in search of the unyielding orb of skull. "He must be engaged," she said, meaning his head had dropped into position at my cervix.

Good, I thought. He, like me, is getting ready.

"I should do a quick pelvic exam," she offered. "Just to be sure."

I'm not a fan of pelvic exams, but I told myself it was a small price to pay. I lay back on the examining table, the paper crinkling beneath me. My doctor pulled on a latex glove, releasing the wristband with a snap. Her hand stretched once as if testing the fit, then moved toward me. I felt an uncomfortable bite of pressure, then her fingers moving inside me, reaching. Suddenly she stopped. Surprise flickered on her face.

"Your baby is breech," she said.

"What!" I was in disbelief. "It can't be."

She stared at me mutely.

"Well," I said. "There must be something that can be done."

Two days later, I was in the hospital writhing in pain while two doctors attempted to manually turn my baby around by reefing on the outside of my abdomen. The pain was unbelievable, but I refused medication. I can handle this, I thought. I focused on the rhythmic sound of the baby's heartbeat monitor and the small, watery figure on the screen of the ultrasound machine.

"You're doing great," one of the doctors said. "We've got him turned halfway."

They reefed again. I closed my eyes and bit my bottom lip as a wave of pain tore through me. Then suddenly, mercifully, the doctors stopped. I gulped big breaths of air, waiting for the pain to subside. As it did, I noticed that the sounds from the monitor were slowing down, the quick pulses of my baby's heart losing momentum. I looked up at the doctors, and they seemed momentarily numb, their eyes impossibly large and full of concern. Riyad's face had gone completely white.

"Quick. Turn him back," I heard the obstetrician say, and the pain swept over me again. I gritted my teeth and squeezed my eyes shut once more. I was still determined to have this baby my way. I'd be damned if I let a foot-first fetus set the agenda.

I look back now and wonder how I could have been so naive. Today, I live in a world of half-formed thoughts and half-finished sentences where there is a running battle between mommydom and me-time. I'd rather have sleep than sex, and guilt bleeds into the margins of every choice I make.

The end of my previous life didn't come immediately. The first months with baby were blissful. I lounged in my PJs until noon. I breastfed and watched Oprah. I took afternoon naps when my son did or went for long runs with my new, high-end baby jogger—inert offspring bundled snugly inside.

Then, at about eight months postpartum, a client called with a big contract, and reality hit. At first, I congratulated myself. I'd put Max on the wait-list for the best daycare in the city before he was even born. Hadn't I done the hard part? I figured there wasn't much more to it than dropping him off and getting back to work.

On his first day, I took him down and settled him in the middle of the bright, kid-friendly space. Max seemed amused at first. He picked up a plastic cellphone and jabbed the colourful buttons. Nothing happened. "We don't replace batteries when they run out," said Elsie, one of the daycare providers. Her bushy eyebrows rose conspiratorially, as if to say, Would you want a dozen toys around beeping and chiming and playing "Twinkle, Twinkle, Little Star" over and over again?

I laughed—a forced, stiff laugh—and nodded. Be extra nice to the daycare provider, I said to myself. Then she will be extra nice to your child.

Elsie was wiry and middle-aged, her frizzy, flyaway hair streaked with grey. It looked as if she didn't own a comb, and though it was only eight-thirty in the morning, she appeared exhausted. Our moment of bonhomie passed, and I was still standing awkwardly in front of her. "So," she said, "we'll see you at five."

I swallowed hard and knelt on the carpet next to Max. "Bye-bye, sweetie. Mommy has to go now." He looked at me blankly, but there was a shadow of uncertainty in his eyes. I hugged him tightly as Elsie looked on.

"Best to be quick," she said.

Hesitantly, I stood and headed for the door. Max immediately started to cry. "Mama. Mama."

I waved and smiled. *Keep walking*, I told myself.

"MaMAAAAA!" He was wailing now, his face twisted with incomprehension. He began to crawl toward me, his pudgy little hands and Robeez-clad feet scrambling furiously along the worn carpet until Elsie scooped him up. My last glimpse of my son was in the arms of a haggard, wild-haired stranger—his body contorted with screams as I walked out the door.

It's like pulling off a Band-Aid, I told myself on the drive home—the pain will be short and intense, gone by the time you sit down in front of the papers piled high on your desk. This is *good*, I said. *You love your work. It's important to you.* But my pep talk didn't wash. I didn't return home buoyant and unencumbered, ready to happily climb the stairs two at a time to my computer. Instead, I lay curled in a fetal position on my living room couch, crying—every inch of my being aching with loss.

There have been many separations since then. There have been intense work projects that I have attacked feverishly during naptime, cursing Max if he awoke early. There have been countless nights when I put the coffee pot on after his bedtime, and worked, bleary-eyed, into the night. I have tried to cobble my work life together, but everything seems fragmented—my desk time, my powers of concentration, my desire.

These days, my most passionate discussions with Riyad are about who does dishes or bedtime. Just as the prenatal exercise with too many Post-it notes predicted, I scramble to fit it all in, the pieces that were there before, the ones added. Time for my husband. Time for my child. Time for me. The canvas of my life is smudged. There are no clean lines. No primary colours. I am continually torn between my desire—even need—to work and my feelings that by doing so, I am depriving my child in some fundamental way.

"Sacred" is the word that immediately precedes "sacrifice" in the dictionary. It is defined as something that is unassailable, inviolable, highly valued and important. Women like me were brought up to believe that our personal aspirations and identities were sacred. So we hang on for dear life, loath to let go of our hard-earned uniqueness of self. Instead, we layer on a new life—the life of mother. And what motherhood demands of us is not just our love and desire but a deep cut into the essence of who we once were. A cleaving apart of the life we were once driven to create for ourselves and our new reality. How could any of us be ready?

Deciding to have a C-section was my first act of sacrifice. I didn't want to be cut open—to let go of motherhood's rite of passage—even when my doctor advised me that breech deliveries were risky.

"Who's stronger," my sister asked when I told her I was agonizing over the decision, "you or the baby?" I should have realized then that I was no longer in control. That there was no going back to my previous life.

I was beaten by a six-pound baby, and it was only the beginning. I still struggle with sacrifice. Some days, I rail against motherhood's repetitiveness and responsibilities. Other days, I feel I might be moving toward a new identity, a new sense of myself as a woman and a person. The predictable progress of my life before motherhood has been replaced by a messier, more ambiguous process of becoming. But I think I am closer to embracing the words of the American artist Charles DuBois, who said, "The important thing is this: To be able at any moment to sacrifice what we are for what we could become."

There is a scar on my abdomen where the scalpel cut into me, a small crease marking the place from which my baby was taken. After my son was born the incision site was red, sore and angry-looking. It hurt to laugh. I walked slowly and carefully then, feeling the pull of tender skin that had been stitched back together. I couldn't carry anything heavy, and I worried that sudden movements would tear the wound open. Today, I look down and see only a thin white line. It will always be with me, but some days I almost forget it's there.

A DIFFERENT KIND OF JET-SET LIFE

MONIKA DEOL

I'm whipping through the airport with three kids and a baby in tow. The lineup to check in looks lovely, and I juggle through with the baby, diaper bag, my purse, my roll-on, and the three assorted bags that are packed with books and other things to do.

It turns out we're all sitting apart. The kids aren't happy, but I assure them that nice, kind people will help us out by exchanging seats. We settle into the waiting area and I do a quick bag and body count. Yes, they're all here. Just then a voice announces the flight is delayed. Oh joy.

Out come the "things to do." I start to nurse the baby and wonder what I was thinking when I told my family we'd be there for a fortieth birthday party this weekend. My five-year-old son lets me know that he needs to go to the bathroom. Now! Okay. I can't leave my eight-year-old and seven-year-old daughters sitting here alone, nor can I leave the bags unattended. So it's hurry, hurry, pack up your things, honey. Now!

Grab the bags. Where's the bathroom? Yes, my boy, you do have to go in the ladies' room because Mommy's not going into the men's. We rush in and there's a line! I love this about women's wash-rooms. All of a sudden everyone has to go. Ah, disaster averted. My son jumps into a stall just as the tap dance he's doing begins to lose steam. People are not impressed as I stand guard while, one by one, my troops file in and out. They then hog a sink to wash their hands. I smile and apologize and get everyone out the door. One more quick bag and body count.

We get back to the waiting area and our seats are gone. So I set up camp in the corner on the carpet and proceed to nurse the baby, who has been very patient.

It's amazing that despite this non-stop action, I continue to adore these little creatures. I love watching how they handle them-selves and observe the world around them. They're constantly bringing a new perspective to even the most mundane events.

The fragrant bouquet of a dirty diaper brings me back to real-ity. Even harsher is the warm, wet feeling on my arm. We don't call my youngest daughter the Master Blaster for nothing. I sit and laugh for a second, until my oldest daughter asks why. I tell her it's the only thing I can do at this point. I glance at the baby, and yes, this is going to be a messy job. So it's back to the washroom with all four kids and all our luggage.

As we return, the lineup to board is starting. It seems we've missed the "business and small children" call. Of course. The kids are being angels with their patience. I didn't even have to resort to the last trick in my bag—Cheerios.

I always love the walk down the plane aisle. People averting their eyes thinking, Please God, don't let that woman and her small tribe be sitting next to me. I can't blame them. When I was single, I was always horrified when a whining, crying, kicking child sat near me. I used to travel a lot. I remember whirling into the plane at the last minute—no baggage to check. My carry-on was always crammed with too much makeup and thigh-high boots. (Now, it's a change of clothes for each child and two sets of sweats for me in case more than one child vomits.) Back then, my travel was booked and paid for by my employer. I had not a care in the world except for the important job I was about to do.

I would sit there calmly and think about the upcoming shoot, what I could buy, which parties I should go to and what celeb-filled club would let me in free. And now, here I was, magically transformed into the person I once dreaded.

The flight attendant kindly informs me that there's nothing they can do about our separate seating until after takeoff. If we'd boarded when they called for passengers with infants and small children, she says, they might have been able to change our seats. I feel like telling her I was not exactly getting myself a latte, but I figure there's no point. We'll just go with the flow here.

I think back to my old life in Toronto, working in television as a host and anchor for MuchMusic and Citytv. It feels like a century ago. At the time, I could never have imagined making the decisions that I ultimately did—giving it all up to raise my children at home. How do women find that balance between self-fulfillment and these small tykes taking over your life? I've gone back to work twice since my first child was born and left after a year each time. I just found that trying to be everything to everybody at the same time was not for me. Something had to slide, and it wasn't going to be my children or my husband.

I used to love the adrenalin rush of all that pressure and all those deadlines: that flying-by-the-seat-of-your-pants energy as you took on way too much, and the huge sense of accomplishment when it all fell into place. I think the magazine editor Bonnie Fuller has it right. It is exhilarating to have much too much. It's absolutely affirming to take on great big chunks of life and revel in the fact that you took it for all it was worth.

I never imagined when I was single that having children would give me the same kind of rush. Life with four kids is full-on, an all-hands-on-deck kind of challenge. Children today live speedy, complex lives, and keeping it all going is as manic and demanding as any successful career. And playgrounds and schools can be just as political as any office.

After we take off, there are nice, kind people who volunteer to move so that I can be close to my kids. My kids are thrilled, their ex-seatmates are relieved and all is good in the world. This is when it always hits me. I imagine my mother, all those years ago, with her husband and three little children, six years and under, on a plane from India, headed halfway across the world to Canada. Forever. I imagine the courage that took. The uncertainty must have been daunting.

My parents were private school teachers in India, and they had teaching jobs waiting for them here. They were arriving in the heady Trudeau years, when immigrants were being welcomed with open arms by a leader who had a global view of the world. But that flight would forever change their lives, and they knew it. At the time, they weren't sure if that was a good thing. They were leaving behind a comfortable, middle-class life in India with maids and cooks and drivers—all to give us a better education. My father taught at the National Defence Academy in Pune, fitting in classes around golf games at the club. My mother taught at a boys' school, one of the very few women of her generation to get a university education and then, horrors, actually use it to work! After marriage! It was their first time on a plane, and it was going to be one heck of a ride.

All these years later, I still marvel at their blind leap of faith. My mother was a working mother in small-town Canada. She had no choice. There were no immigrant families with stay-at-home moms. She was on her own: no household staff, no extended family. She juggled her three kids and career with quiet determination. I always say teachers have the best jobs for the juggle. When we were home, she was home. It never even occurred to us that our mom "worked."

Two summer holidays stand out in my mind. My parents decided they had to do their master's degrees over again in Canada, to keep the competitive edge in a saturating job market. So my father went off to Queen's and my mother enrolled at the University of Toronto to study for the summer. My mother was a full-time student and lived with her three young children in a one-bedroom apartment off Spadina. Remarkably, she went to school all day, spent time with us in the evening and then studied until the wee hours of the morning before making breakfast and heading off to class again. She managed to pull off stellar grades and keep us in line.

One day, I decided to help her by cleaning the carpets. And I did a mighty fine job rubbing the "soap" into the rugs. When she came home, exhausted but smiling, she realized I had actually waxed the carpets. Needless to say we didn't get our damage deposit back when we went back home. But she was very patient and downright calm about the whole thing, something I've yet to duplicate in a similar situation.

In a weak moment, my parents bought a large grain and dairy farm in Manitoba in the mid-'70s. So now my mother was waking up at 5 a.m., helping with all the chores that come with a hundred cows and then teaching a full day at the local high school. After a quick cup of tea at 4 p.m., it was back out to the barn for more chores. Somehow, she managed to keep it all together and still be a loving and reliable parent.

Her three daughters didn't always reciprocate that love. We were too busy giving her a workout with our culture-clash syndrome. The first time I asked my parents to let me go to a concert, I got a firm and resounding no. After much begging, rationalizing and finally threatening suicide, I won, sort of. My father relented and said yes, I could go, but I had to take my mother with me. Miraculously, she said yes. So my mother and I rocked out to AC/DC and Aerosmith: me in heaven and my mother with her fingers in her ears, smiling at me as though she really was enjoying herself. Really. To this day I don't know what's more perverse: my mother's agreeing to go with me or that I didn't even hesitate to ask her in the first place.

NOW THAT I'M A MOTHER, I wonder what inspired her. What gave her strength in the bleak moments?

I try to put myself in her place and think about what I would have done faced with the same challenges. I honestly don't know if I would have had the fortitude. I probably would have stayed in my nice comfortable life in India. I certainly can't imagine picking up my four young children and moving to a different country. Any country. For any reason. I've asked my mother many times why she left, and her answer has always been the same: the adventure, the education, and most important, the opportunities for her daughters.

I settle into my seat on the airplane and I find myself smiling again. My son asks me why. "Because sometimes people think it's so much work for Mommy to run around with four kids and really it's not. Your grandma did so much more with less and never complained." My son smiles back and looks out the window.

I wish I could have told my mother back then not to worry about me. I gave her such a hard time and made so many decisions against her wishes. From being a club DJ, to starting my own rock band, to moving to Toronto alone to take a chance in television. Not the hopes and dreams that Indian parents had for their daughters in the 1980s. She could have relaxed. I would never have done anything to really hurt her or make her feel sorry for the sacrifices she made along the way. Even in my most rebellious moments, I got it. I got that she loved me and that her children meant more to her than anything. I got that there was no safer place on earth than a mother's arms. I got that no one would ever be as proud of me for the smallest things. I knew where to find my biggest ally.

I look at my four children and realize that we are on our own journey. It doesn't take moving to a new country. We're facing our own awesome challenges in different ways and taking risks that are just as breathtaking. Taking a break from my career has felt daunting. I worked very hard to hit a certain benchmark in Canadian media, and I was very happy with what I achieved. When I worked, I gave it 110 percent, and my career was a very fulfilling part of my life. I enjoyed every second of it. But I'm not willing to give my family any less. I love living in the moment and celebrating life in all its big and small glories. I really don't want to outsource the day-to-day experiences I have with my children. I don't want another woman living what should be my family life. And I feel so lucky that my husband and I even have the choice to let the kids be immersed in one parent's full-time attention. It's not just the cuddly, fun stuff: the hugs and first words and being at every school event. It's the discipline and being there to influence their thoughts on who we are, what our culture and values stand for, trying to imprint some sense of character and what's important in life.

Someday I hope they'll look back and realize I made some sacrifices too. I did it because they are the most important things in the world to me and because with careers, you get a second shot. Maybe not the same glory. Maybe not the same glamour. But with your children, you get one time around and then they're out there, taking what you've given them in the short time that you have. And so far I think we're doing all right.

I AM MY FATHER
SHEREE-LEE OLSON

I am my father.

Except my father never cried at work. He'd come home and my mother would pour him a Scotch and he'd shout at us instead. I come home and my husband pours me a glass of merlot, and sometimes I shout at him, and sometimes I tell him I cried at work.

"What about?" he asks.

"What do you think? I want to quit. I've had enough."

This is unhelpful to a man trying to wrangle two cranky boys who have a mixed relationship with dinner and homework. This is particularly unhelpful to a man who would rather be doing anything other than what he is doing now, heating up yet another plate of pasta that is destined to remain uneaten while wolfing down bites of his own dinner and trolling through the day's increment of paperwork from the school apparatchiks. The fact is, a lot of days we both hate our jobs.

"The difference is," he says, raising his voice over the machine-gun fire coming from the shooter game on the computer, "you get to come home at the end of the day, whereas I—"

"Whereas you get to be *alone* during the day," I say. And though I know I'm not supposed to, I wonder what he did today anyway. "Whereas I—Jesus Christ, why is the cat sleeping on my new jacket?"

Some days, it's better for everyone if I just take my wine upstairs.

I TAKE MY WINE upstairs in search of Zen. Sometimes I find Zen in a British mystery or a *Seinfeld* rerun; sometimes I find it lying on my bed watching the shadows of leaves play across the wall. I lie there in a cocoon of guilt and resentment, wondering when the cocoon will split apart to reveal what I was supposed to be: a great mother.

I am not a great mother. Instead, I have become the other parent.

But I am not a twenty-first-century father. I am the father I grew up with, back in the days when fathers were gods smelling of cologne and tobacco, who liked to "shoot the breeze" after work with their good buddies. If they came home late, they were not apologetic as much as amused at their own incorrigibility. They lectured their children over dinner and tickled them mercilessly before bed. They never did dishes.

I never do dishes.

I have not done dishes since I went back to work thirteen years ago. For thirteen years, I have eaten my husband's meals thinking the same thing: that I could do it better. That my boys would be there in the kitchen with me, baking cookies, making omelettes. That their fingernails would be clean, their teeth brushed, their clothes tidy. That they would not cry about school.

It's a complete delusion.

It's a delusion because if I ever really had the skill set required to be that irony-challenged creation, a "supermom"—and I doubt that I ever did—they are certainly lost now. The latest studies from the field of brain science only confirm what our pop-psych prophets have been telling us forever: by doing, you become. My husband when I met him was a charming domestic savage who worked in a bookstore by day and hung out in bars at night. He lived in a basement and washed his dishes in the tub. Now, he is an object of schoolyard respect and envy among my colleagues—a man who has gone the distance. An actual stay-at-home dad!

Behind the scenes, of course, it was kitchen-sink Darwinism, the two of us locked in a struggle for household domination. Mr. Mom never did learn to set the table properly or dust the bookshelves. Just as Ms. Dad—that would be me—never learned to shut up and let him get on with it. We drank resentment in our morning tea and resentment in our wine at night. He resented the relentless drudgery, the social isolation, but most of all he resented my criticism. Nothing in his life had prepared him for the monumental task of keeping two small demanding creatures—underslept, infection-prone imps—fed and clean and healthy and amused. His mantra: *I'm doing the best that I can.* Mine: *Not good enough.*

I resented him for not having to plunge daily into the stress-grind of a deadline-driven job, for not appreciating what I thought he had—time to *think*. But that was not what he had. He was a man under fire, scrambling as the bullets whizzed by. There were close calls he never told me about, like the time our second son was choking and my husband did the baby version of the Heimlich manoeuvre—just as we'd learned in first-aid class—upended him and smacked him on the back until out popped a shiny penny. Could I have done that so quickly and effectively?

My husband is good at his job. He is excellent at the long slog, certainly more patient than I am, and he's had his moments of triumph. Surely my children's prodigious appetite for books has to do with the fact that their father read to them every single night for ten years, firing their imaginations with scenes from the Hundred Acre Woods and Redwall and Hogwarts, sparking their brains with words like *elevenses* and *garderobe* and *animagus*. I can count on one hand the times I read to them at bedtime without nodding off immediately.

But I still resented him, most of all for the fact of his own resentment—for not wanting to be where he was, which is where I wanted to be.

THIS IS WHAT you learn when you grow up: temporary's just another word for permanent. Our house was an ancient semi held together with duct tape and crack filler. Our finances were in the same shape as our roof: occasional leaks, always the fear of a deluge. We cycled through periods of despair and absurd optimism; we still do. It'll be better when. It'll be okay until.

I left my baby with a man who had never held one before his own was born. I left him *until*. Until I could figure something out: go part-time, start a business, sell a novel, any fantasy at all to feed my desperation to stay within that magic circle of first baby love. But we had a mortgage, and exactly one career between us, and it was mine.

Some mothers are happy going back to work, but I was not one of them. I had waited years to have this baby; it felt Kafkaesque to simply walk out the door at the end of my six-month leave, pretending to be okay. There is a surreal disconnect required to resume the role of the competent professional when your breasts are leaking. I felt banished: like the mermaid in the fairy tale who is forced each day to take on human form, for whom walking on land is an agony she bears for love.

Perhaps there is no more potent metaphor for the dilemmas of postmodern motherhood than milk. My employer routinely published stories extolling the benefits of breastfeeding, but there was no quiet place at *The Globe and Mail* in which to pump. (There had been a lounge off the women's washroom known as the "cramp recovery room," but one day we arrived to find the door replaced by drywall.) Supply and demand are well-known concepts to the nursing mother; you cannot have one without the other. My son was getting formula during the day, yet I still entertained hopes that I would be able to feed him morning and night indefinitely, that I would go home and he would be waiting famished in his father's arms, his little legs pumping with excitement, his drooling toothless smile aimed at my chest.

That lasted a couple of weeks. We both tried. But he had never been a strong nurser, and I was not a letdown queen like my girlfriend, my mentor in the baby business. There is nothing more crushing than having a small human tear himself off your nipple in howling fury because he *isn't getting enough*. But he wouldn't take a bedtime bottle from me, because I had followed the advice of the baby books and scrupulously avoided giving him one while I was nursing. Even months later, when I tried to give him one, he would arch and shriek for *Daggy*!

Daddy was the bottle man. So what was I?

There is a term from horticulture: hardening off. You put a plant outside during the day, and you bring it into the nursery at night. Eventually you leave it out all the time. It gets used to the conditions. It gets used to the cold. When I try to explain to myself how I became my father, that is the term that comes to mind. I was hardened off.

The metamorphosis did not happen all at once, of course. There were two distinct stages. I was still hoping for another child, and hope is a kind of hothouse. When my second son was born two years after my first, I was determined to do everything better. But mothering is not a linear process, and the things you learned with one do not always apply to the next. My second son—my last—was both easier and harder to leave. Easier because not only did I feel surer of Mr. Mom, but my second was an easier baby. He was a good nurser, a good sleeper. He walked at ten months. People described him as "merry."

What these words do not convey is the intense longing I felt for him during my first days back at the paper. I know now that I was addicted. That every time we cuddled skin to skin under the eaves of my crooked house, my female brain was being flooded with a bliss cocktail of oxytocin and endorphins. When I left him, I went into emotional withdrawal.

I went back to fresh stresses and expanded responsibilities. We were soon to launch a new weekly section, and I was production editor. It was not unusual for me to be there past midnight, trying to weave all the loose threads into something resembling a stylish garment. That meant morning and night breastfeeding, which had gone better with my second, had to end. I missed Halloween that year because it was a Thursday, and Thursdays and Fridays were a full-immersion race to the finish line. By the weekend, I was toast.

The new work demands meant that not only did my husband have to play the role of mom, but of wife as well. He did not like my long hours, and he particularly did not like the fact that I would sometimes come home and take it out on him. He suggested I'd be better off doing something less stressful, but it was unthinkable to me to back down from the challenge, and unlike the husbands of some of my colleagues, he didn't push it.

My job was what it was, and I think he had decided that his job was to be there for me, just the way my mother was there for my father, through a thirty-year military career. It did not matter if we had been fighting; he would pour me a drink when I got home at night, and in the morning he would wake me up with a cup of coffee and the boys would come in and romp under the blankets. The kids don't come in any more, but the morning coffee in bed is still one of the sustaining rituals of my life.

We made it work, but the cost was high. Recently, it occurred to me that my husband has, in fact, been subsidizing my employer for years, by allowing me to work long hours of often unclaimed overtime that would be impossible for most career mothers with young children. (Perhaps the single-income nuclear family was never about what was best for the kids as much as what was best for corporations.) The more I worked, the better he learned to cope on his own. The better he coped, the less I felt the need to rush home.

After my second mat leave, I missed the children with what was at times a physical pain. I had a regular bedtime call with my two-year-old, but often I would be in some kind of crisis when he phoned, or one or the other of the children would be sick and my husband would forget. Sometimes, on a long night, I would cry over my keyboard. There were times when I would creep into the baby's room when I got home late at night and lie on his floor and cry. But there was no way around our separation, and he was in good hands.

They were in good hands. That's what I told people who asked—who still ask, and not always sympathetically—what about the children? Didn't they miss me? The answer to the question is this: they miss you, but not as much as women want to believe.

Once, when I told my older son that I loved him, he said he loved me too, "but only on weekends." He was two. Then, possibly sensing my disappointment, he added that he was "starting" to love me all the time.

"That's okay," I said brightly, hiding the quaver in my voice, swallowing the lump in my throat. "I love you all the time."

It helped that my children were boys. Every family has its own microculture, and ours was urban geek, a kind of wired monasticism that I have come to find comforting. I am not unwelcome when I arrive home to find the three of them playing *Super Smash Bros.* on the GameCube or watching old episodes of *Doctor Who.* But in the world of boy culture, I am mostly an observer.

And what I've observed in my boys has both surprised and changed me. I love their humour, which is a skill I am still learning from their father. I admire their rebellion. I cherish their secret sweetness, and I regret the stoicism that keeps them from telling me how they feel.

The point is, you don't want them to miss you. You want them to be happy with the person at home, whoever it is: Mom, Dad, Nanny, Auntie, Grandma. Oh, but this is a hard, hard lesson for women who have been conditioned their whole lives, both culturally and hormonally, to be Number One to their children.

However absent my father had been in my childhood, I still loved him passionately. That gave me hope that I could forge a similar bond between myself and my boys. My father knew how to choose his moments. He would blow in with cold whiskery cheeks and hug us hard, and that would answer a week's worth of longing. But here's the other half of that scenario: I was always slightly afraid of my father. When things went wrong, I didn't go to him. I went to the safe parent, Mom.

What my father never admitted, and what I believe is one of the most closely guarded secrets of his gender, is that it is hard for men to be Number Two. I started thinking about that when one of my colleagues let slip how "upset" her husband was when the children would not cuddle with him at night but wanted her. In their house, she said, he was not even Number Two, but Number Three, because the nanny was Number One. This was not a sensitive New Age guy talking, either. This was a hard-ass corporate lawyer with a personality to match. Yet I thought immediately of my father. And I thought, That's why they had to be hard. They have always been hurt by the turning away.

We always knew they were vulnerable, these jolly fathers, that their carelessness was a kind of circus trick made possible by the strength of the woman at home. We knew they were helpless without their wives. But I do not think we've recognized, as a culture, how they pined—and still pine—for their babies, for those small warm dense bodies that carry within them their genes, their dreams. I saw this raw need in the grim nursing homes where we visited various ailing grandparents with our firstborn. He would toddle through the lounge, and they would hold their arms out to him from their wheelchairs, these gaunt old men, moaning like sad zombies in some heartbreaking horror film.

I was still smug then; I was still the mother. I would think, Serves them right. They hid that love when they could have given it, and now it haunts them. I like to think I am no longer smug because now I am Number Two. I would not have known these things if I hadn't become my father.

Sometimes it's good knowing you are Number Two. It makes it easier to be humble. I never missed a chance to snuggle my boys in the morning when they were small, but teenagers are much more parsimonious with affection. Now, when I ruffle their hair, they are apt to shout at me. I don't cry the way I used to. And when they accuse me of never being there, I don't try to defend myself. I tell them if there is something I can help them with, they only have to pick up the phone. I think it's a testament to their father that they never do.

And sometimes I wonder if my father ever came home drunk and smoky and sad, as I did when the boys were young, if he crept into our rooms to gaze at us with choked-up love. I think he might have, for he is a man of depths, but if he did, that truth is now lost.

This is what I hope for today: that young fathers will not learn to hide their longing, but will hold on to that tenderness. That the ones I see in the sandbox at the park, the ones who pride themselves on being equal-opportunity parents, will not one day refuse a phone call because they are on deadline or turn away because a child has turned away, that they will not become their own fathers.

There is a consolation, after all, in being Number Two. And, at least for now, my boys do not allow me regret. On those occasional evenings when we're all sitting around and I'm three glasses into the merlot, I sometimes bring up my shortcomings. "You're not allowed to judge," my younger one told me the other night. "You're not the kid. I'm the kid and I say you're a great mom."

That's just it: I may be my father, but I'm also their mother. Just not a stellar one, their gallantry notwithstanding. I love them fiercely and fearfully and I know that is not enough, but like their dad, I am doing the best that I can. Like all parents, I hope they will turn out fine despite us, that they will understand our choices, that they will forgive us.

PART TWO

Anxiety

TREADING WATER
JOANNA STREETLY

My niece Helen sank down, down, down. Suddenly, there she was on the bottom of the pool, like a lost toy. She's three years old now, but she still remembers the time she jumped in after her brother. Her father turned to pick up her life jacket and when he turned back, she was gone. It happened that fast.

EVERY ASPECT OF my life revolves around water. I own a house in Tofino, on the west coast of Vancouver Island, but I don't live in it. I rent it out. But in the basement, I keep a small suite for myself with an office, shower, bed and laundry facilities. When I go home, I go to a little floating house anchored near an island in Clayoquot Sound. I've lived this way for more than ten years. About half of that time, I've lived alone. More recently, I have been living with my partner, Marcel. When I got pregnant, the last thing I worried about was my unusual living situation. At the time, I couldn't imagine how often I would think of Helen sinking and imagine my own child sinking, too.

By motorboat from Tofino, it takes us about twenty minutes to get home, and every time I walk through the door, I breathe in contentment: it fills my lungs with a stirring mix of joy and peace, something I've never found anywhere else. There's a wood stove for heat, a propane stove and oven for cooking, rainwater in the tap and solar panels for the lights and music. This way of living, quiet and rustic and deeply satisfying, has never stopped me from doing anything. An ardent sea kayaker and lover of the outdoors, I have always found great comfort and inspiration in my wild home, where the water slips in and out of the bay outside my windows and the birds and the animals treat me as part of the scenery.

I discovered I was pregnant on my thirty-fifth birthday. It was near Christmas and I was in England visiting my family. Marcel was in Tofino, feeling broke. He had never been interested in starting a family. For me, it was always something to discuss "next year." When I called Marcel late that night, he decided there was no point being negative. "Right on," he said, after a short silence. "We're having a baby."

As expectant parents, we were confident that our relationship would endure, but we found it impossible to envision our future life. How could our tiny house accommodate the needs of another person? We have thirty-eight square metres of open-plan floor space downstairs, with just a little less than that in the loft. Large windows look onto the water and have always given the illusion of space. But illusions cannot house a growing family. We hashed out a plan, then reverted to a state of vague denial.

I imagined that I would maintain my outdoor activities by hopping into my kayak every evening after the baby went to sleep. I had no clue how much I would rely on naptimes to carry out the basics of survival like meals and cleaning. I didn't think about the rain and the open motorboat and how often I might end up confined to the floathouse during the winter. I fabricated a flotation device for an infant, and I didn't worry about anything. I was being positive.

I wrangled enough work at the front desk of the Tofino hospital to get maternity leave, security that my work as a freelance writer and illustrator could never provide. I wondered what would become of the novel I had written, which was being reviewed by various publishers, none of whom had gotten back to me.

Marcel made lists of things to do before the birth: *make money, cut firewood, build the baby's room.*

When the doctor told me that the baby could come "any day," I fell off my cloud of denial with a thump, panicked, and waddled home to nail in the last boards. Suddenly the whole pregnancy became real. Suddenly, I needed a real room for the baby. Now.

In the end, our daughter, Toby, took four days to be born—an expression, perhaps, of her relaxed personality. The arrival of two of my sisters from England, and daily visits by the midwife, made this a joyous, stress-free time. Since Marcel and I had not been able to imagine ourselves as parents, we had no plan to conform to. We fell into step with Toby's rhythms and marvelled at everything.

We were staying in a house on land with the luxuries of a bath-tub (hot running water!), a washing machine and electricity. Two days after Toby was born, my novel was accepted for publication, so we were doubly celebrating. Brimming with milk and hormones, I joked that I was suffering from postpartum euphoria. But I had another maternal condition developing, too. As I watched my little child grow, ounce by ounce, something else was growing within me: part universal mother, part tigress, part vulnerable woman with child. Like a second self, this radical new dimension of my psyche shadowed all my thoughts.

I remember picking up a newspaper and seeing photos of the Russian hostage crisis: 331 people killed by Chechen rebels, most of them children. Dead children! This was monstrous! Motherhood stripped me of the filters that keep such atrocities from piercing the heart. I wept and wept. I felt as if these were *my* children. What is war, I realized, but humans killing each other's children? Would I be able to protect my daughter from this vile world?

A female salmon lays hundreds of eggs in the hope that just a few will survive. I imagined my daughter swimming up life's river, danger everywhere: war, disease, car accidents, plane crashes, drugs, men. How could I deliver Toby safely to adulthood? My mind reeled at the immensity of my task. Even breast milk has now been found to be laced with PCBs and other toxins. Was I poisoning my baby as I fed her? Or was I inoculating her against an already poisoned world?

Over the phone, my mother referred to the "terrible responsibility" of motherhood. No kidding. The word "maternal" was taking on new meaning for me. How was I going to navigate my maternal course without using fear as a compass point? My own mother never let her fears interfere with her children's lives. Could I do the same?

Small steps. I found that I could keep my anxiety hidden most of the time, even from myself. We arranged to move back to the floathouse, resuming a life that was normal to us. On moving day, the boat was loaded like a Gypsy caravan and the September weather was glorious, the kind that makes you feel as if the best of summer has only just begun. We all enjoyed the boat ride home: the slick water, so full of light, the sun so warm on our faces. The day itself felt like a welcome.

At home, I carried Toby out of the boat and stepped from the garden dock to the floathouse, a distance of less than a metre. And I did what I have done every single time since. I looked down. Dark water swirled beneath me, nothing reflected in it, nothing revealed by it. I thought of the baby—*my* baby—falling, sinking, swirling, vanishing beneath that wordless surface.

IN CLAYOQUOT SOUND, the average tidal variation is three metres. That volume of water is exchanged about every six hours. This means that the view from my house is constantly changing. At low tide, small, tree-covered islands are stranded in an expanse of tidal mudflat. At high tide, branches brush the water and the islands look as if they could pull up anchor and float away.

This same tidal change creates a constant water flow under my house. Sometimes it's like living on a river. When I think of Helen sinking in the shallow end of the pool, I imagine clear, turquoise water—everything in plain view. When I look overboard from my house, I see dark water, moving fast, six metres deep, but seemingly bottomless. Once, my cellphone accidentally slipped in. I watched its glowing green digits for about five seconds. After that, nothing.

As if it is my duty, I visit the dark water in my mind's eye every night before I fall asleep. I try not to stay too long with my vision, but it's always there, waiting for me. For a person who has never been particularly fearful, this is a new experience. I feel as if I am diving into the darkest part of my mind; I don't stay long. The water shows me how quickly my joyful, feverish love for my child can be destroyed. *About five seconds. After that, nothing.*

WHEN I FIRST CAME to Clayoquot Sound, I worked on the water seven days a week guiding whale-watching and kayaking trips, camping on tiny islands, exploring wild, foam-strewn beaches. The water permeated my life. It was a constant drip in my bloodstream. Never before had I felt so alive! Every time my work visa came up for renewal I considered leaving and going home to England. But every time I thought of living away from the water, I feared it would be like closing my eyes and living the rest of my life asleep.

And so I stayed, never losing my connection to the water, instead progressing to a love of the wild places that the water took me to. Then, one winter evening, my dog and I were threatened by a large male wolf. I was so used to being a voyeur of wildlife that it was quite shocking to find myself a participant. We escaped and eventually recovered. I later wrote about the incident for a wildlife magazine: "To live out here, I have to live with wildlife, not against it; I have to experience the beauty and the violence; I have to be part of the cycle."

That was before I had a child.

Now, motherhood has thrown me a new challenge. Now, I worry about protecting my child when we're on the beach or in the forest. Now, my shadow self urges me to join the ranks of those who shoot innocent wild animals "to keep the children safe."

"Don't let *anything* get your child," my shadow self whispers in my inner ear. I resist her, clinging to my über-rational, pre-Toby intelligence.

Once a person has escaped danger often enough, risk becomes more real. I remember my father, renowned for his feats of daring, telling an audience that he never felt fear until his first child was born. Then he went on a mountaineering expedition, a first ascent, and was overwhelmed by his first real experience of fear. Two firsts. As I child, I loved this story, but it didn't prepare me for my own experience as a parent.

When I first came here I treated the ocean as my playground. I took risks and averted many disasters. Now that I am a parent, I stay home when it is windy. I don't drive the boat at night. I try not to travel in the fog. These are risks I avoid for Toby's sake. But just by living on the water I am taking one of the biggest risks of all.

Coastal British Columbia is always susceptible to tsunamis, and is, by some estimates, overdue for a serious earthquake and tsunami combined. Until last summer, I never paid serious attention to this threat.

Then, late one evening, after Marcel and I had finished supper, washed the dishes and were enjoying the summer twilight, my cellphone beeped a message alert. As usual, the noise was an annoyance—an obnoxious intrusion into the calm of the plate-glass-like, light-filled water. I sighed and checked my messages.

There it was: the message telling us there had been an earthquake in California, that a tsunami warning had been issued.

I took a deep breath. I could only think of one thing: Toby, lying asleep in her bed upstairs, eyes closed, arms flung wide. I pictured a giant wave sloshing through the floathouse, taking her away from me, from life. It's an icy feeling, the paralysis of fear, and it's the same feeling I get every time I glance down at the dark water between the docks.

Marcel turned on the VHF radio and we listened to the Coast Guard channel. Just then, the warning was cancelled due to lack of evidence. The earthquake had not spawned a tsunami.

This time.

I KNOW A WOMAN who believes that bad things only happen if you believe they will. Just thinking about these things will attract them to you, she says. She believes she will never have an accident with her bicycle and so her children never wear helmets when they are in the bike trailer. She birthed her second child at home—no midwife, no doula, no doctor, no problems. She exudes confidence and capability. Her technique seems to have worked for her, so far.

Perhaps, as a mother, I need to have more confidence in my fate. "Always trust in your luck," my mother reminds me from time to time. And I do, in a sense. I trust that the general route of my life will be lucky. It's important to be optimistic. But I don't expect luck to see me through poor choices on a daily basis. If I don't put a life jacket on my daughter, I shouldn't rely on luck to stop her from drowning.

Toby fell into the water for the first time at fourteen months. She launched herself out of the rowboat, and Marcel had to haul her back in by the handle on her life jacket. Luckily, I was in town and was spared the whole episode. Marcel said the experience was good for her: she would now respect the water. He proved his point by taking her rowing the next day. "She was so well-behaved," he said. "She really understands."

Because I was not responsible, this incident didn't trouble me. Nor did it trouble Marcel. He doesn't believe in worrying about things that have happened or wasting energy on things that might happen. His personality has an undercurrent of serenity that is reassuring and infectious. Toby thrives as a result of it. And although I cannot deny my maternal anxiety—in fact, I have even decided to embrace it as a normal condition of motherhood—with Marcel as my example, I am inspired to project my old calm self. For all our sakes.

My friend Sharon Carbone raised five children on a thirty-metre boat, the original North Vancouver ferry, anchored in the Tofino harbour. After Toby's saltwater baptism, I asked Sharon how she coped with raising kids on a boat.

"Oh God, they were always falling in," she told me. "And then they'd drift away with the tide and I'd have to row out to get them. The worst was when my eldest boy fell, headfirst, into a kelp bed and his head got stuck underwater."

She sounded so nonchalant.

"They always wore life jackets, that's all," she said.

THERE ARE MEN and women close to me whose children have died. I linger over these stories, turning the pages in my mind, wondering how those parents survived such a loss. My sister lost a three-month-old baby to SIDS. My stepson lost his four-year-old son in a boat accident. His aunt lost her eleven-year-old daughter to a stray pellet from a BB gun. My good friend lost his nine-year-old son to a cougar. In a community this small, there have been many other calamities, all of them horrifying—a sudden ending of beautiful young lives. But life is not beautiful if you live in a prison. It is all too easy for me to build walls around my child, imprisoning her spirit behind a barriers of *what-ifs*.

So how shall I cope with the dark water and the lurking wild animals? I recognize that my undoing could come at me completely out of the blue—unpredicted—but that does not mean that I can ignore the risks at hand. Nor does it mean that I should try to guard against everything.

Mundane safety measures are a start. We have permanent baby gates on the outer doors. There are safety nets stretched over the spaces between the docks. Toby wears a life jacket outside. But we are still surrounded by water, and there are still times when we carry her outside spontaneously, to wave hello or goodbye, to watch an otter or bear or a precious flock of shorebirds that will be gone in a second if we don't see them now. Sometimes, when I wave goodbye as I drive off to my Tofino office, I watch Toby waving back at me from Marcel's arms. I see the water below her. My shadow self rises and I shudder internally, then force myself to "let go." We keep waving until I am around the point, out of sight.

Cellphones and radios are good safety measures, too. I use them to gauge the weather and to cancel appointments if I think it is not safe to travel. If I am alone, I take comfort in the fact that Marcel is just seven digits away.

One windy spring day, when Toby was seven months old, I took her to one of the little grassy islets in the motorboat for a picnic. She was at the age of sitting up, not crawling yet. We sat in the lee of some huckleberry bushes and enjoyed the sun, the mossy grass and an early, exuberant hummingbird. Suddenly, an extra-strong gust of wind whirled around the island and pushed my boat. I had anchored the boat to the island by jamming a seven-kilogram lead fishing weight among the intertidal rocks. I stood up just in time to see the lead ball roll down the rocks into the water—splash!—and the boat was drifting away, anchor and all. I was torn between retrieving the boat and returning to Toby, who was now just out of my line of sight. As I ran back up the hill toward her, she smiled and waved. I waved back at her. Then I saw that she wasn't waving hello to me. She was waving bye-bye to the boat! I laughed and pulled her onto my lap. Together, we waved and waved.

I used the cellphone to ask Marcel to come and get us. But before he arrived, a strange thing happened. Perhaps it was luck. At a distance of about five hundred metres, the boat was caught by counter-gusts. It began drifting back to us. At two hundred metres, Toby began waving again, a hello this time. At twenty metres, she was ecstatic, waving and burbling with glee. I put our life jackets on and put her in the backpack. At five metres I waded out bare-legged to the boat and climbed in. As we began motoring back to the house, Marcel's boat came flying around the point, charging to the rescue.

Before I was a parent, I would have laughed at my situation and probably swum for the boat. Now, as a mother, I felt like a failure. I had been careless in my anchoring because it was difficult to do with Toby in the backpack. And we were marooned, and what was going to happen to my boat? It was a windy day. We shouldn't have come. What was I *thinking*?

When I first saw that chubby hand waving, my sense of humour was still buried by guilt. But when I realized what she was doing, the guilt fell away and I was able to match her delight. And really, that is what a mother should fear the most—quashing a child's delight. For it is children who remind us how to find joy in simple things, and if we cannot encourage joy in our children, perhaps we should call ourselves keepers, not mothers.

I want my daughter to share my love for the water and the wild, but I don't wish to be her keeper. For this reason, I have to teach her well. I have to guard her without seeming to guard her. I have to watch the dark water in private. I have to be honest about my fears without burdening her with the guilt of them.

There is another way in which I could become Toby's keeper: I could imprison her in my wilderness lifestyle. A social child, she babbles endlessly about her little friends. For Toby to have a full range of options in life, to look forward to each day, she will need land *and* water, wild *and* tame, family *and* friends. Otherwise, she will resent her upbringing and reject the very things I want her to love.

Before I moved to this bay, another family lived in a floathouse here. April was eleven when she had to move closer to Tofino to attend school. "I was so shy," she told me. "It was awful. Don't let Toby get that shy."

WHEN THE SUN shines on the West Coast, the open sky promises that anything is possible. Like labour pains, the months of darkness and rain are forgotten, replaced by the joy and ease of summer. Equally, when the rain returns, it dictates our lives. Toby's second winter was a challenge for me. She was very active—walk-walk! run-run!—but storm after storm kept us at home, when previously I would have gone out anyway, rain be damned. Short daylight hours sent me scurrying up the inlet at four-thirty, like a mouse bolting for its hole. A month's travel in January provided a welcome break from the onset of cabin fever.

At my sister's house in London, we went daily to Greenwich Park to see the squirrels and the deer. At Marcel's family home in New Brunswick, we went tobogganing under clear blue skies. We were active. Good electric lights at night allowed me to do so much after Toby's bedtime. I could empty the laundry basket directly into the machine, instead of packing it into the boat and later carrying it across town, along with groceries and everything else. Hot running water meant that I could bathe at home, before bed, one of my all-time favourite luxuries. I felt as if I was being lured over to the dark side. Motherhood became so *easy!*

My mother has always wished that I would live somewhere less remote. Seeing me weaken, she took up her cause again, "for Toby's sake," of course.

While I tend to resist change, I could see that the time was right. Marcel and I discussed the shortcomings of our beloved home. It was a difficult conversation, but we reluctantly decided that we would spend the darkest months of next winter in town. And while life may prove to be easier, things that are easy are not necessarily more satisfying. Also, with kindergarten in the not-so-distant future, this move feels like the first step of many that may send us catapulting toward normality.

The floathouse is handmade, with wood that I helped to salvage and mill into boards, funky kitchen cupboards and driftwood accents everywhere. My townhouse is a regular house on the street, with vinyl siding and linoleum and carpets and drywall and a little patch of grass out front. It is not what Marcel and I dreamt of. We grumble about the clatter of the electric fridge, the noise of cars and the glare of street lights. We pine for the sound of rain on the shake roof and feel lost without the tide slipping past our window.

But as much as we love the water, there is a new drip in our bloodstream now, a new love that eclipses everything else. If we continue to make choices that suit only the two of us, we will lose our daughter as surely as if she were to slip into the dark water. And *that* is worth worrying about.

SEARCHING FOR FRIENDS IN MOMMYLAND (PART 1)

ELIZABETH RENZETTI

London, 2006. We are sitting in Wendy's garden, each of us with one hand on a wriggling baby and two eyes on the shirtless gardeners in the next yard. This is how Wendy lured me to her house—"There are half-naked men next door. Would you like to come over?"

We haven't known each other very long, but we're both foreigners in North London, adrift with babies, our husbands off working through the long days. This is the awkward, first-audition stage of a friendship, when all futures are still possible—will this one be Burton-Taylor fireworks, fizzling to a sorry end? Or a comfortable duvet of a Cronyn-Tandy partnership that we'll sink into for comfort when we're ancient and our children no longer speak to us?

Wendy is a dozen years younger than I am. She's an actress, or wanted to be before her son was born. She's from Winnipeg, a city I know, perhaps unfairly, only from the words "winter" and "mosquito." And the closest I've ever come to an actress is the time that I interviewed Michelle Pfeiffer and she so terrified me with her tinselly, alien perfection and her body the width of a cat whisker that I almost ran from the room screaming.

For the neighbour who introduced us, the differences were inconsequential: Wendy and I are both from that vaguely imagined place called Canada, and we're equally incapable of reading the thermometer of English *froideur*, thus saying the wrong thing all the time. We each have an infant. Of course we'd be friends!

The signs are auspicious, so far. Wendy doesn't talk about her baby constantly, for one thing. Our conversations are rich and far-ranging, from the pontoon-sized breast implants of various Z-list British celebrities to the nasty hairplugs of various Z-list British celebrities. Most important, her mouth is filthy and she laughs like a truck driver.

We are discussing the terrifying Victorian hospital in North London where we both gave birth, when one of the glistening gardeners walks over, holding an extension cord. He is Australian, which just makes it better. "Do you have somewhere in your house I could plug this in?" he asks Wendy. She gives him the benefit of her wide blue eyes and says innocently, "It depends. Exactly how long is your cord?" Ah, yes. This could be the start of a beautiful friendship.

I have a limited facility for making friends. Perhaps it's a holdover from a childhood that seems, in retrospect, to have been spent largely inside my own head. I was shy, although "too lazy to make the effort" is probably nearer the mark. At university, things changed. Either I stopped being a complete loser, or this quality was mitigated by my willingness to pay for endless pitchers of beer with my credit card.

I've been a pack rat with friendships, the oldest dating to the days when I was a candy girl—pardon me, *confectionniste*—at the Eglinton Theatre in Toronto. The most poignant beginning, perhaps, was with Sarah, who befriended me on the first day of university even though she had this exchange with another classmate:

"You know that girl Liz?" said the classmate.

"Yes," said Sarah.

"I think she might be retarded. She's been looking for her locker for *three days*."

Now I am fortunate to be surrounded by friends—relationships that, for the most part, I've carefully tended and maintained over years and thousands of kilometres. In the past seven years, I've moved from Toronto to Los Angeles and back to Toronto, and then to London. Given a choice, I would probably never have left my apartment in those new cities. But I had to go and have a baby, and then another, and that ruined everything. I was forced out into the light, to seek out friendship or be driven off the balcony in my baby-crazed solitude.

It is an odd fact that once you have small children, you no longer choose friends based on compatibility or fellow feeling or a shared interest in cooking, reading, travel or tequila. You choose them based on a shared loathing of head lice and those disgusting turkey nuggets shaped like football players.

"Have you seen those things, the nuggets they have at lunch?"

"Absolutely vile."

"I couldn't agree more."

LONDON, 2005. On certain days after I pick my son up from school, I see the same man on a bench in the park. I burn with envy for this man. He sits, oblivious to the Chernobyl of after-school energy exploding around him, and reads a magazine. I think it's *The Economist*. He appears not to notice if his own children are falling out of trees or failing to make the crucial early-year attachments that will lead, with a little careful guidance, to the right high school, then to Oxford or Cambridge and worldly success, and thus to a smug and honoured death.

Around him, of course, the mothers are busy plotting this very trajectory. We can't help ourselves. On all sides, there are mini-Yaltas being conducted over playdates, vacation plans, the job list for the school summer fair. We talk about the difficulty of finding dentists in the National Health Service who aren't former South American torturers. We trade information about which football camps still have available places. We never talk about ourselves. I know the intimate details of many of these children's lives: this one needs to touch the doorknob four times exactly before he leaves home; that one still wets the bed. But I often don't even know the mothers' names. Mothers are just the people who take the kids to the park, vestigial fleshy bits of the past keeping watch on their shining young lives.

LOS ANGELES, 2001. I had always thought of Cedars-Sinai Medical Center as the place famous old Hollywood comedians go to die, but it also does a brisk trade in the birthing business. A dozen new mothers are gathered in the hospital to talk about the difficulties we're having, to seek advice on breastfeeding, to pour our troubles into the nice nurse's ear and have them flow back, alchemically altered, as soothing advice. Some of us are just there to kill two hours in a very, very long day.

We are such newbies, holding our babies gingerly, unwrapping them like howling Fabergé eggs from their too-many layers. This insecurity binds us, but it's about all that does. Otherwise, these are not women I would run into during the course of my normal life in Los Angeles—that is, in the daily run between Ralph's supermarket, packed with fledgling rock stars and specials on Jack Daniel's, and the park, where crack vials crunch under the wheels of my son's stroller.

One of the mothers talks about how she no longer recognizes herself since the birth. She misses her daily trip to the gym. I have not been to the gym since high school, and even then I showed up twice and forged notes to excuse myself. Another mother in the group points to her baby, a lawyer presenting evidence. She is worried about his size, that there's too much of him. "My pediatrician told me that if a baby has fat cells, he can carry those fat cells into adulthood." I almost laugh, but then I realize she's serious. The poor little bugger—he's heading for baby Atkins already. I try to push my son, who weighed almost ten pounds at birth and now wears Super Jumbo Sumo diapers, behind a nearby ficus. There's no telling when they'll turn on us like the villagers in Shirley Jackson's story "The Lottery," chanting "Fatties! Fatties! Make them die!"

Yet they don't turn on us. In fact, the mothers decide to carry on with an informal group outside the hospital, and they invite us to join, although the only thing we have in common is the fact that we've all shot a squealing pink stranger out our birth canal. Yet I'm beyond chuffed—the cheerleader girls have invited me to a sleep-over. At this point, entirely friendless in Los Angeles, I'm willing to go just about anywhere in search of someone who will laugh at my stupid jokes and admire my boy's fine auburn hair.

We meet at a house in the Hollywood Hills, a showpiece of mid-century modern furniture and luminous oak floors. My knees pop as I lower myself and the Michelin baby to the floor. I've got one eye on the pastries, but I'm only going to make a move if one of the other moms goes first.

"I'm worried when I bathe her," says a woman with sleek dark hair. "I'm always afraid I'm going to drown her."

"That's good practice, though," I say, "because one day you will want to drown her." A dozen pair of eyes swivel my way. Even the babies look horrified. I'd really better work on my material.

It seems unlikely that I'll hear from them again, but a week later one of the moms phones to ask if I'd like to host a baby meeting. I look around our tiny two-bedroom apartment, and imagine them visiting my building, which in a clearly absinthe-inspired moment of madness was named the St. Tropez. What would shock them more—the Russian family who barbecue entire animals in an oil drum on their balcony? The giant transvestite in the purple track-

suit who is so fat that she rides around on one of those scooters usually reserved for the elderly? Or Victor, our building manager, who
would be a rock star if the CIA didn't keep stealing his songs? "I'm
moving back to Canada," I lie. "Good luck with your babies."

The fruitless quest for a friend continues. In the park are the
Russian moms, who arrive in sky-high heels and blue fingernails,
and the Hasidic moms, who do not. They stay in tight formation
with their children and their old people and admit no outsiders.
Then my luck changes and I meet Karen, a fellow Canadian living
in L.A., and I build my own little ethnic enclave.

Karen is sitting behind us with her husband and son on a flight
from Toronto. Our boys, it turns out, are almost the same age. She
tells me that her son was born on July 27. I point out that his birthday is one day after Mick Jagger's, and this detail, pulled from my
nearly limitless store of useless trivia, provides the key to our friendship. We are off and chatting as easily as if we had met fifteen years
earlier sharing a bottle of Southern Comfort in the parking lot
before a high school dance.

Now I know why those Russian mothers cling together. There
is just an ease, a sense of comfort and relief, when you're hanging
out with someone who grew up in the same place, at the same time.
When I make a Bruno Gerussi joke—a rare occasion, I admit, but it
does come up—Karen laughs instead of looking blank. She knows
about Dr. Tongue's 3-D House of Stewardesses and believes, as I do,
that the only cure for a hangover is the uniquely Canadian concoc-
tion called a Bloody Caesar. Most important, she shares the sense of
humour that is unique to Canadians, or maybe just Canadians living
abroad: a dry, rustling thing that creeps along under a conversation
and rears up at unexpected moments.

"Waxing," she says one day. "Specifically, getting a bikini wax
on the way to your C-section. That's what happens in L.A."

"Get out."

"It's true. Apparently out of consideration for your doctor."

You see how valuable it is to have a like-minded guide in such a place? As we sit on the fake bit of grass in front of the fake pond at the Grove mall, Andrea Bocelli booming on the loudspeaker, we squeal about the latest absurdity to hit town: the baby showers where the host provides valet parking but doesn't allow children; the mother-and-daughter plastic surgery offers; the toddlers stuck on two-year waiting lists for nursery school—and even then having to pass "auditions" before winning the right to fingerpaint next to the stars' tots.

In short, Karen kept me sane for those few years in Los Angeles, when the unfailingly cheery weather threatened to drive me mad. (My favourite weather forecast on local TV was Zen in its brevity: "Nice again." I still think it might have been satire.) Eventually, though, work calls my husband and me back to Canada. When it comes time to pack up our tiny apartment and bid farewell to the St. Tropez and the big old trannie in the purple tracksuit, I dread telling Karen.

"That's it. No more Canadian friends," she says. "You keep leaving and breaking my heart."

LONDON, 2005. New city, another new baby, same old foot in mouth. I miss my old friends at home terribly and bombard them with grumpy emails about the social Siberia of North London. One day in the playground of my son's school, my baby daughter in the stroller, I set out once again to build bridges. I've tried before. I have the frostbitten fingers to prove it.

"Those are nice pants," I say to the mother waiting by the door. I have spoken with her before. Our sons are in the same class, and I'm convinced that the relentless drip of my Canadian cheeriness is wearing away the granite of her English reserve.

She looks at me as if I've handed her a dead vole, and, sinking heart, I realize what I've done wrong. "Pants" is the word the British use for underwear. I have just complimented her undergarments, which is surely a no-no in most parts of the world. "Trousers," I say weakly. "I like your trousers. Although I'm sure your pants are nice, too. Not that I can see your pants, of course, but if I could...." It's too late. She's scuttled away, grimacing, as if I'd produced a very bad smell neither of us could afford to acknowledge.

Clearly, personal overtures, or indeed anything that requires me to speak to other human beings without giving offence, is not my strength. Once again, even though every fibre of my being resists the idea that I will forge a friendship solely over children, I turn to the mommy network. My neighbourhood has a parents' association, and I volunteer to host a morning tea.

I spend a ridiculous amount of time worrying about the details. If I put coffee cups on the table, am I running the risk of scalding a toddler? Does the cat have fleas? Should I serve scones or cookies—biscuits, they're called biscuits here, for God's sake remember that!

An hour later, there are six women and their babies in my living room. No one is scratching and the children remain unboiled. The conversation has moved, haltingly, from baby food to baby vomit to baby waste—a thrilling journey from one end of the baby to the other. Someone brings up a reality show that's been gripping the country. It features, among other things, a transgendered former pop star in a monkey-fur coat and a controversial politician forced to wear a red leotard and act like a cat. For a moment, the conversation brightens. It feels giddy, rebellious: Look, we're not talking about our spawn!

Then, the most schoolmarmish of the mothers—in my head, she is Posh Granola Queen—snaps, "I don't watch television," and asks me for a tea towel. I hand her one without question. She flicks it open on the floor and proceeds to show us how to fold a cloth diaper, should we ever chuck our earth-destroying, landfill-clogging disposable diapers. Nappies, I mean. Damn.

If there's potential friend material among them, I can't see it. How do you know if someone will make you laugh, watch your back, endure your rants, when all conversation has been restricted to children and nothing else? We drink more tea. Silence. "So," asks one of the mothers, a young German. "Has anyone seen the poo that is orange?"

My mother, who is visiting from Toronto, passes around biscuits and scones and says little. Afterwards, though, she shakes her head. "I can't believe you all sat around for two hours and talked about nothing but babies. In my day if you talked about baby poo for hours on end people would think you were crazy."

She was trained as a nurse at a large Catholic hospital in Toronto. She had only four children, making her a laggard among her classmates, who all spawned five or six or, in one memorable case, eight. Fifty years after they went into training, they are all still friends. "But didn't you get together with them," I ask her, "and sit around and talk about what you should feed them and how they were sleeping?"

She looks at me as if I have spoken to her via satellite from the planet Venus. If she says Jesus, Mary and Joseph, the closest she comes to profanity, I'll know she's really exercised. But she only says mildly, "No, dear, we didn't sit around talking about our babies. We were having babies and working and getting on with it."

She does admit that she once looked after seven of her friends' children while their mothers were out at various appointments and things went swimmingly until my brother David tied her, using her apron strings, to a chair, only setting her free when she threatened him with death, and she realized that the only way she could keep everyone safe was to lock all the children in the basement until their mothers returned, which she did. To quote Archie Bunker, those were the days.

From my perch in privileged London, I watch the sorties of the modern mommy wars: the mustard gas filling the air, the bayonets fixed, the crazed eyes of the materfamilias going over the top. One mom has fallen out with another over the issue of a Kinder egg given without permission; another is sending out emails addressed to her "FWOCS," Friends Without Children.

On many days, I fear I've become just as demented as the rest of them. I find myself droning on about my kids to old friends, the ones who never had children, and I wonder later whether this pains them or bores them or causes them to roll their eyes in some far-off living room. Do I need to share the news that my son runs through the house screaming, "I am the king of bacon!" which I, as a pork-o-phile, find amusing, but they may not?

In the middle of winter, I'm on the phone with an old friend in Toronto, a poet whose life is wild and storm-tossed, holding my infant daughter in one arm while my son and his little buddy roll by and almost into the fireplace, howling like monkeys. "For God's sake, don't actually wrestle in the fire," I scream at them—and into my poor friend's ear. I apologize, tell her I've turned into a horrifying Frankenmother constructed of giant lactating breasts and eyes in the back of my head. Worse, I'm Erma Bombeck. I've become the woman I used to read in the toilet. "Yes," she says, "except for the part where you drink way more."

When I hang up I'm deflated—I'm a shrew, a shrieker, not the partner in crime and cross-city fun she once knew. A few weeks later, lying in bed reading her latest book of poetry, I come across the story I told her about my son. She has remembered, treasured it, fixed it in time. Maybe we aren't lost to each other after all.

The teas are a washout. Wendy is a stalwart, willing to show up for even the most dreary tea parties, but I can't rely on her for all social interaction. She continues to be a lifeline, but there's still no escaping my incredible lameness at making mommy friends.

Just as I'm resigning myself to my lonely fate, my luck changes again. One morning, I'm talking to my son before class begins when

I hear someone ask, "Are you Canadian?" I look up to see a blond woman smiling at me.

"How did you know?"

"Well, I heard you say 'out.' Can't fool me."

Viki, it turns out, is another expat. She tells me she came to London for a party and never left, and I think, Here's my new Karen. We're in the children's playground, but I feel as if I'm eight years old again, thrilled that the cool girl has singled me out for attention. Viki moves deftly among the other mothers, chatting, laughing.

"It must be so easy for you," I say enviously.

"It's not easy at all," she says. "It doesn't come naturally to me. It takes a lot of effort."

That's the question, isn't it? Am I willing to make the effort, to build those mommy bridges that will lead me deeper into the community, give me some sense of belonging in this foreign land? There are times, as the conversations about our kids stretch into the next century, when it doesn't seem worth it. But then there are times, when my kids lead me to Wendy or Karen or Viki, when it absolutely does.

Viki and I are out shopping for shoes for our kids. The elderly shopkeeper tries to put all our purchases in one bag when Viki stops her and says, "No, two bags, thanks."

"Oh," says the shopkeeper, startled. "I thought you two were a couple."

Outside the shop, Viki doubles over with laughter, stopping only long enough to insist that I was the one to give off the Ellen DeGeneres vibe. Stuff like that just doesn't happen when you're alone.

One afternoon my son's teacher tells me that she's slightly concerned that he often prefers to play by himself rather than join in the other kids' games. For a moment I'm terrified: have I passed on my anti-social curse? Have we ruined his life and his networking skills by dragging him around the world?

It takes a second to regain perspective. He's only four years old. It's his character, not an illness. He may simply have inherited the loner tendencies that led his father and me to become journalists, a profession best defined by the phrase, "Doesn't play well with others."

"Do you like school?" I ask him one day.

He seems mystified and says he does. I ask him if he likes his friends at school. He thinks about it for a minute. "I don't have a lot of friends," he says. "But I have two." Sometimes I think I couldn't possibly love him more than I do, and then he proves me wrong and adds another drop to the bucket. Two is great, I tell him. Two is all you need.

SEARCHING FOR FRIENDS IN MOMMYLAND (PART II)

KATRINA ONSTAD

I live in *Toronto,* and since *I've* had children, the city looks different. Where I used to see alleyways and unexplored neighbourhoods and darkened cafés in which to feel arty, I now see an endless shopping mall overrun with kid-sized versions of our adult excesses: mini-manis, mini-Hummers, valet parking at Holt Renfrew for $1,200 Bugaboo strollers. A multi-million-dollar baby industry has sprung up in North America over the past decade, turning motherhood into the new wedding, a formerly sacred life-changing event whose significance is now measured in dollars. Motherhood will make a consumer out of you, and therefore a sucker. It will make you feel like that $1,200 stroller is the choice of the better parent, like releasing doves from cages is the choice of the better bride. That borrowed stroller isn't just stained with old baby puke, but with neglect. It means you don't love right, you doveless loser.

When I had my first child in 2003, I didn't need a statistic to tell me that I had been hurled into a demographic as desirable to many retailers as the eighteen-to-thirty-four-year-old flock I was finally leaving. I felt it all the time. I went to a mommy–baby movie and they tried to sell me shit. I went to a mommy–baby workout class and they tried to sell me shit. I considered, very briefly, a mommy–baby massage class, but I could practically hear the massage oil salesmen panting at the door. Plus I was disappointed to learn that mommy–baby massage is all about you massaging the baby, as if that lazy baby aches like his mother, with her Mayan-brick-hauler's back pain. The thing is, when you have a kid, you stand still and baby shit— literal and figurative, fecal and in the form of beeping, squawking toys "previously loved" by friends and acquaintances—sticks to you. And there's no need really to pay for any of it.

But free enterprise, like the women's magazine industry, only succeeds when the consumer is crippled by feelings of inadequacy. And no one feels more inadequate than a new mother. This is obvious: the leaking, scabrous breasts and the melting mass where the brain was and the sudden damping-down of a career years in the making. I anticipated the enormous physical and professional dislocation that motherhood would cause, at least intellectually, but I hadn't realized that the emotional isolation would be so hard to break out of. Somehow, I had it in my head that the transition from autonomous being to "mother" would resemble in social magnitude the transition from high school to university. I would open the gilded gates of a world heretofore denied me and find myself afloat on a sea of fascinating women who made me more fascinating by association. Together, we would bob together in warm waters of intellectual exchange, only this time we'd be lubricated not by alcohol and music, but herbal tea and Baby Mum Mum crackers.

It gets harder to make friends once you leave university. Somewhere after twenty-five, the common ground is less visible than when you're eighteen and meeting the eye of someone in a Bible and Western Culture seminar, sharing a simultaneous thought: Wow, you made it to eighteen without knowing anything about the Bible either! Let's hang! Later, the workplace is a potential friendship well, but that's risky. Do you really want Phil from HR to hear about your St. John's wort abuse? And anyway, I make a living writing, and writing is painfully solitary.

By the time I hit my early thirties, I deeply missed my friends, both women and men, my most intimate confessors, close friends whose input required daily telephone debriefings. Each of us always knew what the others were doing every night, and when one would call and say, "What's going on?" something always was. But the slow drift of adulthood took many of them to other cities and countries, or deeper into relationships, and I moved away, too, into my own relationship and my career, and into a sadly adult sense of independence that wasn't just financial but emotional. I was hardening. I was learning not to need anyone but my partner, and just then, I had my son, and I understood need in its most derailing, fantastic sense. What I wanted more than anything when he was born was to know that we were part of something bigger, that he was loved from all directions as much (or almost as much) as his parents loved him. I wanted a community of voices and arms to help raise him because our little family, cool as it is, could hardly contain and nurture his wonder. Thus, I fully intended to make friends off the back of this motherhood thing. I knew that meeting the child would be great, sure, but the prospect of meeting grown-ups had me almost as excited.

Like a postpartum Goldilocks, I tried three times to find some kind of human connection within my flourishing neighbourhood mommy culture—posters for baby sign language classes had begun to outnumber band stickers on local lampposts. But each time, I left feeling more isolated, and poorer. The medicinal phrase "postnatal workout," written on the schedule at a chic boutique gym, appealed to me more than the flyers for "Mommy and Baby Fitness Classes" I'd seen in other mother-hunting territory, like kiddie toy stores and my midwife's office. I'd come to notice that the word "mommy" was shorthand for the infantilizing of mothers, as if we ourselves were babies, easily suggestible vessels prone to irrational spending sprees: I-want-I-want-I want—a Kate Spade diaper bag!

Still, medicinal is expensive, too: the postnatal workout cost $12 an hour. When I walked into the gym, a second-floor wood-and-mirrored loft space overlooking a Starbucks, I noticed immediately that all the moms seemed to know each other. Like the kid who was sick on the first day of school only to find that everyone has paired up by Tuesday, I panicked. How could this be? The babies had just been born. Weren't we all new to this? Why did they look so experienced, so pre-friended?

Babies in Madonna-toned arms, the super-fit moms in sleek yoga workout clothes bounced up and down on giant balls before class started, talking to each other about cottages, a row of cellphones resting on the window ledge. I don't have a cottage. I do go to the park a lot, though, and I intended to bring that up if anyone asked.

I set up my step near the back and laid my son down on a mat, immediately noticing I hadn't brought any toys for him to play with. Most of the kids were surrounded by toys that appeared educational, brightly coloured and somehow cerebral, even though shaped like octopuses. I had never seen toys like this before. They looked expensive. What kind of mother was I, anyway? I gave Judah my keys for fun and easy self-blinding.

When class began, the moms somehow already knew the moves, stomping and shaking it across the steps like a row of "In Living Color" backup singers. When that was complete, they casually and simultaneously returned to sit and bounce on the giant balls with so little exertion that it appeared as if they were testing mattress firmness. There was only one other mom who looked as out of place as I felt. She had a bit of a belly and a face as if she'd been mugged and thrown in an alleyway, say, thirty-seven times. This is called sleep deprivation, and I could relate. I tried to catch her puffy eye, setting my face in a manner I hadn't had to employ in years—

not since high school, or the first day of a new job—a wide-eyed half smile, consciously not too desperate (I am a vibrant, interesting person. Get to know me!) that I call my Alone but Not Lonely Face. Later I checked this face in the mirror, and it's a bit fiercer and more fraught than I'd intended, a little less Mona Lisa, a little more Steve Buscemi. My maybe-friend left quickly after class, and so did I.

Jude was a Christmas baby, born into a long cold winter, but that wasn't the problem. My dark periods didn't fit the definition of postpartum depression. They matched in tone the general modern alienation that had snaked in and out of my life since adolescence. At first, the old dullness had been vanquished by the sheer oomph, the weight of joy that arrived—smack—with my son. And yet, after the early weeks of romance, the evenings gazing at his miraculous digits, the head-spinning marvel at this great, glorious fortune, I was surprised to feel at once profoundly changed, and still me. And being me, I was a little bit bummed. I have always been good at this. I listened to a lot of Smiths in my life, and read too much Sylvia Plath, and I saw the movie Ordinary People six times when I was ten. Having a child shoves every truth about yourself wailing into the light. Motherhood didn't change the nature of my loneliness, but it helped articulate it as an imperfection in me, as an unbecoming youthful indulgence, something I needed to conquer for my child's sake.

Were other mothers feeling these things? Who could I talk to about this? If the yuppie moms at a $12-an-hour fitness class seemed inured to the dark moments, surely mom-and-baby yoga would be filled with fragile, caring souls. But on my first day, waiting in the cramped foyer outside the studio with a dozen hysterical babies caught up in the crying-domino effect, I heard two moms—makeup-free faces glowing with new motherhood, one possibly wearing a smudge of whole wheat flour across a cheek—discussing baby transportation. "I'm not really into the whole stroller scene," said one. She wore her baby in a flower-patterned sling. Not just any sling—an Ergo, a $100 carrying device I would hear about many times on the playground, as in, "What? You don't have an Ergo? Doesn't your back hurt like a Mayan brick builder?" The other mom had hers in a Baby Bjorn ($110). She nodded, and said, "I look at strollers as a form of... well, abuse is too strong a word...." From beneath the torture straps and pulleys of his car seat at my feet, Jude managed a strangled cry.

Baby yoga ($15) is retarded. The first few times, Jude just slept and I felt a little smug as the other babies fussed and whined, their mothers forced to interrupt shavasana to breastfeed or soothe. And then, at around two months old, my son woke up. He hollered, he turned purple, but I felt there was time to finish one last tree pose, right? A mom shot me a dirty look. I picked up my squirming, angry child and the instructor told me to keep him between my legs as I stretched. Doing yoga with a baby between your legs is uncomfortable. It's like trying to do yoga with a baby between your legs. The baby disapproved too, and soon I was sitting with my back against the wall for one third of the class ($5 worth), nursing.

Perhaps my mistake had been moving too far from the known. Yuppies and hippies with babies are still yuppies and hippies. Stick with your own kind, I thought, and around then, a neighbour with a new baby, someone I didn't know well but who had always seemed funny, bright and hip, told me about a moms' group she belonged to. I liked this idea: get together, nosh, let the babies roll around in the middle of the floor. And it was free.

I pictured a kind of '70s consciousness-raising gathering, and I was ready. I was ready to bitch it up and take down the patriarchy, man. Domestic labour was my new obsession: how to divide it up and how it would be when I went back to work. I wanted to hear the wisdom of these elder sisters (their babies were all about four months older than mine, which is like twenty years in baby time).

We looked the same, these women and I, and a yuppie mom walking in would probably have smirked at the safe aesthetic sameness of our group. But I was optimistic. Here, at least in terms of real estate choice, was guaranteed commonality. And yet, when we gathered in our similarly decorated living rooms (semi-vintage, a hint of a past life that included "exotic travel," half-renovated, a preference for the old, a utilitarian appreciation of IKEA), we didn't actually discuss consciousness. Instead, we fanned the flames of maternal anxiety: sickness, vaccinations, daycare—all the things that could go wrong. Most of all, of course, we discussed where to buy baby shit, though status in our group was around second-hand shit. The women were very nice, but what did we have in common outside of children? Efforts to bring the conversation to books or films fell flat. We returned, always, to the children and the ways that we might be failing them. Everyone looked a little bored, and though I sensed that among their own friends, they might have behaved entirely differently, in this group, under the rubric of Mommy, we were our most narrow, insecure selves.

Sharing mother status alone is not enough to build a friendship, it turns out. Within months of my son's birth, I gave up on the mommy industrial complex. When I really did need to laugh, when I was desperate for an outside perspective, I realized I still had my friends from the Time Before, scattered and busy as they were. None of them had children yet, and some of them were even men. It didn't matter. As they had for years, they could still listen to my whining, empathize, and tell me about the world in all its breadth and chaos. I was calmed to be heard, and to hear of something outside motherhood. As Michael Ondaatje wrote in his poem "To a Sad Daughter," "This was not what I expected, but I like this better." The community was always here, and very rarely do we discuss shopping.

LEAVING PEMA

JAMIE ZEPPA

When my son turns two, a new anxiety comes over me, different from the initial anxiety ("Oh my God! A *baby*? How did this happen?"), different from nursing anxiety ("If I'm doing it right, why does it hurt so much?"), different still from sleep-deprivation anxiety ("When you die from lack of sleep, do you fall asleep first or do you just drop dead folding laundry and listening to 'Itsy Bitsy Spider' for the 114th time?").

Those anxieties disappeared, and for a while, I believe I've entered an anxiety-free zone that will last from age two to twelve, or the discovery of a joint in my son's pencil case, whichever comes first. Then this new anxiety appears—separation anxiety.

I tell myself it's normal to be anxious about taking my child somewhere and leaving him. New mother, old instincts, the primal urge to protect offspring in a world beset with dangers: strangers, unsafe vehicles, dioxins, toxins, freak events, flukes. There is no knowing. You can never tell. Et cetera.

Besides, I come by it honestly. My grandparents, who raised me after my parents split up, were great worriers. You were in grave danger the minute you stepped outside your door: robbers, drunk drivers, lightning, stomach cramps. And you weren't so safe inside either. Someone was always going to put out an eye or drink Javex from the unmarked bottle under the sink.

I remind myself that we are in one of the safest places in the world, the Himalayan kingdom of Bhutan, Land of the Peaceful Dragon—extraordinarily low crime rate, so few cars there are no traffic lights, no guns, no gangs, no serial killers. It is my theory that Bhutan doesn't grow serial killers because you need isolation to become that kind of psychopath, and there is simply not enough privacy here. Doors are rarely closed. Everyone knows everything about everyone else, and wants to tell you about it.

Still, I walk my son to his nursery school, counting the dangers: open drains, ruptured sidewalks, a car that veers too close to the side of the road. At the school gate, I kiss Pema goodbye and stand around, watching, counting. The dog across from the school barks itself into a hysterical fury behind a metal gate: someone could leave the gate unlatched, the dog could escape, charge into the schoolyard if someone left *that* gate unlatched. The coat hooks in the front foyer: someone could slip and put out an eye. The jagged stone steps in the playground: someone could fall. (And indeed, someone does fall—a six-year-old boy who lands on the spike of some bush that has been cut close to the ground but not uprooted. The spike pierces his stomach and grazes his intestine. A freak fall, a fluke spike! In the end, he is fine. But still. Still!)

I know I am being ridiculous. I tell myself, "You are being ridiculous. You are in one of the safest places in the world." A jeep with a red flashing light pulls up behind me, followed by a dark blue Land Cruiser. Pema's classmate, one of the youngest princesses, climbs out of the Land Cruiser, her long black hair pulled back in a ponytail. Three royal bodyguards follow her into the school. They are big men in army boots and fatigues and maroon berets. One has a walkie-talkie, another holds a clipboard and the last carries the princess's pink Little Mermaid knapsack.

I can't stand out here all day. I have a job, and besides, what will people say? I don't want to be one of the people that everyone wants to tell everyone else about. ("Crazy woman stands outside the school all day. No idea why.") I eye the Jeep with envy. That's what I want for Pema. Three burly protectors who will follow him everywhere and guard him against dogs and hooks and falls and lost knapsacks and every other sorrow in the world.

I don't worry about the things other mothers worry about. I let Pema finish eating the candy he's picked up off the floor. ("It's too late—he's already sucked all the germs off it.") I let him splash in an icy mountain stream in the cool spring sunlight. ("If he gets cold, he'll stop.") I let him walk to town with his cousins, children themselves, to eat dumplings dipped in chili sauce at a rickety shop. ("The chilies will act as an antibacterial agent.") Children in Bhutan are hearty and sturdy, with strong legs and sunburned cheeks. They stay up late and get up early and eat what their parents eat. At the age of eight, they have all sorts of skills that continue to elude me to this day: They can cook over a kerosene stove, skip down an almost vertical slope, sharpen pencils with razor blades. So I am not worried about germs, cold creeks or a proper bedtime routine. And I don't sit at home and count the dangers. But as soon as I have to leave him somewhere, I am sunk in dread.

I counter the anxiety by throwing myself into my work as an editor for the World Wildlife Fund. When I am editing, I am quieted. I am a humming machine of nouns and verbs. I can ignore the sharp whistles of pressure cookers and Hindi film music from the surrounding apartment buildings, the car honking in the street below, the students playing soccer in the open field behind the office. I am almost finished a donor report one afternoon when a baby in a nearby apartment begins to cry. It is that intermittent, just-woke-up fretting that will soon be crying, and the closer it gets to crying, the harder I clench my teeth. I know this is not *my* child crying. This is a baby cry, not a two-year-old cry, and besides, my child is on the other side of town. But suddenly I can no longer edit the paragraph in front of me. I can't even read it. I pick up the phone. The babysitter answers on the third ring. "Is Pema okay?" She says he is fine. "What's he doing?" He is playing in the garden. "He's not crying?" No, he's digging with a spoon and a fork.

Now the crying is full and insistent. I get up from my desk and pace. What is taking the mother so long? I try to imagine what she might be doing that is more important than picking up that baby *right now*. What? What could be more important? I cover my ears.

The baby's cry becomes a desperate wail of unimaginable desolation. The baby is alone. There is no other explanation. My heart is pounding, my chest hurts and a thousand tiny insects are crawling under my skin. I run outside and stand in the parking lot facing the apartment building. What do I intend to do? Bang on every door until I find the crying baby? And then? Demand to know why the baby is still crying, why no one has picked her up and comforted her? Deliver a lecture? Yes, that is exactly what I want to do. I visualize it briefly: the bewildered mother or babysitter, her hands covered with flour or her sleeves soaked with water from the wash. I imagine what she will say to the neighbours after I leave: "Crazy woman, comes barging in, face all blotchy, starts shrieking at me. Shrieking!"

It's a good thing I care so much about what everyone will say. At this point, it's the only thing saving me from full-out, bug-eyed craziness.

Then a friend needs surgery in Bangkok, and I have to go with her. Now *I* am leaving Pema and I can hardly stand it. "It's just four days," I tell my husband, Tshewang, hoping he'll say, "Four days? You want to leave your two-and-a-half-year-old son with his father and his father's family and an entire town of kind friends and help-ful neighbours for four whole days? Are you crazy?"

He says, "Sure."

I say, "I feel sick. I don't know what's wrong with me."

Tshewang says, "Maybe this reminds you of your childhood."

But it doesn't really. My mother left my brother and me when we were very young. Her marriage to my father had just imploded, and she left, hoping my father would come to his senses and ask her to come back. He did not. Every step took her farther away, and when she finally did come back on her own, she had lost custody of us to our paternal grandparents. She went to see a lawyer, but he was not encouraging. It would be an expen-sive case, and he didn't think her chances were good. She stuck to the terms of the custody agreement and saw us one Saturday a month, from ten in the morning until seven at night. There was no provision for extra days—birthdays, Christmas, summer vaca-tion. I would be a teenager before I saw her on a day that wasn't a Saturday.

But my mother and I managed to develop a relationship in spite of this. She waited patiently until my grandparents relaxed their vigilant anger, and then began to take back her role as my mother. She took me shopping for school clothes, paid my rent through uni-versity, drove eight hundred kilometres to bring me a sofa she had recovered herself. And over the years, she has tried to explain the past, even though her eyes still fill with tears when she talks about it. I understand that she was young, just twenty-two, and desperate to get my father to come back to her. I understand that she has suf-fered the bitter and corrosive consequences of leaving. I have told her numerous times that I forgive her for leaving. I am proud of the way I have come to terms with the past. It's over, it's done, and I'm over and done with it. So I do not think this anxiety with Pema has anything to do with my childhood.

In Bangkok, I call home every evening. Pema is a breathless whirl of cheer and incomprehensible news. "Mommy! The dog is eating my rice! I drawed a spider and then the spider drawed me. Talk to Dad." I miss Pema, but it's not just missing him. It's something else, something worse.

My friend finds out she needs to stay seven more days. When I call home, Pema says, "Mommy, aren't you ever coming home from the office?" I feel as if my heart has been ripped out, as if my child has been taken away from me, as if I will be stuck in Bangkok forever and I will die—no, literally die—from this longing.

He's only two and a half, I keep telling myself. He doesn't know where I am. He thinks I'm at work. He thinks I've left him. He thinks I'm not coming back. I wake up at night gasping at the horror of this.

Tshewang says, "He's fine. Of course he knows you're coming back." He calls to Pema in the other room, "Pema! Do you want to say hi to Mommy...again?" I hear Pema call back, "No." Tshewang says, "He's playing with Norbu."

I say I will call back. I go out to sit on the balcony, in the wet blanket of smog and humidity that is called air in Bangkok. "He's only two and a half," I say out loud, and then I realize who I am talking about.

The hole that opens in my head is so shockingly big, I cannot believe I won't fall into it and drown. Nothing my mother told me about leaving makes sense. She was young. So? The court case would be expensive. So? My father didn't love her. *So?* I know my mother as a good person, a kind and responsible person, but this makes it even more incomprehensible.

The leaving makes no sense because my attachment to Pema is written in my very cells, and leaving him—running away, giving up, relinquishing custody—is unimaginable. Maybe my mother did not have the same story written in her cells. Maybe something interfered with that initial writing—depression, trauma, some fundamental biochemical misfiring. What got written later—the custody agreement, the doing of duty, the standing-by—was not enough to overwrite the tragedy of that first story.

I sit up most of the night and then fall asleep. When I wake up, I call Pema and tell him when I will be home. He asks for Spider-Man. "The good Spider-Man," he says. "Of course," I say.

I hang up and take a deep breath. Things I do not know: I do not know how my mother could have left us. I do not know if I will ever understand it. Or forgive her. And I do not know what kind of relationship we will have after this realization.

Things I do know: I know my son is fine at home. He is not feeling inconsolable grief and terror at being abandoned. That was me. Is me. I know I am going to need some serious therapy to figure this all out. I know that in seven more days, when I get off the plane deep in the mountains of Bhutan, I will be the happiest mother in the world. And I know that tomorrow I will walk all over Bangkok looking for the good Spider-Man.

PRESENT IMPERFECT

ALISON KELLY

This is how I assumed things would go: I would have a carefully planned conception, followed by nine months of pregnancy, during which I would shine and be held up as a fine example of how women today can have it all. I would work throughout my pregnancy, arriving each day full of energy, exuding calm and joy, dressed in a flattering array of outfits suited to my lifestyle (hip, chic, sporty). My clothes would celebrate my changing body yet leave no doubt in anyone's mind that I remained a sexy, attractive and competent woman.

Two weeks before my due date, having tidied up all loose ends at work, I would begin my maternity leave. I would spend the final two weeks nesting: cleaning and putting nutritious meals in the freezer for those busy first weeks after I had the baby. Having participated in prenatal exercise classes, I would be in great physical shape. And having attended birth classes, I would be informed, relaxed and in charge of my birth process. My husband and I would have a birth plan that would guide and inform the attending doctors and nurses, who would hover in the background, humbled at the gift of being on this journey with us.

I had always assumed (that damn word again) that children would be part of my life. My husband and I had talked about "when we have kids…" but we hadn't actually said those magic words "Let's make a baby." I was out of town when I started getting a few niggling worries. I made my living as an actor and was on a tour of B.C. and Alberta schools. Pregnancy was not on my mind. Besides, we used birth control. When I called my husband to tell him of my suspicions, he was, understandably, surprised.

"What?" came his puzzled voice, "How sure are you?"

"Well, I've missed my period and my breasts are huge and sore." I answered, trying to sound calm yet enthusiastic.

"Oh," he replied, not attempting to match my mood. "Let's not jump to any conclusions until you've seen the doctor."

Far from the fantasy night of wild sex, neither of us could even recall the event that had caused this predicament. A week later, I came home, saw my doctor and my suspicions were confirmed. I was happy, if a bit shocked, to be pregnant. My doctor calmed my fears about how much drinking I had done over the previous weeks, assuring me things would be fine. And I calmed myself. Sure, I had strayed from my plan, but all was not lost. I would get back on track.

As an actor I had no loose ends to tidy up at work. And since I was self-employed, I wouldn't be getting maternity leave. My choice of career also meant I didn't have the kind of salary that allowed me to buy those great maternity outfits. I made do with hand-me-downs from friends and sisters that, for the most part, did not flatter me. But then again, I am not sure much would have.

I didn't spend hours contemplating the miracle growing within me. I didn't glow with a mysterious and womanly aura. I didn't radiate calm or look the image of an earth goddess. I didn't feel beautiful or sexy. I was crabby and awkward. For every centimetre I gained on my belly, I gained one on my butt. I waddled. The only parts of my body that hadn't been affected by the pregnancy were the few centimetres between my elbows and wrists and between my knees and ankles. Everywhere else, I was a swollen, doughy lump of stretch-marked skin. I had a bad case of acne, which on a good day subsided to angry blotches. I was hot and itchy. I had cut my hair into what I hoped would be a perky, low-maintenance, trendy style, but it only made me look pinheaded, stern, and threatening. I felt passionately about things and cried often in joy, anger, frustration, and sometimes simply because it was the best way to express some indefinable feeling. My husband, ever the trooper and never one to run from emotional outbursts, would console me with tender phrases of understanding.

"You know you're feeling like this because of the hormones," he would whisper while rubbing my back. And then look hurt and confused when I would cry harder and tell him to leave me alone.

Frequently, I would find myself fantasizing about divorce. I was cranky from lack of sleep. I lay in bed each night obsessing over how exhausted I would be the next day if I didn't get a decent amount of sleep. I fought with my bedding, trying to coax my pillows into the magic position that would prevent heartburn but not put a kink in my neck, casting off the blankets in order to cool down, only to reel them back in moments later to warm up. I rolled around, trying to ease my aching hips and lumbered downstairs regularly to empty my ever-shrinking bladder. Sex was a thing of the past. If my husband so much as looked at me, I would snarl. If he accidentally brushed against me in bed, I would swat him as if he were a bug.

Occasionally, I would remember how I had envisioned my pregnancy and panic about how little time I had left to get back on track. I would make a promise to myself to look into an exercise class or at the very least go for a regular walk, but somehow neither ever happened.

I performed in a show that ended three months before my due date. I had incorporated my bulging belly into the show so I didn't have to pretend I wasn't pregnant. I was going to use those last three months putting my plan into action: get the house ready, make food for the freezer, research and sign up for birth classes. A highly organized friend said she was going to give me a week off and then take me Christmas shopping as I would be too busy with the new baby, who was due mid-December, to deal with Christmas. I added shopping and wrapping to my to-do list.

One week after the closing of my show, on the morning my plan of action was to begin and eleven weeks before the birthdate, I awoke early to answer the call of my bladder. Sitting on the toilet, I noticed a trail of blood on the floor. My heart stopped. My husband was out of town. Out of the country. Off the bloody continent! He was certainly not going to be any help. Having my first baby almost three months early when my husband was away was not part of my plan!

I made a panicked phone call to my doctor who advised getting myself to the hospital. Bent double, I scuttled around the house collecting my toothbrush, pyjamas, book, brush, wallet, all the while moaning a prayer to any god or goddess who would listen to "please, please, please make things work out." At the hospital, I was examined. I was not in labour. Assured. The baby was fine. I was kept for observation, just to be safe. All was well with the world. I was back on track. Back to the plan. Back to striving for perfection.

Ten hours later, I gave birth to a two-pound baby boy. The delivery room was noisy with teams of doctors, specialists, nurses, technicians. I had yet to sign up for birth classes. There was no birth plan to follow. My husband had been reached and had been on the phone with me during the height of the labour, making helpful and encouraging statements like "Can't they stop it?"

My son was alive but very ill, very fragile. I did not get to hold him or nurse him. I saw him briefly before he was whisked off to be intubated. My husband made it home twenty-four hours later, and we began our immersion in the bewildering world of the special care nursery. Three and a half months later, we emerged with our son, who was still frail but healthy enough to come home. My plan was shattered. I had not managed to do a single one of the things on my list. How would I ever deal with motherhood?

Easy. I just needed another plan. My manifesto: I will welcome and embrace my role as a mother but not lose sight of me the woman. I will stay in touch with the world, my look, my childless friends, my husband. I will not become one of those mothers who can speak of nothing but her children, who becomes nothing more then a walking heap of outdated, ill-fitting clothing that does double duty as a snot-swiper, puke-catcher and hand-wiper. I will not be a woman who sees her husband as nothing more than the father of her children.

I had spent four years working as an early childhood educator. I knew how to make several different kinds of playdough. I knew all the right songs and finger plays to stimulate and entertain young minds. I understood the importance of outdoor play and unstructured time. I knew that children thrived when they had a routine and clear boundaries. What more did I need? A schedule.

I was a stay-at-home mom. Work was out of the question with such a needy little fellow. The least I could do was maintain the home, create meals and take care of a baby. I would have a weekly plan posted on the fridge.

Weekly

Mondays: grocery shopping (a few extra minutes the night before would ensure I had a menu plan for the week so I would only have to shop once a week)

Tuesdays: laundry, including the sheets

Wednesday: clean the bathroom (there was only one so that would be easy)

Thursday: vacuuming

Friday: sterilize baby toys, clean out the car

Saturday: yard work and gardening

Sunday: hang out, enjoy life and my family

Daily
–an hour of general clean-up should keep me on top of the clutter and surface mess
–dishes and kitchen: no dishwasher, but if I do dishes with each meal I will stay on top of things
–an hour of "me time" to do whatever I like
–every other day I would get to the gym
The rest of the time, other than meal preparation, will be spent at the park, the library, visiting with family and friends, attending play group, and lots of quiet time so he learns to entertain himself.

Monthly
–wash the kitchen and bathroom floors

I HAD BEEN in the homes of people who had these schedules. They were the kind of people who sent out hundreds of handmade Christmas cards stuffed with newsy letters. They never forgot a birthday, made interesting and time-consuming gifts, sewed wardrobes for themselves and their children, exercised regularly and never complained about their husbands. I was determined to be one of these women.

First, however, I needed to get some sleep. The problem was my baby was a remarkably noisy sleeper. And I was a remarkably light sleeper and very anxious. If I had felt sleep-deprived during the pregnancy, a new term had to be invented for what I felt now. I was nursing, so it made sense to have the baby in our room despite his continual snuffles and grunts, squeaks and squawks. Being so little he needed to nurse a great deal. I slept in tiny fragments. At six-thirty each morning, he would wake up ready to take on the day. My husband would take him, and I would get my only two hours of uninterrupted sleep.

My husband is a musician, so he is out of town a great deal. He would call home happy to hear my voice and wanting detailed updates on our son. How was his health? What was he doing? Could he roll over, sit up? I would answer his questions as best I could, struggling to make my tiny world sound interesting. I would half listen as he told me about his life, so much bigger in scope than mine, so much more stimulating, full of creative people and events. My voice would become flat, monotone. I had nothing to contribute to the conversation. How could I explain that folding doll-sized preemie undershirts would put me into a state of bliss or the miracle of discovering if I sang 'You Are My Sunshine' to our son he would stop crying? I would break off the conversation claiming I had to deal with an overflowing diaper pail or some other equally necessary but outrageously boring task. Later, I would promise myself to make more of an effort to include my husband and to validate my world, but later never came.

As for my schedule, it never made it to the fridge, let alone to paper. Piles of toys, books and gadgets littered the already cluttered house. It seemed such a colossal effort to put them away when I would only need them again an hour later. So they just stayed heaped in corners, mounded on furniture. I'm sure I cleaned the floor when my son was an infant, but I can only remember doing so once. He sat happily in his bucket seat on the counter while I scrubbed away, crying with relief at actually accomplishing a concrete task and singing to him and praising him for being such a sweetie and letting me get something done.

I was haunted by doubts about my abilities. Here I had this sweet, good-natured baby who despite the odds was thriving. I looked at him and was overwhelmed with the depth of love that I felt. Here was the perfection I so badly wanted. Why wasn't I satisfied? Why wasn't this enough? Why was I worried about the chaos around me? Why was I unable to accept my life, my limitations?

I had been raised during the women's movement. On an intellectual level I knew that as a woman I did not have to think of the house as my domain or assume people judged me by my homemaking abilities and skills as a mother. If they did, they lacked enlightenment and I didn't want them around anyway. I had a husband who supported me in being a stay-at-home mother but did not assume or expect that I would do it all. He wanted to be a hands-on dad and was more than able, if not always eager, to do housework and cooking. Yet somewhere in the dark corners of my heart, a little voice whispered that it really was my job to do it all. After all, he earned the money, so I should take care of the rest—happily, easily, and well. I struggled on.

Four years later, after being assured that I wouldn't have another premature baby, I found the courage to get pregnant again. This time I would get it right. I was sent to a specialist (just to be safe) who promptly popped my euphoric bubble by telling me there was a one-in-four chance of repeating the nightmare. On the outside, I took this information maturely and calmly. Inside, I was chanting, Oh fuck. Oh fuck. Oh fuck. I gritted my teeth and smiled. I could handle this. I could. Days ticked by and turned into weeks and then months. I blossomed. Not into a flower but a beach ball with flabby tubes representing my legs and arms. At five months, strangers would smile and wish me good luck, thinking I was ready to pop any day now. I held my breath as the six-month mark loomed, then passed. Then the seventh and eighth. I was out of the woods. I had done it right! My husband and I even took the birth classes we had missed the first time around. Some of the other couples thought it odd that we already had a baby and were in the class. I made a mental note not to include them on our Christmas card list.

Three weeks to go. My husband was ending a month-long road trip with a concert two hours outside of town. I joined him. Despite the success of the show, I forwent the after-party, opting instead to go back to the hotel to put our son and myself to bed. Early the next morning I awoke to a funny pain. A possible contraction? I nudged my husband awake. Having celebrated till the wee hours, he was not thrilled to be woken up. His suggestion on hearing my concerns was to go back to sleep. I got up to start packing when another contraction wrung my body to a standstill. I lovingly yelled my husband out of bed. There was still time. We would head home and go straight to the hospital.

While my husband took a load of stuff to the car, I shuffled down the hall to a bandmate's room to let him know what was happening and that he would have to do that day's interviews alone. His wife answered the door. With an unearthly moan, I dropped to my hands and knees and began to push. I crawled into the room and my water burst. "This is so wrong," I muttered as I was wheeled out of the hotel and loaded into an ambulance, stoically trying to ignore the startled faces of hotel staff and guests. I was adamant that I would not have the baby in the ambulance. Every time the attendant tried to examine me, I would press my legs together, hit him away and holler, "Just drive!"

We arrived in time to get me through the doors and into a delivery room seconds before I pushed the baby out. A film crew who were doing a documentary on my husband's band arrived, hoping to catch the final intimate moments, thinking it would make great footage for the end of their film. They were shocked when I refused to let them in.

Once again, I hadn't done things according to plan, but I comforted myself with having gone almost to term and having produced a beautiful, healthy little girl. After a luxurious three-day stay in the hospital, I was sent home. I didn't know what hit me. What had I been doing with all my spare time? "Busy" took on a whole new meaning. I would really have to get down to it now. Get on top of things and stay there. The problem was that she just wanted to be held every waking moment of every single day, and I just wanted to stare at her perfection. Also, I had an incredibly active four-year-old who welcomed each day with questions, chatter and an energy that took my breath away. My husband still travelled a lot. My flat voice continued when he phoned home.

My life was fuller then ever, busier then ever, and I had become the person I had vowed not to become: I had not stayed in touch with the world. The rare time I read a paper or listened to the news I felt depressed, helpless and fearful for my family. I spoke to friends on the phone, but unless they had children around the ages of mine I rarely saw them. Gradually, I stopped hearing from friends with no children. I didn't blame them. I had become one of those people who could speak of nothing but her children. My fashion sense was dubious. I chose my wardrobe based on what was clean and least likely to show grime. I used my clothing to mop spills, clean hands and wipe snot from runny noses. More than once, I horrified some unsuspecting restaurant worker by pre-chewing food and then feeding it to my baby. I was not interested in my husband's life beyond knowing if he was making enough money to support us, if he was going to be in or out of town and whether he was able to relieve me of child care so I could have a bath.

Some days life trickled by. Some days it flew and the kids grew bigger, the way kids do. They fought a lot, despite my thinking that having them four years apart would mean they would be each other's best friend. My son's frequent trips to the hospital lessened, and he was followed by fewer specialists. I began to sleep more and was able to freelance. Life no longer fell apart when my husband left town. I started to enjoy some of his phone calls home, and our conversations had some energy. I could contribute to them. When he came home from a road trip, I was usually happy to see him and could hear about his much more exciting life without feeling overly resentful or comparing it with the often thankless, mundane routine of home life.

Occasionally, we would go out on a date, and these dates no longer consisted of wolfing down a meal and then trying to think of things to talk about in order to distract each other for an hour before hurrying home to see if the kids were okay and hadn't killed each other. And as we left behind those early years, I was sure this meant I would, at last, blossom into the organized mother I was sure was hiding inside me. It was my time.

I waited. At first patiently, then restlessly, and finally I took action. I came up with a new plan. It was the best plan yet. What my family needed was a colour-coded wall chart. Every summer, from the time my children were in grade school, I had fantasized about a wall chart that would divide household chores, cooking rotations, yard work and a weekly bedroom shakedown. We would schedule in fun family time too. But each summer came and went and I never got around to making the chart.

My children are now thirteen and seventeen. I have had a lot of years to plan and fine-tune that chart, but not once have I followed through on making it. I am forty-seven, and I've stopped worrying about fashion, opting for comfort and clothes that suit me. Sometimes I look pretty put together. I am still married. Somewhere along the way, we have found that we do still have things in common beyond being parents. We like spending time together, especially over coffee and crossword puzzles. He makes me laugh. He thinks I'm a good mother and beautiful. I have friends who have children and some who don't. I can talk about things other than my kids, but I've made a career of shamelessly exploiting their lives in my writing and performing.

Motherhood has been a slow journey for me. It has taken me years to accept that I'm not perfect and never will be. Perfect would be boring. If I were perfect, I wouldn't need a plan, and plans are what give me hope and energy. Here's is my latest plan: once the kids are gone I will have a house that is clean all the time. I will be active in my community, taking classes, volunteering and continuing to be a financial contributor to the household. I will stay on top of current affairs and throw magnificent parties. I will find joy and simplicity in all I do. I will do yoga every day and remember to take my vitamins. My garden will be beautiful. I will not experience any negative effects of menopause. And when I am blessed with grand-children (not that I would ever pressure my children to take that route), I will be a fabulous grandmother, adored and involved in my grandchildren's lives. On Sundays, I will gather my offspring in my tidy home and we will have a family meal. We will converse and revel in the joy of having a well-adjusted multi-generational family. My husband will adore me, always seeing in me the woman he mar-ried. That won't be difficult as I will have kept my figure, maintained my health and still be considered sexy.

One morning, well into my eighties or early nineties, having buried my husband several years earlier, I will simply not wake up. My family will be sad but not devastated. I will have taken care of my finances such that I can leave a sizable inheritance to each of my grown children, allowing them to put their children through post-secondary education without depleting their own finances. I have made all my post-death wishes known and prepaid the whole event so there will be no work to be done or financial burden to incur. And if they peek in the freezer, they will find all the food needed for the reception. Having had a premonition of my death, I will have done all this in advance. All they will need to do is warm everything in the oven and put the food on platters, which are stacked by size in the cupboard above the stove. A selection of lovely wine, beer and champagne will be chilled in the fridge. Toasts will be made to a lovely woman, a fabulous mother and grandmother and to a life well and not so perfectly lived.

THE OTHER SIDE
OF BRIGHTNESS

DENISE RYAN

As editor of the softer sections of a major market newspaper (*Body & Health, Style, Food, At Home*), I am bound to take pitches from writers, or anyone with a computer or a phone, for that matter. In particular, I must endure the constant and ringing tones of mothers who think their experiences are interesting, unique, even extraordinary; women who think the new otherness of motherhood is entertaining, or that motherhood, somehow, is news.

They send emails signed with pulsing smiley faces, or mail eye-catching lime green envelopes of carefully typed sample columns. With cheery cover letters they introduce themselves as the new Erma Bombeck or worse, as aspiring "real" writers (did I know that Alice Munro wrote at the kitchen table while she baked bread and her children played around her feet?) who want to balance work and motherhood.

Some simply materialize in my glass-walled office, dozing tot parked in the Peg Pérego outside the door. They chatter, grinning and sheepish, ply me with Starbucks and apologies, but they've always wanted to write, and motherhood has just given them so much to say! You're a mother too, aren't you?

Yes, yes. I'm a mother too. But when they ask why I don't write about motherhood, I bring things to a close and ask them to leave their pieces. I promise to get back to them. (I won't.)

The columns they submit sound frighteningly similar, as if they've all come from the same mommy factory. There are the standbys: spit-up on unwashed clothes, lack of sleep, unwashed hair, mommy brain, unwashed floors. There is plenty of cheery ruminating on the tug between feelings of frustration and the absurd pleasure of it all, and there's always some variation on the theme of "my milk-duds are a-flapping and I'm too tired for sex."

As I toss these wastes of paper onto the teetering stack of an in-basket, I wonder why it is that motherhood seems so damn fascinating to them, so slapstick, so winning.

I wonder why motherhood suddenly matters so much. When did motherhood become "a thing," like achieving your dream of singing at the Met, circumnavigating the globe or soloing Everest blind, on one foot? When did it become something other than the dark, complicated, terrifying thing we were born to desire and then doomed to endure, like adulthood itself?

As I toss these spunky little efforts away, I'm aware I'm waiting for the one thing I know to be true about motherhood to reach me, like a small cry in the dark, the one that wakes you from the deepest sleep, that seizes you from even the most pleasurable dream, that reminds you of what it is to be human and, as my own mother would have said, "goddamn-well trying to get somewhere, somehow."

Mothers, when I was growing up, were not something to be interested in. They were a rather sorry lot, and I spent a good deal of time—like most young girls—tottering around in their sling-backs trying to be like them, hoping to better them, or spying on them through the French doors while they lounged on couches smoking menthols and drinking gin, as if I was peering through the bars at zoo animals in their cages.

I pawed thoughtlessly through their drawers while I babysat, tried on their wigs and garter belts, sniffed their lipsticks and rolled around on the bed in their fur coats. I dug into jewellery boxes to unearth their secrets (a newspaper clipping of Sophia Loren because she had miscarried too, a dried rose tucked inside a matchbox, and once, under the glued velvet lining of the ring compartment, a photo of a man I had never seen before). I handed over fresh Kleenex and cleaned wadded ones off the bedspreads of my friends' mothers whose husbands had left them for someone else.

When my own mother left my father—sometime before she gave up on motherhood entirely and left us too—I cowered at the back of the bank as she railed over the institution's refusal to grant her access to her husband's accounts and a bloodstain bloomed on the back of her pink-flowered skirt because she could not afford to buy Kotex. She made a scene, sobbing, as if anyone cared. "I've got three children to feed. Please. Please."

That my brothers and I were three surly teenagers by that time, with safety pins in our ears and dime bags in our pockets, made no difference to her. We would always be what she carried around, marsupial pups permanently attached and leeching from some dark pocket of her being. We made her desperate and, I'm pretty sure that at least for a time, we ruined her life.

In the newsroom, I think of my mother sometimes, especially when I open one of these motherhood pitches (I want to write about the greatest challenge, most exhausting job, most fulfilling experience, the day my uterus dropped out, ha, ha...), and when I do there is an image I have of her that I cannot shake.

She stands at the window of a bungalow in a California suburb where we lived while my father was overseas during the Vietnam War, looking out. I can see her as surely as if I were an adult already, not a twelve-month-old baby girl sucking her fist. I see the rest of it: the gold brocade carpeting, the animal-chewed legs of the sofa. I smell the two dogs, their breath hairy and warm; I can feel the sheers that brush against her cheek as she stares out at the street from the darkened room. The room is darkened because it is afternoon and achingly sunny outside; we are supposed to be napping, but we are fighting the heat, awake.

There are three of us, all born embarrassingly close, within months of each other, Irish triplets. My newborn baby brother lies prone in a soggy diaper, his wails getting louder and louder. My legs are rashy with prickly heat. My older brother, two and a half, detached as always, occupies himself with the tail of a dog that flips through the bars of our shared playpen.

She stands there, hour after hour, looking out, wearing pedal pushers and bare feet, her golden hair limp around her shoulders. She can feel the darkness of the room, how close it is. She can see the car in the drive, the MG that is no longer big enough to hold her and these three fat, wobbly things that must be carried with her everywhere. She sees the road that my father used to take her down, toward the Pacific Coast highway, where they used to drive, listening to Clarence "Gatemouth" Brown on the radio. They'd drive all day past Santa Anita, through Carmel and San Diego to Tijuana, where they would go to the dog races and drink cold soda and surf the Tijuana sloughs.

Now he is gone to plan some invasion, some offensive in Vietnam she knows little about, and she stands at this window alone; invaded by us, overtaken, she has surrendered. As the weeks tick by, she stands in the same spot. She gets thinner and thinner. She can barely get out of the house for groceries or anything else, and if she could, why bother? Where would she go? The wailing of the smallest one is like a constantly skipping record, one note that repeats itself and fades, repeats itself and fades, a kind of hypnosis that has dulled her.

When her parents call, they can hardly hear her. They ask questions and guess at her answers. At first they think it is the telephone line. After all, it is a long way to call from Canada to California. They don't know that she doesn't eat any more—sometimes a grape, a piece of Melba toast chewed in careful, small bites. She might have a cup of sugary tea, but only when it doesn't seem like too much to boil the water. Sometimes she moves us from our pen, sometimes she doesn't. The German shepherds prowl around us like hungry wolves; she neglects to feed them too. Finally her father, unable to get her even to pick up the phone any more, gets on a plane and arrives to find her as scrawny as a nine-year-old and wandering distractedly through a house boggy with diaper pail, dog hair and baby breath. He feeds the dogs and finds them homes, takes us all away, up to Canada and to our grandmother who is warm and capable, who gardens and goes to church and cooks. He rescues her, and us. After a year, my father returns and order is restored, barely.

She gets on with the business of mothering—sewing clothes, baking cakes, birthday parties, carpools, boiling crabapples for jelly. In between, she doodles a lot of hearts on pads of paper, all of them with long trailing tails. She traces over and over the lines of these hearts with her pen, pressing until the ink is so thick that the paper falls apart. She leaves these papers everywhere, this trail of broken hearts. At night, she bathes us and puts us to bed. Afterwards, she sings listless lullabies from the hallway so we all can hear, each of us in our separate rooms, our eyes fixed on our own starless ceilings.

Sometimes, when I slice open the brightly coloured envelopes that tell me how to think of motherhood, I think of her tuneless voice coming from out there somewhere a little too far away, and then fading as she moves inexorably farther from us and down the stairs, my brothers and I drifting carelessly off to sleep. Sometimes I don't open the envelopes at all.

Besides, I have other things to think about. That veterinary column I am supposed to put in place, more recipes for the food section, shoes and handbags for Style. Work.

Perhaps because of my own mother, I had always incorporated work into my motherhood plan. It was what she didn't have. For her, there was nothing but the relentlessly growing pile of laundry under the bathroom sink (she couldn't be bothered with hampers), the water pooling in the crisper drawers of a fridge that needed to be repaired again, and a constantly irritating feeling that there was somewhere— maybe in Paris, Argentina or Egypt—under some glimmering, lemon-scented sun, an experience she would never reach.

In between the meals she made, the lessons she dragged us to, the meetings she distractedly sat through at our private schools, smoking, tapping her foot, she took art classes, did macramé, learned pottery. But still.

When I became a mother, I had a plan. I would take care of myself by taking care of business. Work, I knew, was necessary. It was not something to be cunningly fitted in between naps. It couldn't be—and I didn't believe that stuff about Alice Munro pounding out stories while her children played around her feet. Surely she shooed them, booted them away, the rats. After all, work had a function, and it was not about motherhood. It was about motherhood's opposite—some kind of linchpin connecting me to all that was solid and sane and onward-moving. It was the drive that would take me down the road to the Tijuana sloughs, sodas and sunshine and dog races. I would never be standing there on the dark side of some invisible glass window, unable to break through. Or so I thought.

I remember being slightly embarrassed by my pregnancy at work. I felt Victorian about it and disguised it until it was impossible to hide any more. Although properly married, I felt like some errant teenager when I confessed the situation to my managers. I thought I read grim resignation in their tight smiles, a hint of disappointment. I would have to go away for a while. I would have to be replaced. I fielded calls from friends on the outside: Would I take a maternity leave? Would there be a posting? Could they have my job?

I was already as good as buried and I sensed the chill of something no one talked about, the threat of some unnamed spectre that persists and terrorizes by constantly changing its form—that childbirth would be the death of me one way or another.

Still, I was determined. I would take my maternity leave as planned. I would take on motherhood. I would get the job done. I would survive. I was going away, but I imagined on the other side something bright and welcoming, something to cross over to, another mother standing there, not mine, welcoming me to some new heaven.

Sometime before the birth, just in case, I inform my doctor about my mother's history. She provides me with emergency numbers, brochures that list warning signs of postpartum depression, the location of a clinic I can attend if. If.

I shove it all in my in-basket at home, sure I won't need it. I'm a professional, after all. I'm a grown-up. I'm going to exercise and take walks on the beach, get it done. And I do.

After a blurry, one-year maternity leave, I return to work as scheduled, to a new job managing the so-called good news sections (what is more often, and less flatteringly called "the back end" of the newspaper). Keep it light! Keep it bright! I could do that, I was sure.

AND SO I DO. I put a new food columnist in place. I get interested in fashion. I run series about hip replacements and articles about weight loss. I show up at news meetings and before we get to discussing Air-India, Iraq or the dead women on Vancouver's Downtown Eastside, I present my editorial plans for the next day. I announce, Pink Is the New Beige! Sex Is the New Exercise! Pomegranates Are the New Apples! I keep it light. Day after day, section after section, I get the job done.

I don't tell anyone that at night, after all those long hours of being super-capable, I stare numbly out the window of my second-floor apartment, stare at the pool of orange lamplight beyond the closed windows and think of nothing. I take my son from his crib and into bed with me. I curl my body around his, determined to mother him by osmosis, to love him in his sleep. Night after night, I sleep like this, holding my child in a dark room, holding on for his life, and mine.

Only once do I confide in a colleague about how hard it is—though I'm not even sure what I mean to identify as difficult, so I reach for something and zero in on dinner. You know, I say, after a long day, and the trip to the daycare, and laundry and husband and so on, to get a meal together, it's not so, well, it's not...

Even as I say it, I trail off. I worry that by naming it I will make it so. My thin shell will start to crack, my crisp suit of resolve will unbuckle, my Pink Is the New Beige cleverness will fall away and I will be exposed as someone sunk in the swampy depths of the diaper pail. I will be relieved of my responsibilities, my big glass office, my linchpin. My only recourse will be trying to hack my way back in with cheery columns about my num-num bunny, my mommies' group, my unwashed whatever. I will become what I most fear I am—one of them. Trying to convince myself. Trying to convince everyone else.

My colleague, who is dedicated and hard-working, efficient in ways that I will never be, and who just as efficiently mothers a handful of children I have never seen, immediately closes the door to her office. Here's how I do it, she says. Her eyes are bright, her face animated, her voice full of enthusiasm. I take a chicken first thing in the morning. I take a chicken that's frozen solid. Rock hard. I stick it in the pan, stick the pan in the oven and set the timer. It thaws through the day, the oven goes on at five, you get home at six, or six-thirty, your chicken is done. Saves me every time.

Don't you have to thaw it? What about salmonella, food safety? What about lemon and salt and rosemary, a leaf of bay? Of course,

I don't ask. I do not acknowledge what is unspoken, because that is not within reach here in the dead air of the glass office. I do know this. She is not giving me a recipe for chicken. She is letting me in on a secret: the real job of mothering is the job of just getting it done. That's what mothers do. Chop-chop. Doesn't matter what it tastes like.

The next morning, I open the freezer and take a Safeway chicken out, rip it from its plastic, unpeel the Styrofoam from its gut and remove the little diaper there to absorb its pale, icy blood. This chicken, I think, will save me. I hold it stripped and frozen in my hands, the bare bones of it. I wonder how to use the timer on the oven, whether the house will catch on fire while I'm at work, whether I will misjudge and the salmonella will proliferate and poison us all. I stare at the frozen yellow fat, the factory-white flesh, already tasting its flavourless meat and I wonder, What did I expect? But this is getting it done. This is motherhood, after all.

I REMEMBER THE day I noticed my mother had stopped getting it done for the second time around. It was after school. I was in Grade 6. She was in the kitchen, where she always was at about four o'clock in the afternoon. I stopped dead when I saw her—maybe she had been like this for weeks, maybe months, but until then I hadn't noticed. I was beyond being interested in mothers to even notice her at all. I was too preoccupied with combing through my hair for split ends or staring at myself in the mirror wondering whether I could ever write like Dostoevsky, and if not, could I hope to be a model on *The Price Is Right*. But there she was, suddenly all ribs and bones. Every sharp edge of her jutted out. She looked like some grey skeleton that had been unearthed and assembled, without flesh or life. She must have stopped eating again sometime before. Her hair hung limp and oily around her face. One hand held a cigarette with a long ash. With the other hand she leaned against the sink. In front of her on soggy pink butcher paper, a pile of fatty ground round lay unwrapped, sitting in a pool of its own blood.

How long had she been leaning there? How long had she simply stood and stared? How many kilos of ground round had she slapped into a meatloaf pan with her bare hands? How many quick spaghetti sauces had she made? How many pots of chili?

I don't remember if we had dinner that night, what happened to the beef or what we did instead, but I do know it was a long time before she cooked for us again with anything that resembled joy, and by the time she did, she had long since left the family.

I would never be like that. I would never. And yet.

All day long I do my job. I read the wires, but no matter how I try to keep it light, I am dragged under by stories that bleep by across my screen. *Mother who drowned her five children hopes for appeal. Toppling large-screen television sets biggest cause of emergency room visits in children under four. Toddler left in car dies of heatstroke while mother gambles. Children in daycare more aggressive than normal. Teen boy kills mother.*

I shake my head, get a coffee, go to the afternoon meeting, tell the requisite jokes that keep me on the good side, return to my desk, open mail, skim through queries. Some piece about a child's first day in kindergarten, a mother turning forty, reflecting rites of passage, meant to be touchingly universal. I drop it in the in-basket. At night, I dream of a woman whose teeth are falling out. I dream of murder. I dream of confessing. I dream of jail.

Most days I get through, putting distance between me and what might have been, ticking off the weeks and months that could be described as postpartum until I think I am safely on the other side. But one day I pick up my two-year-old son, and his daycare provider asks to speak to me privately. He has bitten someone. The other mother shows me the two rows of teeth marks on her daughter's back, the tender imprint of my son's looming delinquency. I apolo-

gize, but later the mother calls me at home to say she doesn't think
I have taken the situation seriously enough. She wants to speak
Mother to Mother. She wants me to do something about my son.
His teeth. She wants me to do something about my attitude. She
doesn't understand why she can't get through to me, why I don't
seem to care. I hold the phone away from my ear as I grit my teeth
and hold my breath. I refuse to let her hear me cry.

That night, I sit in my chair, staring sleeplessly out the window.
Another story from the newswire surfaces through the murky,
shapeless waters in my brain, about a mother who threw herself in
front of a train. How she stood on the platform for hours, clutching
her infant, while all around her commuters came and went. There
was a picture of her, golden-haired, a doctor. A woman, friends said,
who had it all. A woman just like me.

Later that night, in bed, I clutch the solid, breathing body of my
son. He sleeps so sweetly, unaware. I imagine the other mother holding her son as he slept sweetly, unaware. *That* is a nervous breakdown,
I tell myself. Not this. Never this. I think about the beautiful doctor,
that other mother, how lonely it must have been to stand there, at the
edge of something and never to have found her way to the other side.
I see her golden hair streaming in the hot rush of air from the train as
it screams into the station and how her body arcs, the child held close
in her arms going down with her, warm, willing.

I think of my mother, how still she held herself at that window
in California, waiting for something to get better. I think of what it
must have taken not to leave us then. To take the MG, top down,
warm wind in her hair. To leave us there, German shepherds cir-
cling, our cries ringing through the empty house at first and then
fading. How there must have been something keeping her near.
Grim will. Hope.

So you see why, when the queries come in, with their amusing
anecdotes and annoying but endearing toddlers, those mothers

who, for some reason, think the world needs another Erma Bombeck, I cannot take these balls lobbed from the other side of brightness. It is because I have learned only this: motherhood is an uneven passage through all that is precarious and terrifying in life; a body flung toward a light that seems to be eternally shimmering on the other side. The child, clung to at night, is a life preserver in a sunless room; we float, while up above, the plum-dark ceiling, star-less, keeps its cover over us.

PART THREE

Guilt

UNHINGED

JEN LAWRENCE

Before I had children, I was the perfect mother. I had a loving husband and financial stability. I had scaled back my career to accommodate a more family-friendly lifestyle (heading a children's museum, no less!). I did yoga, meditated, ate organic food and took my folic acid. I was ready.

Unfortunately, my uterus didn't get the memo.

So my husband and I met with a fertility specialist. While I sat in the clinic waiting to have my blood taken each morning, I listened to the stories of women who had been there for months, even years. I promised myself that if I was fortunate enough to become pregnant, I'd be the best mother in the world. I would breastfeed. I would make my own baby food. I would get rid of the TV. I planned to make those peaceful mothers rocking their babies on the cover of those *What to Expect* books look like rank amateurs. To my surprise, I became pregnant during my first cycle at the clinic. Now all I had to do was keep my promises.

Things started out well enough. I made sure I took my progesterone at the exact same time each day so that I would not miscarry. I ate seven to ten servings of organic fruits and veggies daily. I did not work, in order to avoid stress. I did my Gentle-Yet-Effective pregnancy workout every morning. I avoided gardening and cats. I avoided soft cheeses and mosquitoes. I did not take hot baths and I slept on my left side. I was a perfect incubator for my unborn child.

Sadly, and somewhat predictably, I also went crazy.

The depression I'd dealt with on and off throughout my life reared its ugly head, this time manifesting itself as acute anxiety. I was positive I had lead poisoning. I was positive I'd been exposed to toxoplasmosis. I was positive that the strawberry I ate had been sitting uncomfortably close to a piece of listeria-ridden brie. I was sure I would come down with West Nile virus or SARS or mad-cow disease—perhaps all three. When I told my obstetrician my concerns, she referred me to a perinatal psychiatrist who, in turn, recommended that I start to take antidepressants immediately. She assured me that they were safe to take during pregnancy and I did in-depth research to confirm that she was right. But antidepressants were not on the list of Must-Dos in the Healthy-Earthy-Perfect-Natural pregnancy books I'd been devouring, so I said thanks, but no thanks. I'd consider the meds once I'd stopped breastfeeding—in about two and a half years.

My anxiety continued to worsen. I saw everything as having the potential to harm my unborn child. After a while, I was afraid to leave the house and dreaded my now frequent appointments with my obstetrician and psychiatrist. Finally I agreed to start taking antidepressants a short time after I delivered. Secretly I hoped that the depression and anxiety might simply lift with the joy of giving birth. Not long thereafter, I delivered a beautiful, healthy baby girl. And I was a mess.

The post-delivery hospital stay did little to help my mood. It was simply assumed that I would be breastfeeding exclusively, and so even though my risk of serious postpartum depression was written all over my hospital chart, the nurses insisted that I wake every two hours to nurse my daughter. And when they were not waking me to pump, they were flicking on the lights to see if I was asleep.

Now, I'm no medical expert, but it does seem to be a rather odd way to help a clearly depressed and exhausted woman recover after a painful delivery (my daughter had a *very* large head).

The nurses seemed obsessed with my ability (or inability) to breastfeed and with each shift change came a new onslaught of often contradictory advice.

"Use the football hold!"

"No, no. Who told you to use that hold? Use the cradle hold!"

"Baby should make a fish face while eating!"

"No, no! No fish face! No fish face!"

The only things that were clear were that (1) breastfeeding was the most important thing on earth and (2) I was bad at it.

I was told I needed to attend the hospital-run breastfeeding class and was left with the impression that if I didn't go and get myself sorted out, they might not let me take my daughter home. While on the one hand, the thought of being entirely responsible for my daughter terrified me, I figured that my chances of getting some sleep were better at home. Besides, the food was killing me. (What kind of sadistic mind comes up with a breakfast of corned-beef hash and a lunch of chili for new mothers whose digestive systems are, for the most part, shot completely to hell?) So I picked up my daughter and my breastfeeding pillow and shuffled uncomfortably to the class.

The session was led by a lactation educator who was a strong believer in extended breastfeeding. No matter what question was asked, her answer was "breastfeed more." No milk supply? Breastfeed more. Sore breasts? Breastfeed more. Someone asked about taking medications while breastfeeding, and the woman stated that she could say "with confidence" that no one in the room would be taking a medication unsafe to take while breastfeeding. One woman let out an audible scoff, picked up her baby and her doughnut cushion and walked out of the room. I should have done the same.

I had planned to wean my daughter right away so that I would feel comfortable taking the prescribed antidepressants, but suddenly I was not so sure. Were I to stop breastfeeding, I would potentially compromise my daughter's IQ and resistance to infection, and increase her potential for asthma, life-threatening allergies, obesity, and heaven only knows what else. And yet, I could not get comfortable with the idea of taking the medication while breastfeeding. Even though my extensive research had turned up no long-term adverse effects, I still had the contamination fears I'd experienced during pregnancy. The thought of taking a drug that the manufacturer suggested be used with caution while breastfeeding was simply too frightening for me. Because ethical considerations prevent clinical testing of drugs on pregnant or lactating women, and because the risk of lawsuits is so high, very few drug manufacturers are willing to declare their drugs "safe" during pregnancy or breastfeeding even when the medical community thinks the benefits of taking the drug outweigh the potential risks to the baby.

Besides, mothers are supposed to be willing to die for their children. Was I not willing to feel down for a while longer in order to give my baby the best chance in life? How selfish was I?

I was discharged from the hospital with my antidepressant prescription still unfilled. The fog of new parenthood settled over me as soon as I got home. When I wasn't breastfeeding, I was attached to a breast pump. When it became clear that in spite of my efforts, my daughter was still not gaining enough weight, we began to supplement with formula on the advice of our pediatrician. The guilt of giving her a less than perfect food, of giving in to Big Formula, made me all the more determined to continue my breastfeeding efforts. So I continued to feed and pump, pump and feed, growing more and more anxious and depressed.

In truth, I don't really remember a lot about those early days. In photographs from that time, I'm the ghost in the corner while other people smile and coo at my daughter. I kept a written record of my moods to share with my doctor, and in it I wrote about being terrified that my daughter would die. I feared that she would stop breathing in the night or that I would drop her down the stairs accidentally. I was convinced that I was not a good enough mother to keep my daughter safe, and that she would be better off without me. After all, I reasoned, if fate had intended me to be a mother, I would not have required the fertility clinic. If I had been meant to be a mother, my breast milk would flow like the mighty Mississippi.

I started to drift away emotionally from my daughter. My thoughts were consumed with self-harm. I remember standing out on my front steps on a cold November night, hoping that the chilly air would help clear my head and stop the Iago-like chatter running through my brain. My daughter was a few weeks old and needed to feed every couple of hours. I was beyond exhausted and feeling wholly incompetent. I honestly believed that if I gracefully exited the picture, my husband could remarry and find a better mother for our daughter. I looked down our street toward the bridge that runs over the ground-level subway tracks. *Do it now, before she gets attached*, I remember thinking. I started to walk down our front path, trying not to think about the pain my actions might inflict on others in the short term, when suddenly I stopped. There was a dusting of snow on the walk, which had melted beneath my feet and had seeped through my thick socks onto my skin, reminding me that I was not wearing any shoes. I started back toward the house with the intention of grabbing the shoes that lay on the mat just inside the front door. A little voice urged me to forget about the shoes and to turn back to the darkness of the street. I knew that once I opened that door, I would lose my nerve, that I would be trapped with the ache and the worry. But it was too late; my hand was already on the worn brass door handle; the moment had passed.

The incident rattled me. I knew I needed help. I knew I needed medication. So three weeks after giving birth, I weaned my daughter and started taking antidepressants. I assumed that the weaning process would be painful and imagined I'd need to wrap myself in cold compresses and drink strong cups of sage tea. I think I secretly hoped that a physical pain might numb the psychic ache. Instead, my milk supply dried up quickly, further proof of my ineptitude. I felt that I had officially failed my first test as a mother.

A few weeks later, I found myself sitting in one of those mom-and-baby classes. The medication had started to kick in, but I was still quite fragile emotionally. Every time I burned my fingers on the fresh-out-of-the-sterilizer bottles or spilled some formula, I beat myself up over my perceived maternal failure. I had wanted to skip the class—it was the dead of winter and getting to the class meant a twenty-minute walk uphill, pushing the heavy stroller through the slush and snow. But my doctor and family thought it might be good for me to get out of the house. When I arrived, most of the other new mothers were sitting on the floor. A number of them were breastfeeding their babies, and I felt a stab of envy as I watched how competent and content they seemed. I was still sweaty from the walk and regretting wearing a turtleneck as the place had the heaters turned up full blast. My daughter had woken up as soon as I took her out of the stroller and was starting to fuss for some milk. I tried to pour the tin of ready-to-use formula into the freshly sterilized bottle while jiggling my increasingly noisy daughter on my lap in an attempt to soothe her cries. I spilled a little of the milk and found myself growing flustered. I considered simply getting up and leaving, but by this point the program leader had handed me a blank name tag and a pen, and I figured I might as well stay.

After a brief hello, the facilitator introduced herself. She made it very clear that she was a fan of attachment parenting and believed strongly in extended breastfeeding. She talked at length about how breastfeeding was such a wonderful bonding experience. She described breast milk as not only the perfect food but also a magical elixir curing everything from cracked nipples to eye infections. Babies, she told us, thought breast milk was more delicious than ice cream. She asked each of us to talk about our own experience with breast- or bottle-feeding. Given that I had already popped open a can of ready-to-use in front of the class, I had outed myself as a non-breastfeeder. I really had no desire to get into my tale of postpartum depression and acute anxiety with a bunch of strangers. So when it was my turn to share, I simply lied and said I was using formula as a supplement to breastfeeding. The instructor commented that formula could be quite convenient. She did not mean the comment to be hurtful, but I still felt its sting. Motherhood was about sacrifice and sleeplessness and breastfeeding through three bouts of mastitis. Convenience ought not play a role.

Many months later, I was taking the subway home after a visit with my psychiatrist. My medication was working well, and I had told my doctor that I was starting to feel good again. I stared at the ads up near the subway car's ceiling as a way to avoid eye contact with my fellow riders—one of whom appeared to be wearing a homemade tinfoil hat. There were ads for career training, a new soft drink and birth control pills marketed to college-aged women. And then there was this: a brightly coloured poster sponsored by the city's public health department featuring smiling cartoon babies and the caption, "Every Baby Deserves Breastmilk!"

Every baby, of course, but mine.

By the time I got home, I had become unhinged. I wondered how I could have been so stupid as to think that I was doing well.

WHEN I GAVE BIRTH to my son, twenty-one months after birthing my daughter, so much had changed. I had decided that I would continue to take my medication throughout the pregnancy.

Now that I was no longer consumed with worry, I could make a decision based on the actual risks rather than on a wild-eyed feeling that any level of risk was unacceptable. The medical community continued to believe that my medication was safe to use during pregnancy and breastfeeding, and there was mounting evidence that untreated depression during pregnancy was harmful not only to the woman but also to her unborn child. Plus, I had to consider my spirited toddler. I could not simply put my life on hold for nine months—my daughter needed a mother. I did not make the decision to take my medication lightly and I did not live with my decision without guilt. During the course of the pregnancy, I developed a small placental tear and was barred from lifting anything. Then a routine ultrasound uncovered a choroid plexus cyst on my son's developing brain. In spite of my doctor's assurances to the contrary, I could not help wondering if my medication was somehow to blame. I've since been told that the cyst will disappear and will have no lingering effects; the only reason it was flagged in the first place is because it can be an indicator of a serious genetic disorder that my son clearly does not have. But still, my son has been late to walk and has a very large head, prompting frequent monitoring by his doctor. I'm not entirely convinced that the cyst has gone away or that, from a blame perspective, I am off the hook.

This time around, I was fairly comfortable with the idea of breastfeeding while taking my medication and planned to give it another try. This time, however, I would not pump. If my milk came in and my son latched well, fabulous, but I would not undertake any heroic measures. And irrespective of my breastfeeding success during the day, at night we would use formula so that my husband could take over the late-night feedings.

My doctor had arranged for me to be part of a pilot postpartum program: my son would stay in the hospital nursery at night so I could sleep and decrease my odds of another depressive episode.

The nurses, for the most part, were wonderful and supportive. Breastfeeding seemed to be working out better this time around. My son was a healthy eater and had no trouble rebounding to his birth weight, and I was so much more relaxed about the whole situation.

Then, the nursing shift changed. A new nurse came in while I was feeding my son and started to shake her head.

"You need to go to the breastfeeding clinic," she barked.

I told her that this was my second baby and I did not need the clinic.

"No, I don't believe this is your second baby. The way you breastfeed, this is your first baby," she stated bluntly as she started to flip my baby around and jam my breast into his mouth. I started to protest.

"Baby needs to eat!" she exclaimed.

"We're using formula," my husband interjected and briefly explained what was going on.

"Oh, you are using formula," she said. "You will need to meet with a social worker before you are discharged."

That's when all the old anxieties started to flood back. I couldn't breastfeed. I had no interest in learning. I was crazy. Clearly they wanted me to see a social worker because I was such a terrible mother. I had planned to stay in the hospital another night, just to make sure I was feeling strong before we went home and started around-the-clock feedings, but now I just wanted to get out of there. Luckily, the social worker on call knew my psychiatrist well and was surprised that the nurse thought I ought to see her. We signed the discharge papers and gathered up our stuff and left as fast as we could.

And then we were home and, as everyone tells you, it is so much easier with the second one. This time around I wasn't terrified, and I could sit and rock my newborn son and drink in his milky smell until he drifted off to sleep on my shoulder. Having missed out on so much with my daughter, I was bound and determined to enjoy these first days with my baby boy. I knew that taking care of myself was a big part of making that happen. So when I realized that I no longer enjoyed breastfeeding my almost-one-month-old son, when I felt that it was taking away from the bonding experience, I simply stopped.

Weaning my son was more difficult than weaning my daughter had been. Since my milk had come in, I experienced the discomfort of engorgement. So I used the cold compresses and drank the sage tea. I also took a lot of ibuprofen; the last thing I wanted was any more pain.

Now, it seems like such a long time ago. My son is one and my daughter is three. Most of the mothers from the playdate circuit have weaned their children. My bottle-wielding children are no longer an oddity at the park.

And yet I'm not completely over my failure to breastfeed my children. When my son was diagnosed with asthma (a condition both my husband and I share), part of me wondered if breastfeeding might have prevented it. Whenever my daughter gets a patch of eczema, I feel a pinch of guilt. I keep my eyes open for studies that refute the absolute benefits of breast milk. I'm ashamed to say it, but when I read that trace levels of toxins can be detected in breast milk, it made me feel a little bit better. And, as a feminist, I was thrilled to read an article arguing that bottle feeding was good because it allowed for more equal participation in child care. When I read these things, I can tell myself, See, I *wasn't* so bad.

The truth is, I don't think any mother can be perfect. And the definition of a good mother seems awfully narrow these days. Have your own identity but don't seek paid employment. Breastfeed for at least a year, but don't be seen breastfeeding in public. Be close with your children but not too close or you will smother them. Eventually, we all set foot in the bad mother camp. We find ourselves shouting at our kids in the supermarket. Or using the television as a babysitter. Or giving up breastfeeding too early. Feelings of guilt seem unavoidable.

For me, the answer lies in facing one's perceived deficiencies head-on, and then moving forward. I know that I'm prone to depression. That I need far too much sleep. That I need a lot of me-time and solitude. That I swear far too often in front of little ears and that I buy too many handbags. I also know that I love my children truly, madly, deeply and that I'll always do the best for them that I can. And that is what keeps me afloat.

I wish I had been able to breastfeed. I wish I had been able to give my children the perfect food that all babies deserve. But as the days of rocking my babies to sleep are drawing to an end, mainly I wish that instead of spending so much time feeling guilty and berating myself, I had simply embraced the bottle and spent that time on cuddles and stories and kissing their sweet downy heads.

ONLY ONE
LISA BENDALL

I have only one child.

Her name is Emily, and as I write this, I'm picturing her standing up one day at an Offspring Anonymous meeting declaring, "My name is Emily and I am an Only Child." There would be nods of condolence all around.

Emily is beautiful and bright and the core of my life and she is growing up without brothers or sisters. Regarding this last point, I feel guilty, saddened, wistful—and often (let's admit it) wholly liberated.

This family structure is a far cry from the one I knew as a child. I grew up among a motley crew of four siblings, all born within six and a half years. My mother was homemaker, peacemaker and "pacemaker." Our family lived in the countryside of the Ottawa Valley. We had no close neighbours, so playdates were prescheduled or we resorted to each other's company for amusement.

Sibling rivalry was fierce. We were like fellow castaways trapped together on a desert island, suppressing our murderous feelings. I try not to dwell on that now. That would unfairly downplay the delights of playing together: building forts, fishing and skating, climbing trees, or playing indoors with Tinker Toys and dolls. I recall with chagrin my brother tossing one of my dollies over the fence, where it landed freestyle in a cow patty. There were other similar torments. But then again, I know how to build a river raft and tie a fishing lure because I had siblings.

As I grew up, my opinion about having children of my own vacillated. I genuinely liked kids. I babysat them, tutored them and taught them the rudiments of piano playing in exchange for a modest contribution toward my university fund. But I also had my heart set on a rewarding career, one that I felt would somehow eventually define me. And this I knew I would not sacrifice or compromise for anything. I didn't know if that life path would be compatible with kids.

It certainly wasn't for my mother, who found child rearing and corporate-ladder climbing mutually exclusive. In any case, by the time I was in my early twenties, I was fairly certain I would never have children. Well, I would either have no children or a clutch of them. These were the only two possibilities I thought to consider back then.

And look at me now: I am living neither reality. I've been married eleven years, and my family life is nothing like I ever expected. I never imagined I'd have an only child. For that matter, I never pictured myself married to someone who comes with a set of wheels.

My husband, Ian, is an intelligent and passionate man. He's easy on the eyes and he can make me laugh. He is also quadriplegic from a spinal cord injury many years ago. He can't walk or use his hands well. For a long time he wasn't even sure he'd be able to father children. When we got married we didn't care, but after two years and two advancing biological clocks we put in our bid for parenthood.

It turned out Ian could knock up a girl with the best of them. But it takes more than fertility to make a family work. It takes a first-rate juggling act. And we soon discovered there was a cap on the number of balls we could keep in the air at one time.

When Emily was a toddler, we both worked full-time outside the home. I punched the clock as a magazine editor. Ian had a frenzied management job. On top of that, my husband spends up to six hours a day just looking after his personal needs. We liken that to a part-time job—albeit a sadly underpaid one.

Attendants arrive at our house most mornings and many evenings to assist Ian with tasks like washing and dressing. Usually, he would be competing against the clock, not wanting to make us late for work, not wanting to make us late for bed. The only time I heard him curse was when he fumbled at the sink in his haste and his toothbrush landed on the bathroom floor.

On a typical weekday morning, I'd take responsibility for feeding and clothing the baby and myself, and periodically hassling my husband about being late. Throw in some outdoor snow clearing if it was winter, some slathering of sun lotion on a squirming child if summer, and I'd be lucky to get time to pack a lunch. Then, my husband would drive us all to our respective destinations: daycare, my office, then his office. We worked like dogs, and then the day would end in a reverse pattern. Ian would do the pickups and we'd charge home. I'd scramble to get a decent dinner on the table in the shortest amount of time possible—no apricot-basted, oven-roasted quail here! Our goal was to finish our meal before an attendant arrived for the evening shift. Ian would push through his nightly routine while I tended Emily through bathtime, reading and bed.

By the end of the day, we were both exhausted. Often, our pillow talk was not much more than a pragmatic reminder to set the morning alarm. I'd love to say we refreshed ourselves on the weekends, but any mom would know I was lying. Weekends meant fiendishly early wake-ups, multiple loads of laundry, expeditions for diapers and groceries, and usually a full-out siege with the mower on a back lawn that had somehow managed to grow past my knees when I wasn't looking.

Of course, most of the physical tasks of household management necessarily fall on my shoulders, always have. That's not to say

Ian isn't a typical twenty-first-century superdad. He chauffeurs Emily to gymnastics, oversees her daily piano practice and reads aloud her favourite books. On more than one occasion, he has stoically allowed her to pin his salt-and-pepper hair into a pompadour using a dozen pink barrettes. But one fact remains true: he can't change a single damn diaper. When Emily was a fussy infant who could not merely be held but had to be bounced in a very specific choreography requiring working arms, Ian was helpless to calm her. I adored my child, but babyhood exhausted me. My responsibilities exhausted me.

Another drawback of disability is that it's bloody expensive. Ian and I spent more of our disposable income on his needs than we did on daycare—in the heart of Toronto, that's saying a lot. When we thought about footing the bill for a second baby, we were confronted with the brutal reality that it might mean trading in the mortgage. And as for the sleep deprivation that routinely comes with a baby, let's just say it's that much harder when you're already dealing with a chronic condition. When we considered another newborn, my husband was blunt about it: "I don't think I can go through that again."

If we had any doubts at all about the impracticalities of a second child, they receded after the absolute apocalypse that befell our household when I was down with the stomach flu. Suddenly meals weren't getting cooked, laundry wasn't getting done and various family members were going completely unwashed. Our home wasn't shipshape at the best of times, and at the worst of times, like this, it felt about to capsize.

Still, we lobbed the idea of multiple children back and forth like a hot potato, but the ultimate decision was obvious. It was a sensible choice to stick with one child and delight in her alone. But sometimes what is sensible and rational to the head can be wrenching to the heart.

I know that only children are out there. But it still seems painfully apparent to me that two children—preferably one boy and one girl—is the most commonly sought-after ideal for moms and dads in my particular demographic. Without question I'm in a minority. I remember having lunch with a colleague who visibly glowed as he crowed about his impending fatherhood. His pregnant wife's ultrasound had confirmed the genders of the twins she was carrying. "They saw one hot dog and one hamburger," as he put it. Then he trumpeted, "It's the instant perfect family."

I would venture to say now that our own family structure is perfect for us. But I certainly haven't always managed to view it that way. And it doesn't mean I don't still, even now, wallow in the what-ifs.

When I gave birth to Emily seven years ago, all my friends were having their first children as well. Our camaraderie became powerful. As every mother knows, having a baby gives you de facto membership in the Club. As it happens, you don't even know the Club exists until you have a baby. But once you're a mom, you instantly belong to a sisterhood of women who share tales of diapers, colic and chapped nipples. These shared experiences unite us. And they insulate us from non-parents. We wouldn't dream of discussing our battered perineum with someone who's never had a baby. But mention it to another mom, and without batting an eye she's recommending her favourite brand of vitamin E oil. We are allies.

Then, when my daughter was about two, a shift started to happen. Many of my mom friends became pregnant for the second time. Outwardly I cheered, but as I observed them trying to assuage their first-trimester fatigue while dealing with an active toddler, I began to realize this was outside my own experience. And when they had to buy two sizes of diapers, source out a double stroller, explain to Child Number One that Child Number Two wasn't ever going away, I began to feel like a Club outsider. What did I know? I had only one child.

There were a few other holdouts like me, parents whose children reached the ages of three, four, and five without a sibling. Many of them eventually went over to the other side, one by one their bellies swelling in betrayal. A colleague with a preschooler faced removal of certain reproductive parts; she had one last chance to have a second baby and had to make up her mind fast. Her daughter was born a year later. A daycare dad talked about the indecision he and his wife were grappling with regarding a second child. "Of course, if we want another baby, first we have to start having sex," he commented wryly. We all laughed. We'd been there. But his wife was pregnant within weeks.

As my friends steadily expanded their families, I felt as though my own was somehow incomplete. In my gut was a stubborn yearning for a second baby. I told myself we'd never have another, but I longed for one anyway and thought about it all the time. What would it look like? Would it be a boy, to whom we'd probably give the boy name, Thomas Harry, that we'd had on standby the first time around? Or would it be another girl, who would be called Sarah or perhaps Kathleen, after my mother-in-law? Would Thomas/Kathleen be as profoundly wonderful as Emily—as lovely, as smart, as healthy, as active? What were the odds of creating a great kid twice?

I felt Thomas/Kathleen's absence most acutely when I watched other moms hold their second babies. Sometimes the ache throbbed almost physically, just as it had been painful to see pregnant women back when my husband and I were riding the roller coaster of we're-still-trying. Instead of hoarding the crib and the clothes and the infant swing and the designer stroller, we distributed them among sisters and friends who were still building their own broods. Every time Emily outgrew some piece of equipment or clothing and it disappeared from our house, it was another tender reminder of the end of an era.

I battled feelings of inadequacy on many levels. Did people question our ability to bring another child into being? Did they wonder at my proclamation that it would be too much to handle? Did they judge me? In conversations, I often downplay my domestic workload because I don't want others to view Ian's disability as a burden. He's a hands-on husband and father in so many good ways—why should the fact that I do many things for him be allowed to obscure his contributions? But the result of this positive PR campaign is that when friends who have hordes of kids confess that they're frequently flirting with the edge of reason, I feel as though I have no right to commiserate. I have just one child. How can my own cargo compare?

When Emily was younger, I'd sometimes laughingly justify my motherload by claiming my feisty, spirited, strong-willed child was as demanding as a set of triplets. I recently read in a parenting magazine that although ten babies take up all your time, one baby also takes up all your time. There's some consolation in that. But the truth is, my now school-aged child is not so needy, is more often onside. The fits and fights are fewer. I feel a growing fellowship between us, which delights me to bits.

In our newfound peace, Ian and I now read the weekend papers again. That is delectable. These days, our daughter can become engrossed for an hour in a project involving paper, scissors and four rolls of Scotch tape. That's a whole hour of calm. When I prepare meals, she is a help rather than a hindrance, dragging ingredients out of the refrigerator for me instead of dragging me away by the leg. Because Emily is now old enough to undress and bathe herself, even a parent without properly working hands can oversee the bedtime routine a few nights a week. That means the other parent is free to do as she pleases—in theory it sounds liberating, although in reality it usually means paying bills and folding laundry. Unlike our friends with two kids, however, we're not doing a double-parent evening marathon. So why, at moments like these, couldn't I just treasure the tranquility of our household?

And it wasn't just me. Emily was about three when she started to notice the trend of baby brothers and sisters sweeping through fellow daycare families. She let it be known that she was waiting rather impatiently for her own baby. I was blunt with her. It's just not going to happen. "You're an only child," I explained to her.

"A lonely child?" she echoed, flabbergasted and forlorn.

I have never studied the stages of acceptance when it comes to single-child status, but obviously bargaining is one of them. In begging for a baby brother, Emily pledged never to quarrel with him, promised to get up in the night to feed him and swore she'd share all her toys right down to her last piece of Lego. "I want a baby in your tummy," she decreed emphatically. I felt I was letting her down. I felt guilty. She wanted a baby sibling. It was a natural and reasonable thing to want. It would have been a good thing for her to have and I was refusing to supply one. I felt selfish.

I worry about the message we are giving Emily as we repeatedly repudiate any notion of a second child. How do you tell your child you don't want more like her? "Our family is just right," we tell her. "We love being your mommy and daddy."

And we highlight the goodies, which she can now, a few years later, parrot back to us without even pausing to gather her thoughts. "I don't have to share with anyone when my friends go home. I get lots of attention. My mom and dad can play with me more." She's been well programmed by her guilt-ridden parents. Except for the "but." There's always a "but." "But," she'll add thoughtfully, "but sometimes I would still like to have a brother or a sister." Owwww.

I understand the ambivalence. By the time Emily, about age five, realized it was futile to keep asking for a baby, I was still secretly unresolved. I'd dip my toe into an ocean of possibilities— my husband the pragmatist never failed to grab my arm and haul me back to safety before I could drown in an unexpected tidal wave. I wondered aloud about adopting. This way we could skip the challenging infant stage. "Are you crazy?" Ian asked mildly. Maybe a child with special needs, since we have all that disability experience? "No," he said flatly.

Not that he's callous. He too has wrestled with a desire for more kids. He grew up with siblings, and he knows what we're denying our daughter. But Ian knows all too well that it falls to him to pull me together whenever I come apart at the seams. And come apart I would, assuredly. I just didn't acknowledge it. It's like, before parenthood, disbelieving a baby really is a twenty-four-hour-a-day job.

Then came the turning point.

After resolutely rejecting the idea of having more babies, adopting older children and becoming foster parents, my husband the stalwart finally caved. I had suggested a puppy and, surprisingly, he agreed. "After all," I'd pointed out reasonably, "Emily will be six. She'll be old enough to help." And I was preparing to leave my magazine job for a new life working at home as a freelance writer. I was convinced that we finally had room in our lives for an extra dependant.

I lasted two weeks. Actually, if truth be told, I was in a swamp of tears by the end of week one. But it took a full second week to send our poor puppy packing. Like much else in our household, puppy-tending fell wholly onto my roster of responsibilities. Emily preferred to adore her teething (read: incessantly nipping) puppy from a safe distance, and Ian was dealing with some unexpected health problems. I was overwhelmed.

As I struggled to balance doggy needs with family needs and household and work duties, it occurred to me that there wasn't much difference between a new puppy and a new baby. Except for a couple of important imbalances: I wasn't on maternity leave and nobody was bringing me casseroles.

The balls in the air began to rain down. Having an additional needy creature was more than we could handle. In the throes of this painful epiphany, I fully understood—for the first time—that if we had two kids, vital parts of our lives would suffer more than I could imagine. Our marriage. Our household. Our minds. And unlike getting a puppy, the choice would have been irreversible. Finally, my head caught up to my heart. A second child didn't—couldn't—make sense. It would require sacrifices I was not prepared to make.

After we said goodbye to our puppy, a load lifted. I was so happy to have those few cherished moments of peace back. I want them. I need them. I need to not be filled to capacity. I need a reserve, something I can dip into when someone gets sick, when guests are coming or even when I'm close to the end of a really good book. The puppy finally helped me accept that my lifestyle is the one I want. I can breathe in it. No regrets. This family is complete. Really. I've made my peace.

THE NANNY COMPLEX

RANDI CHAPNIK MYERS

*B*efore I stepped down the stairs, I peered around. With my husband at work, the kids off playdating and Myrna cleaning my parents' condo, I was, amazingly, alone. The silence prickled my skin. It was now or never. I felt like a girl about to unlock her sister's diary—knowing full well I shouldn't but powerless to resist. At her closed door, I stopped. *This is her private room, I warned myself. Cross that threshold and you're as good as a thief.* But my gut urged me on: *It's your house, your kids, your right.*

I twisted the knob.

What I remember most about my very first nanny was my brother's fury. I was six, he was eight. Our little brothers were still in their pyjamas at noon, watching *Scooby Doo*, brain dead on the corduroy couch. I came into the kitchen when I heard shouts. There was Lynn, her face so black that her eyes and teeth kept appearing in my dreams. She was balancing a Kraft cheese slice on her chalky palm.

"That's not cheddar!" Brian shrieked.

"You'll eat it!" she yelled in her Island accent. For a second, I thought she might grab him in a headlock, pinch his nose and shove the rubbery square down his throat.

The next thing I knew my brother let his foot go. It landed smack above Lynn's knee as he unleashed the terrible words he

164

couldn't contain: "You're not my mother! You, you—chocolate bar!" And so ended number one in a string of nannies who unpacked her things in her own room of our house, then eventually packed them up again, as my brothers and I grew up.

In her classic ambitious fashion, my mother popped us all out in a quick six years. Then, it was either one more child—five was sure to keep her busy enough—or back to school. That year, she bought a briefcase and placed an ad in *The Toronto Star*. "Nanny Wanted. Four kids. Ages 2–8. Babysitting. Cooking. Cleaning." Basically, she was willing to pay for what she used to be: our mother.

At first, oblivious to the nannies' effect on us, we were infected by Mom's enthusiasm. It was the mid-'70s, and even with Women's Lib marching in full force, most thirtysomething women (whose own June Cleaver moms taught them to tuck hospital corners around a bed) were content to decorate their suburban dream homes in feisty orange-reds. Sure, some other moms worked—as teachers, nurses, hygienists. But only mine, it seemed, was applying to Osgoode Hall Law School. Related to her by blood, I considered myself something of a pioneer. "My mom's going to be a lawyer," I'd slip in every chance I got.

Pretty soon, I was enjoying the perks of having a nanny around. A British woman named Margaret bought me a pair of silver earrings for my birthday. Lucy ironed every item of our clothing—underwear too—as an excuse to simultaneously jabber away the day on the phone. Pearl from Jamaica turned me into a soap-opera addict. Instead of practising piano, I'd tear open a bag of potato chips and join her in tsk-tsking the stupidity of the married woman being duped by her own daughter.

Best of all, with a nanny in charge, we kids had free rein to do as we pleased. We'd read Archie digests until supper, crunch candy into cavities and crank the hi-fi full blast. We lived like sloths. Mornings, we'd abandon our gaping beds, leave soggy towels on the bathroom floor, stack our breakfast plates by the sink. It wasn't that we were lazy; there was just no need to clean up after ourselves. No idiots, we figured out fast that when we came home from school at four, everything, magically, would have found its way back to its rightful place.

Still, such freedom had its dark side. When puberty hit, I learned the hard way that adults aren't interchangeable. Without our mother to stop him, Brian nicknamed me Ug and would punch my budding breasts. Our younger brothers lived in a tangle of wrestling legs and pummelling fists. Heading a household of six, plus a dog, the nanny was simply too busy to deal with any emotional pain. She was perfectly capable of tackling our physical needs—mopping spills, bleaching stains, cooking macaroni and cheese. But when we came through the door after a pressure-filled day at school, she wasn't the one we wanted to hug.

One afternoon, Petrona was baking my mother's cornflake chicken when, from the upstairs bathroom, I screamed. On my panties sat a dark purple stain. At eleven, I'd read *Are You There, God? It's Me, Margaret*, and had a fairly sound idea what lay ahead. But purple? Seconds later, I heard a knock. Already, my cheeks were darkening, aware that my brothers were somewhere in the house. Petrona looked from my face to my stain and back.

"Yep." She sighed. "That sho' is yo' period, girl."

She reappeared minutes later with a pad in her hand.

"What do I do with it?" I asked, trembling.

"Just shove it in there to catch the blood," she said and left.

"You're a woman!" my mother gushed at eight o'clock that night, after I whispered the shameful news in her ear. I had never, ever felt so young.

A few short years later, I was acting all grown-up. Our parents' high-powered jobs bought us an impressive custom-built home that quickly earned a rep as party central. As a result, my high school popularity soared. With Mom and Dad off at conventions, my brothers and I hosted pool bashes in summer, billiards games in winter, while Nettie—expert at making evidence such as beer caps and cigarette butts disappear—agreed to keep mum.

Weekends, my friends got high on the freedom of my house, but after school, I loved heading over to theirs. We'd slip through the side door and line up our shoes. Mothers stirring meat sauce or reading the paper would greet us with a plate of cookies or a pot of tea. We'd sit around a kitchen table, chewing or sipping, answering questions about our day, then we'd pull out our homework and finish it before supper. Despite the fact that I was a wiseass teen, the structure in these nanny-free homes felt as secure as a fence locking childhood in and strangers out.

At the same time, I was taught to believe exactly what I now teach my own daughter: that I could aspire to become anything I want—a lawyer, a doctor, a teacher, the prime minister of Canada. Witnessing my mother's success—even if it did lure her from the tasks of motherhood—was intellectually inspiring.

My mother always said that women can have it all, and I believed her. Surely I wouldn't have spent three years studying for law exams, another articling, a fifth writing bar exams, a few years arguing in court and another two obtaining my master's degree if I didn't expect to emerge both an involved mother and a hard-working professional at once. In fact, it wasn't until my first child promptly attached himself to my body (and soul) that I asked myself, *Who on earth is going to raise my kids if not me? And when do I plan to do it: on my lunch hour?*

As I stroked my son's cheek as he nursed, all those years of mentoring left me with just one clear realization: it was simply impossible to shun this magnificent job of mother, and I refused to trade it for any amount of income or prestige.

Having seen the light, I was like a religious fanatic: smug in my choice, brutally judgmental, astonished to find myself so alone. All around me, working moms who counted on having it all—my colleagues, cousins, girlfriends—handed over their poopy infants to strange women, along with bottles of synthetic milk, while I slept and swept, rubbed and scrubbed, shopped and mopped myself. In my humble opinion, these working mothers paying slaves to raise their kids were traitors, unworthy of the title "Mommy." Of course, I recognized that finances forced some to work. But I couldn't shake the belief that most women I knew had a choice. They just made the wrong one.

Nonetheless, mom judgment stung me right back. I had been scooting along the fast track, and now here I was, singing about sunny days sweeping clouds away, pulling out my battered nipples and brushing diarrhea off toilet bowls. To working moms, I was, in effect, a nanny. Without pay. *What a waste*, I could hear them think, knowing somewhere in my consciousness that I was judging myself. That deep down, I too subscribed to the modern view that raising my own kids made me a throwback, a disappointment.

Well, I'd tell myself, *at least I'm enjoying milestones they'll never get back: first smiles, first steps, first lost teeth. At least those nannies gabbing on their cellphones, half-watching tots hanging by the monkey bars, are not my concern.* But every time I spotted one pulling a wagon, I felt like shouting. Not just at mothers who put their own interests before their child's but also at society for applauding them while scoffing at the essential role of the full-time mom.

The questions I dodged made me want to choke the people who dared ask them. Like "What do you do all day?" as if maybe I just lolled around in bed OD'ing on truffles, still hooked on soaps. Or "So, when are you going back to work?" to which I'd silently steam, I AM BLOODY WORKING! It's not that I wouldn't have benefited from the confrontation—ah, sweet catharsis—but I didn't trust myself not to throw a punch. So I taught my muscles to just smile, shrug and keep pushing my double stroller.

When I tested pregnant with twins, though, my faith began to crumble. I had just started writing stories and daydreaming about a career as a freelancer, where my hours would be mine. Where I could squeeze work into my schedule of driving carpool, preparing lunch and keeping the fridge stocked. Now, out of nowhere, I'd have four kids under four, and suddenly all I could see ahead were endless days of milk, sweat and tears. And as I neared thirty-five, an age when my contemporaries were banking their bucks, I realized in horror that if I waited to work until my kids were in school, I might never catch up.

To free up a couple of hours each day, I had a few options. I could drop my kids at the local daycare and let them battle over grungy, germ-infested toys. Nope. I could arrange playdates at their friends' homes, but then I'd have no idea who was in charge. Nope. I could pay a cleaning lady to do the dirtiest work and a neighbour to babysit some evenings. But that would get pricey. In the end, my husband and I agreed the most cost-efficient solution was to sponsor a nanny from the Philippines who would live in our basement for two years.

I would give up my claim-to-fame housework and hand over the reins while I took one or two kids to the grocery store or to programs, and if I could snag a few minutes alone, I would write. The catch was I would no longer be Supermom. Nor would I be Super-working-mom. Worse, I'd be your average suburban princess with no real job and full-time live-in help. Out of nowhere, I'd embrace everything I'd been repulsed by, everything I had sworn against.

Before Myrna arrived, I lost the twins. But soon I was pregnant again. And after all the paperwork it took to bring her to Canada, with the promise of citizenship, I felt bound to follow through. So we set up a bedroom in the basement and welcomed our newest arrival: a nanny.

I'd be lying if I said I didn't enjoy a spotless kitchen floor. Or grateful for the hours that used to evaporate as I folded T-shirts into warm, tall stacks. Having taken on her load of tasks before, I respected Myrna's job. Even so, I squirmed at the thought of telling another adult what to do.

I had no choice. Except for the odd teen sitter, and to a limited extent my husband, only I knew the kids' routines. To get Myrna up to speed, I sat down at my keyboard and began typing *The Lists*. The lists were divided in two.

The House details were straightforward: "Wash towels in hot; switch immediately to dryer; never use fabric softener."

But when it came to *The Kids*, I was retching minutiae in a mad, panicked fury. I was convinced that if Myrna didn't heed my each and every word, my poor babies would starve. "Lunch: yellow (not orange) macaroni (7 minutes on stove, just 2 drops of milk), in a bowl (plastic) with a spoon (no forks), and remember: NO butter/margarine!!"

In addition to full menus for each child's loves, likes and hates, I outlined their schedules, their habits, even simulated dialogue for putting them to sleep. But when it came to discipline, Myrna wouldn't need instructions. That was my territory.

It turned out that just about everything to do with my kids was my territory. Although poor Myrna's eyes bugged out when she saw *The Lists*—as if I was a teacher demanding she memorize the whole year's worth of work overnight—she might as well have pitched them straight into the trash. Although I didn't realize it yet, I was just playing the role of employer. No way was I abdicating control of my kids to a stranger. Not a chance.

Delegating would have been simpler if I worked outside the home. Apparently, once you're on the other side of the door, your expectations shrink to the prayer that your kids don't eat poison or break their necks before you can make it home to kiss them good-night. Without time to second-guess their every activity, you have no choice but to trust. But I had a different set-up. A tug-of-war, if you will. These areas are yours: cleaning house, babysitting, feeding kids (limited to slapping sandwiches together, mind you—the real cooking, and kudos for cooking, was mine, all mine). Discipline, outings or any teaching whatsoever was strictly off limits. And most crucial of all, my Golden Mama Rule: *if I'm around, you're not.*

The problem was I was always around. Having a nanny actually proved harder than doing everything myself because, like an ego-bloated two-year-old, I had no idea how to share. I told the kids Myrna was part of our family, but I really wanted them to want me more than they wanted her. To combat the jealousy I oozed when I heard her playing Barbies or reading books aloud, I'd stop typing mid-sentence and race to relieve her.

It must be natural to resent the Other Woman in your kids' lives. To feel inadequate that they're cozy inside lemon-fresh sheets laundered by Her. To blame Her for the disdain from nannyless moms who ship their toddlers to daycare with the conviction that at least school teaches them the alphabet. I fought these feelings with pity. Here I was, an educated wife with three kids in private school, living in a 335-square-metre house, while poor Myrna, a single woman with no kids of her own, had left her life across the ocean behind.

My mother always gave nannies more than just a bed to sleep in. They had autonomy to set their own schedules, all the steak they could eat, first pick of our hand-me-down clothes. For a while, my brothers and I would watch as our nanny beamed with gratitude. But inevitably, the thanks would turn flippant, almost inaudible amid general ennui. Soon after, alerted by shoddy housework clues—dusty mirrors, bath scum, crumbs under the rug—my mother would reappear at odd times of day to catch her employee napping on the couch, trying on her dresses or even pilfering tins of tuna. "Give a finger, they take a hand," my mother would say, shaking her head, but she'd be sad—we all would—that this fringe member of our clan, who had spent a couple of years coming to know our habits and our hurts, had betrayed us in the end.

In the beginning, I watched Myrna's every move. When I left for a lunch date or a quick workout, I felt like a cad. Complicating my worry about what was happening in my absence, I felt I was robbing both my kids and my work of my time, as if I had no right to take a break. In a constant state of checking my watch, I couldn't let myself relax.

Eventually, it became clear that my frequent interruption of Myrna's work meant that neither she nor I was accomplishing much, and slowly, very slowly, I started coming around. One afternoon, as I hurried to meet a looming deadline, the glorious sun splashed through the study shutters, and I couldn't deny that the kids should be at the park. For the next awkward twenty minutes, I gave Myrna a safety refresher that even my four-year-old had memorized—*Hold hands! Stop at stop signs! Look both ways before you cross the street!* At last, my grip was loosening.

To steady my guilt about mothering less, I began giving Myrna time off without docking her pay. Since I didn't want her around when I wasn't working, this new arrangement seemed the perfect solution for both of us. Soon, my nanny was the best dressed on the block, working the shortest hours, even cleaning my parents' place one day a week on top of her regular paycheque.

My husband saw the signs first. He complained that the toilet stank. Then a generation of bugs infested our pantry. But when someone lives in your house and you feel forced to trust her, you make excuses. She had a busy week. She may not realize. I'll speak to her.

Then one day, I drove into the garage at noon. After unlocking the door to music blaring, I wandered down the hall, wondering where I'd find Myrna: the bathroom, the kitchen, the laundry? I didn't have to look far. Comfortable in my office chair, my nanny sat, immersed in images on my computer screen. Behind her, my son was fussing on the floor as she muttered sharp, nasal sounds to quiet him. Stiff, I stood there, my bewilderment rippling to shock and then to fury, but I didn't speak. I just picked up my child and held him against my chest, behind the back of the woman to whom I had handed his life, waiting for her to turn. It took seven stretched minutes.

My mother never gave nannies a second chance. Once the trust had been severed, she said, there was nothing left to go on. But by now, the kids loved Myrna and I considered myself a fair employer, someone who could empathize. So she wanted to upgrade her skills. So she was curious. She had learned her lesson. In some sense, it was a welcome wake-up call. For so long, I had restricted her hours with the kids. Now I could pat myself on the back, knowing that I was the only person fit to raise them, that I had been right all along. To keep the situation in check, I'd make sure Myrna focused squarely on the broom while I spent as many hours as possible with the kids out of the house.

In spite of my efforts, the state of our home continued to deteriorate. Suspicion itched. If strands of hair lingered in the shower after five hours of supposed cleaning, what was I paying my nanny to do all day? Friends suggested I hire a nannycam company to catch her in the act, and in the quiet of my study, I Googled them. But I couldn't pick up the phone. What I could do was play I-spy solo.

Though I knew she wasn't there, I knocked as I had many times before: to ask if she wanted to taste my cabbage borscht, to say we were off to a movie, to wake her because I was in labour. Now, feeling small, I entered the room inhabited by furniture from my husband's old bachelor pad. *This is your home,* I reassured myself over and over, yet if the door had flung open just then, I'd have hung my head in shame. I started on the drawers fast, pulling them out and rifling through them. I don't know what I was hoping to uncover. If I found nothing it would mean I had invaded someone's privacy without just cause. And something? What could I do? Didn't breaking and entering mean that I was coming to court with dirty hands?

When I found the porn tapes, I slammed the drawer shut. They were clearly adult content, the ultimate in sexual secrecy. My mind exploded with conflict: where is she watching this smut? In your family room? And who are you to judge?

Slinking out, my stomach in shreds, I sealed the door behind me. While our house was Myrna's place of employment, it also contained her bedroom, her own intimate space. Then again, didn't I owe it to my kids to hire a nanny who wasn't obsessed with sex?

For the next few days and nights, I kept silent, strangled by the burden of having snooped. My new knowledge kept me chained to the house, scrutinizing Myrna's steps. I couldn't live like this, I knew, feeling like a secret agent armed with key information I felt scared to turn over to the authorities.

I didn't have to agonize for long. The next week, my mother surprised Myrna by coming home early from work. Sitting right in her front hall was all I needed to finally fire my nanny: six bags of soon-to-be-stolen items—bathroom supplies, handbags, a plant— waiting idly by the door for the vacuuming to end.

The ensuing mix of remorse and relief plagued me for months. I had fallen prey to a common trap: trying to please the nanny at my own expense. Now, reclaiming my domain, I rose to queen again, able to ensure once and for all that it ran the way it should. But as fate would have it, the laundry began to pile up at the same pace as my writing assignments. Something had to give.

It was a tough choice. I felt freer without the stress of another person around. The kids were pitching in again, cleaning their rooms for allowance, setting the kitchen table. Their future seemed steadier this way, with a slice of family responsibility heaped on their plates. But my own future felt bleak without the hours of writing that had come to feel as important, as necessary, as breathing.

I closed my eyes then, and instead of envisioning the future, and dreading it, I found myself looking back. In my mind's eye, there I was, politely asking Lynn for a glass of milk, sitting on Margaret's bed listening to tales of her all-girls' school, sneaking a forbidden cigarette with Nettie in the yard. There was grief in the memory that my mother wasn't always around, but there was also nourishment in the bonds I forged with these women who helped me navigate the rough road to womanhood.

And then it struck me. Hiring a nanny poked at my fear that I might never strike that elusive balance between giving my children what they need and giving myself what I need. If I went to work and let another woman take my place, I might vanish. It wasn't the nanny I feared. It was the possibility that if I allowed myself to succeed, my kids would lose their mom.

I suddenly saw my youth with adult eyes. Maybe, just maybe, it was possible to share the workload, and the satisfaction, of running a household, and still be home to answer the bell most days at school's end. Maybe I could nurture a career, with a little help from the nanny, without the guilt that too many mothers find crippling.

When I interviewed Helen for the position of nanny, I couldn't yet see that she would become a lifelong friend. Or that I would rely on her cleverness and calm to keep me focused on deadlines without losing sight of my kids. Or that we would develop a sisterly give-and-take—me offering advances and cast-offs in return for her extra hours when everyday details get out of hand. I did recognize, though, her kind mommy eyes.

I have only seen photos of Helen's children, but she has held and soothed mine when I could not be home. And we both hold tight to my sponsorship pledge, which in three years will bring her family to Canadian soil. In the meantime, while I prattle on about missing my daughter at sleep-away camp, for my nanny the separation of mother and child is torture.

Some nights, when our house should be safely asleep, I follow Helen's tears to the basement, where I know I'll find her curled on the couch. In the dark, without the preoccupation of shirts to starch or floors to wax, the ache of yearning for her babies, who are growing up with another woman in her place, cuts so deep that she can only sob. I sit down and hold out my arms. When she falls inside my embrace, I wrap her firmly and rock, the way every mother, near or far, instinctively knows how to do.

CONFESSIONS OF
A SEXLESS MOM
DOROTHY WOODEND

During labour, my son got stuck, and stuck he stayed. Labour hadn't been that bad. I'd hummed my way through every contraction, but as the night drained into dawn, it was clear that things were not progressing. I pushed until my legs trembled uncontrollably. At 6:30 a.m., my midwife fetched the doctor. It was only when the room filled up with doctors and nurses, all staring fixedly at the bottom half of me, that I began to think there was a problem. Until that point, my brain had been mysteriously absent. But now it strode back into the room along with all the medical staff and started pushing me around. You will feel scared now, it said. But it's okay. I can figure this out. Just stay calm. I hadn't realized how much quieter it had been without its constant chatter.

When the doctor brought out the vacuum extractor, he said, "This might hurt a little." That is doctor's code for "this will be the most unbelievable pain you've ever felt in your life." I began to feel really afraid, but by then pain and fear seemed beside the point.

Everyone screamed, "Push!" all at once, and I screamed too, and inside that huge roar of sound my son was born.

No one talks much about the brutality of having a child, that pushing out a baby can rip you apart, your skin and flesh as flimsy as paper. The doctor sewed me back up and congratulated me for losing so much blood in one enormous rush. He told me my dangerously high blood pressure was now back to normal. No one warned me that when I first climbed out of bed, blood would come pouring out and puddle on the floor. I went down like a nosediving airplane with the tiny pilot desperately pulling at the throttle to no effect. Pull up! Pull up! my brain screamed. The nurse came and put me back into bed, and my brain muttered and pouted in the corner while my body curled around itself like a hurt animal.

The next day, the hospital sent us home. The midwife told me to wait for my milk to come. "Sit in the bathtub," she said. "That will help." For the first few days there was nothing, and then one evening, as I sat in a puddle of hot water in my mother's house, the milk arced through the air like spray from twin nozzles. It is oddly thrilling when your body does something that your mind has no power over, but the thrill was short-lived. What stayed much longer was the pure physical misery of smelling like sour milk while sporting enormous wet patches on everything I owned. I'll spare you the intimate details of stitches and other physicalities. Mostly, for the first few months of motherhood, I was so exhausted and often desperate just to rest, even go outside, that I didn't notice the absence of sex. In fact, sex was the very last thing on my mind.

Before I gave birth, I don't think anyone mentioned that my sexuality would completely vanish with motherhood. Or if they did tell me, I wasn't listening. What I was learning with new motherhood was that desire and love can exist quite independently. My body and mind split up; they waved their goodbyes and went their separate ways.

Despite my exhaustion, I thought that the resumption of our sex life was a good idea, a necessary thing, and part of me did try. But whatever it was, perhaps the physical discomfort, or just the idea of going back again to the mess and bother of contraceptives, it seemed like too much work. So I put it off. I was busy, utterly pre-occupied and often completely stricken with terror over the sheer size of the responsibility involved in caring for another life, a life so small and fragile that I was convinced the first moment of my inattention would end in tragedy. I thought desire would come back eventually, and I would feel like myself again. Weeks and months went by. Life was full of the ordinary stuff of cooking, cleaning, taking my child to the park. My son learned to crawl, totter unsteadily and finally to walk. I fell asleep every night so quickly it was as if someone had snatched me sideways into the darkness. And all the time I assumed it would come back. One day I'll feel like doing it again, I thought. I would look at the man I married and remember why I'd been so desperate to get married to him in the first place.

But a creeping thought, not even something articulated, just a dark shape in the water, started to intrude. Maybe I don't want to. I didn't want to admit it even to myself, but the stone truth of it remained. Hard, bleak, and deeply sad. The thought appeared time and again, like the discomfort of a sore tooth or, rather, like a painful absence, a place where something had been that was now nothing, with pain at the edges. I would imagine what it was like for my husband, and the guilt compounded daily, like bank interest. I felt it every night when we climbed into bed together: his confusion, anger, resentment, and ultimately his fear. Losing this sense of togetherness was like a small death, a harbinger of things to come, the things of youth falling away and the glacially slow but constant approach of age.

We had cold, arctic fights, heavy as a storm, in which we circled endlessly around the problem.

"You're the most selfish person I've ever known," my husband said.

Really? I thought. Is that possible? Am I really such a terrible person?

I worried over this for days, and then I worried about worrying so much.

We got married in the middle of an extended argument about whether we should get married at all. It wasn't the fairy-tale convention—no big diamond or white wedding gown. But that didn't really matter much. Marriage seemed a Brownie badge of adulthood, something you ought to do. A step to be climbed on the winding path up toward acceptance and propriety. A baby seemed the next logical step.

Before we had a child, our life was pretty simple. Or as simple as life ever gets. We both worked. We both had money. There was a relatively equal division of power and responsibility. Our sex life was good. It was the before-time. I can recall it, but only in the way you remember the past, blurry and indistinct. You know you were once there because the frozen images in the photo album tell you so. But you can't really recall what it felt like. I look at my husband and think, He is good, he tries so hard to do the right thing. So what's wrong with me? Is it hormones, guilt, patriarchal condescension? Or is it just about sex? And if so, what does that mean exactly? Can you love someone without actually loving him? Or is the act indivisible from the condition?

Desire, to me, seems to live in the thin line between love and fear. Perhaps not fear precisely, so much as tension, excitement, unease. No single word seems exactly right.

I am my body. Nothing hammers this fact home more deeply than having a child. I have fulfilled my biological function, my Darwinian duty to pass on my genetic material. It is both banal and miraculous all at the same time, like so much of life. When I was trying to have a baby, sex became a job, full of planning, schedules, and precisely timed everything. Once I started paying attention to my body, I was startled by its precision; like a clock, every twenty-eight days, the chime sounds. During ovulation, my perception of the world changed entirely. Sex coiled in my belly like a serpent and radiated out through my eyes. It was discomforting, like a form of violence, disrupting the normal routine of life.

It's amazing how simple it is: the body wants or it doesn't want. There is no tricking it, no way to make it feel something it doesn't feel. Herein the great war between the mind and the flesh, one riding the other, like a beaten horse, the body twitching under whip of the almighty brain, tyrant that it is.

This split between lust and love is not foreign to me. I used to get crushes. Every time a crush arrived, unbidden, often unwanted, a part of my brain would think, Oh no! Not him. Not that jerk who lectures you about French film. Not the weaselly one with the heavy-lidded stare, who makes your heart hammer in your chest. Oh Christ, here we go again. My history carved patterns in my brain, as deeply as a knife into the living wood of a tree, so that the cut became part of me. After a while, I didn't think of it as wound any longer, merely a path taken.

I've always been drawn to the Rochester type—dark, fierce, endlessly unpredictable. When I was a little girl, I listened to operas alone in my room, drawing and writing to the music of stories of women who died, were killed, walked into fire or jumped off the parapets of Rome for love. The otherworldly beauty of their songs captivated me: these dying, gutted, disembowelled, murdered, bloodied women. I was enamoured of Tosca, stabbing Police Chief Scarpia as he tries to rape her. And Norma, walking into the sacrificial flames. Or Mimi singing her dying song of love, drowning in her own lungs. Story after story of woman sacrificed, of pain, suffering, sorrow—all for love. But it was all so terribly, terribly beautiful. The music gave me moments of joy so piercing and glorious that they radiated through the whole of me and showed me the thinness of the barrier between the physical world and something else: the barest glimpse of beyond.

But tucked inside the cozy harbour of marriage and children, I thought I was safe from these storms, and for a while I was. But sometimes they still come, take over your mind and disrupt all your carefully laid plans. No one has ever been able to say why love comes and why it leaves. Maybe there is no answer. No one ever consciously decides to feel one way and not another. Emotions arrive at your doorstep like hungry relatives and refuse to leave. They settle in, make a mess of things and generally upset your previously quiet life. I felt divided. I felt terrible.

So I ran. I mean, really, I ran. Every morning in the dark, even before the sun came up, I laced up my running shoes and headed out into the darkness of predawn. Most often, I ran with my sister. While my body plodded along, the spiders in my brain spun endless questions. We talked, panted, ran up and down hills. We talked and talked. What should I do? How to make things better? Am I doing the right thing? Should I hunker down and endure? Isn't this what life, largely, is? Or is it? Is this normal? Is this what happens to other people? Can I live the rest of my life this way? Can I wait until I'm simply too old for it to matter any more, or should I take up a revolutionary banner of liberation and sign a sexual manifesto? I was split in two with both sides screaming. One said, Be good, you are a mother, an adult, a woman with debts, responsibilities, dishes to wash, laundry to fold. The other wanted to run the streets at night, head into the darkness, testing the limits of possibility, screaming and singing.

Most mornings now, I tie on my running shoes and head out the door into the dark and empty streets. This is the only time when the division between my mind and body eases. One is occupied and the other is somehow more restful for it. My sister and I dissect every possible problem, and by the end of our run I feel whole again. Mind and body are one.

Operas end in death or passion, but this story has no end, no happily ever after. No curtain comes down; it just keeps going because there is no end, only the ongoing fumbling effort to try to do the right thing. I'm still not sure what the right thing is. If only there was a means to jump the intervening years and look back to say that's where I went wrong, that's where I should have gone left when I went right. If I could somehow gain an overview, a map, where I could move the little figures around, like a board game. But of course it doesn't work that way. You can only know what you know when you know it. But sometimes the very act of trying to put words on paper allows me to suddenly see a truth I never knew existed. Words require a certain clarity, a certain remove that can be useful in trying to sort out the murky strands of want and need. Not in this case. The truth is I still don't know what to do. I wish to God I did.

My past stretches out behind me like a dark road, all the things I did and didn't do. All the small hurts, the little victories, but the whole time I was only looking in one direction, always planning ahead, thinking when I get this thing it will all be good—a man, a marriage, a baby, a house. But what you think it's going to be is never actually what it is. I read endless books to make sense of life, theory, art, looking for lessons. Most days, I feel as if I am floundering around, drowning in choices, decisions—stay or go, hunker down or run. In my mind's eye, I can see my flying feet making a pattern in the air, like the wake in the path of a boat when the water splits apart in opposite directions. Eventually the swirling chaos is lost in the greater patterns, a minor disruption after all, but a permanent change, a different path taken.

ME, MY RAGE AND MY HIGH-FUNCTIONING HUSBAND

RACHEL MATÉ

There's more than one way to become a parent. Sam's approach was to take a deep breath and jump right in. Not me. That first morning in the hospital, just hours after I'd given birth, I lay there completely rigid with fear. I was terrified my new daughter would wake up; I didn't know what to do with her. After all the anticipation and hype focused on the birth and delivery, I was suddenly aware that I was woefully unprepared for what it actually meant to *have* a baby.

Sam, though equally clueless, mastered without assistance the diapers sticky with meconium. He dutifully ran after the nurse to remind her not to use shampoo and helped manipulate our squawky bundle into a sleeper, which while unbelievably small was still too big. It was as if he had somehow already processed the feelings of unease and insecurity. He later recounted to me that ten months earlier, right after we had first had unprotected sex in a deliberate attempt to get pregnant, he rolled over thinking, What have we done? And yet, none of that indecision or doubt was present once the baby arrived.

When we brought our baby home and she was inconsolable in the middle of the night, Sam perfected the one-handed soothing jiggle while watching the World Cup broadcast. He even claimed to be able to unload the dishwasher while maintaining the rhythmic motion she required to sleep. He lay motionless night after night while she slumbered on his chest and later when she was moved into her own crib, he rose zombie-like to retrieve her for her nighttime feeds. He dutifully strapped on the Baby Bjorn and puzzled through the intricacies of the various baby contraptions that are now considered essential accessories. Although he railed against the maddening snaps and buttons, Sam gamely dressed her in the cute but impractical sleepers that I preferred over the purely utilitarian ones purchased at the Bay.

When it came time for our prenatal class reunion, Sam didn't want to go. He accused me of only wanting to show off our daughter, which was partly true. But in the end, he humoured me and we went. We were asked by the instructor to go around and say a few words about our new babies. One after the other, each couple enthused about what a good baby they had. When it got to our turn, Sam deadpanned, "We got ourselves here a ba-ad baby." Only the instructor laughed.

Through my bleary, sleep-deprived eyes, I somewhat begrudgingly conceded that Sam's confidence was not simply bravado, but also a competence that stemmed from the principles of equality on which we had entered into our marriage. I had expected that Sam would be fully involved when it came to caring for and raising our children. I saw this as part of his commitment to me and would have viewed anything less as a betrayal.

Where Sam fell short, I could not fault him for lack of effort. I knew many couples who, whether by design or not, slid into a more traditional pattern of child care, with the woman assuming the bulk of the responsibility. Not many of my new baby-toting acquaintances were able to hand off their charge at four in the afternoon each day. Sam was eager, willing and apparently more than equipped to fulfill his role as a true co-parent. I suppose I should have been relieved and grateful to be blessed with such a supportive partner. But what I was surprised to discover was that in spite of this, I was feeling a strong undercurrent of rage that threatened to disturb our tidy equilibrium.

The differences between us were subtle, at first. I started noticing them right after we brought our daughter home from the hospital. Sam bustled about greeting the hordes of well-wishers, answering the telephone and throwing in loads of laundry. All I wanted to do was sit on the couch with the sunlight streaming in and hold my baby. I was instructed to sleep when the baby slept, but my growing fatigue was overtaken by my desire to stare and marvel at this new being I had created. I wanted to eat toast slathered with peanut butter and bask in my sense of accomplishment and pride. I wanted stillness and peace and quiet.

I have always enjoyed occasions that force a change in routine. I relish the infrequent snowy days when everything here on the West Coast is quiet beneath a cold, white blanket. Before we had kids, I would deliberately wake up early on a weekend morning just so I could have a few hours to do nothing when I knew most other people (that is, those without kids) were still sleeping. I was also a consummate organizer. I prided myself on being able to accomplish a number of tasks at the same time. When I was pregnant, I even created a spreadsheet to chart all the new baby things I needed, organized into columns: "To Buy," "To Borrow" and "To Gift."

Now, suddenly, the clank of dishes placed in the dishwasher was an assault; so was the unrelenting churning of the dryer or the insistent ringing of the telephone. Sam's efforts to create order incensed me. I was insulted by his multi-tasking, wanting his attention fully focused on me and on the baby. As Sam tried to create a sense of normalcy, I struggled to maintain the womblike unreality that had defined the birthing experience and the emergence of this new presence in our lives. It irritated me even more that I had to articulate to him how and why I was feeling this way. Unlike Sam, I wasn't ready to pick up the normal hectic threads of our lives and get back to business as usual. It was incomprehensible to me that he didn't understand that.

Breastfeeding was another site of our differences, beyond the obvious biological ones. In private, we self-righteously discussed the moral superiority of our choice to breastfeed. After all, breast is best. Sam would often marvel at our daughter's creased thighs and announce proudly that it was all milk. I, too, was proud of my ability to sustain this new life. I was prepared to weather blistered and scabby nipples, oval-shaped milk stains on the front of all my shirts and the surreal experience of exposing my breast and trying to force an uncooperative and screaming mouth to open wide in the middle of a coffee shop.

Once I got the hang of it, breastfeeding became extremely convenient, so much so that I put off introducing solids until she was practically grabbing the food off my plate. The breast was a fail-safe soother. Sometimes after a feed, I would debate whether to burp her, reluctant to disturb the drunken, blissful sleep. It was also something only I could give to her. Although slightly irritated when someone would suggest she was still hungry just minutes after I fed her, I would always take her back and offer her a top-up. I was lulled by the contented cooing and rhythmic sucking—one little hand reaching up, aimlessly caressing my neck, the other one securely wrapped around my lower back. We spent countless hours in that close embrace, like lovers.

The nightly pattern that emerged was that Sam would bring her to me when she cried. I would feed her to the sound of his snores, and when she was done, I would nudge him awake. He would then attempt the transfer back to the crib, the anxiety of this transaction being too much for me to handle. If the transfer was unsuccessful, he would take her downstairs and employ various methods of rocking, pacing, and positioning. We both understood this to be so that I could get some sleep.

This rarely played out as planned. She would scream bloody murder and I would lie in bed getting more and more tense and more and more angry. Didn't Sam realize that I couldn't sleep when my baby was hysterically crying? Why couldn't he get her to stop? Why was he not able to distinguish between the type of cry that meant she would soon fall asleep and the type of cry that meant she needed her mother? I would lie there using all my mental power to transmit the message to him to bring her back up to me. But he rarely did. Not because he was being stubborn, but because he didn't want to disappoint me. The standoff usually ended with me storming downstairs in a martyr-like huff and grabbing the baby. Most times, all she needed was for me to hold her. I was smug in the knowledge that I was the chosen one. Sam would say ruefully that the problem was she just loved her mommy too much.

We were warned about the magic six-week marker before which the introduction of a bottle can cause nipple confusion and after which it is simply too late. Anxious not to squander the promise of freedom, I borrowed an electric pump and attempted like a good cow to stock up our freezer. I found pumping, even with a fancy pump, extremely difficult and frustrating. The machine would suck away at my nipples and produce a meagre amount. I never experienced what I heard other women describe as the distinct let-down reflex, and the suction was never quite right. Once I had painstakingly secured a few precious drops, there was the problem of how and whether she would ingest it. She flatly refused to take the bottle from me, and it was touch and go with Sam. Either she would gulp it down in seconds, or worse, she wouldn't take it at all and the baggie of frozen milk would go to waste.

Eventually, I gave up and accepted that at least for the duration of breastfeeding I would need to be constantly accessible. Unlike other mythical babies discussed at playgroups and drop-ins, my baby didn't easily conform to a schedule. Her naps were irregular and her feeding was frequent and unpredictable. She seemed to be in a constant growth spurt and I felt as if I was always feeding. I was nervous about leaving her for any extended length of time.

I calculated that if I fed her right before I left, I could drive to the community centre, go for a swim, shower and change and be home within an hour and fifteen minutes. Although this was supposed to be "my time," I resented the rushed and pressured pace. I couldn't really relax because I was worried she would wake up while I was gone and need me. It galled me to no end that Sam could leave without any of the same emotional encumbrances. No wonder he couldn't relate to my feelings of entrapment: he could take a break whenever he needed one. It didn't make any difference to me that he rarely took advantage of the freedom that I imagined him to have. I laid on the guilt anyway. If he could leave without being concerned about the baby, I made sure he would be concerned about the emotional fallout from me on his return. I became a victim of my own twisted logic. I liked the power of being the only one the baby wanted, but at the same time, I raged at Sam for not being able to take my place.

The intensity of my feelings of rage and resentment was scary for both of us. For his part, Sam really couldn't understand where these feelings were coming from and perhaps justifiably felt perse-cuted and victimized. He couldn't change the fact that the baby wanted me or that he couldn't breastfeed, and because I was the one on maternity leave, he also wasn't given the opportunity to know the baby in the way that I did. When he came home from work, he had no way of knowing the intimate details of her day and therefore what would be most likely to soothe or please her. I knew all this, yet my formerly logical and organized brain could not seem to rec-oncile the churning emotions, and Sam was an easy target.

For every milestone I fretted and worried about—introducing solids, moving from the crib to the big-girl bed, toilet training—Sam would remind me that things had a way of working out. Sometimes this was reassuring. Other times, his quiet confidence was infuriating. It trivialized my anxiety, which, even as I expressed it, I recognized as symptomatic of my more general concerns about how to be a good mother. I marvelled at how conveniently he positioned himself as the relaxed, chilled-out parent while I felt myself slipping into the uncomfortably familiar role of the hypersensitive, overanalytical one.

THAT BABY HAS now turned four, and we have a second daughter, who is two. The past four years have been a time of incredible growth and change for our relationship. My identity has become irreversibly meshed with being a mother. I have trouble remembering what it felt like to be just Sam and me. In our own messy, confusing and often volatile way, we are what we are and we are nothing like what I expected.

I now know that there are certain things like making doctors' appointments or buying gifts that if I don't do, will never get done. I am the one who thinks about whether there is enough food in the house for lunches and babysitter treats. I am sensitive to the ever-shifting list of who is and who isn't a friend. I anticipate the need for new shoes or clothing. Sam gets pale at the thought of having to plan a birthday party, let alone attend one, so I take that on as well. I register for gymnastics and swimming lessons, sign up for field trips and comb out nits when necessary. As the somewhat reluctant social coordinator, I orchestrate our numerous plans and engagements.

Sam, on the other hand, does things I would never do and don't particularly want to. He putters around the garden with the girls for hours. Too cheap to pay someone to clean our house, he'll turn vacuuming into a family activity. He conducts jam sessions in the living room and sells tickets to the daddy train up to bed. He is the official fingernail cutter, car-seat installer and nighttime bather.

Four years into parenting and the deeper differences between us are still there. But somehow I am less aware of them and the intensity of my anger has faded. There are many reasons for this change, not least of which is the realization, likely obvious to anyone else looking in on the situation, that being angry takes a lot of energy. As a working mother of two, I have limited reserves and I simply can't waste that energy resenting Sam.

My expectations have also shifted. I don't see this as settling for something less or compromising what I want. I see it as an acceptance of the complexity of the feelings that emerge as Sam and I attempt to sort through the layers of our sometimes competing and conflicting realities. I no longer feel that I have to cling to a simplistic notion of equality in order to stake my space in our relationship. It is not easy but we are working toward a balance in which our differences can actually complement each other.

Once I was able to stop viewing Sam's strengths as proof of my own inadequacy, I was able to appreciate him as a source of support rather than competition. I needed to block out the barrage of unsolicited advice, free myself from my own expectations and listen more carefully to what my baby was telling me she needed. I needed to trust my own parenting instincts. I also needed to hear from Sam that he appreciates and admires me as a mother.

There are still moments when both kids want only Mommy and I feel impossibly stretched and frustrated. The old resentment and anger comes flooding back. I feel that familiar spark of impatience and I have to clench my jaw so as not to completely lose it. On nights when both girls want me to put them to bed and Sam throws up his hands in sheepish defeat and retreats downstairs, I find myself lying in bed with one of them reading a story while periodically yelling through the wall at the other to stop banging or throwing toys around the room. Even as I'm reading aloud the words of *Goodnight Moon*, I'm having a different conversation inside my head, viciously berating Sam for his inability to take my place.

Sometimes I lash out at Sam simply because I feel overburdened with responsibility and somewhat bewildered at how all these demands have grown up around me, as if I had not played a direct role in it all. I have mornings when I lie in bed mentally going through all the steps and struggles it is going to take to get the girls up, dressed, teeth brushed, fed, packed up and in the car to daycare. The reality is usually much easier than the anticipation, but often the anticipation is daunting and I just want to curl up and avoid it all.

Once I actually manage to deliver the girls to their respective daycares and negotiate the goodbyes, I am incredulous that I actually have to go to work. Our lives are so precariously coordinated that if any part should become unhinged, I fear that it will all fall apart. The pressure of keeping it all together is at times overwhelming. Some give is inevitable; I have been forced to relinquish some of my need to control.

The shift in my feelings is also attributable to the fact that the girls are growing up. Their needs are not always so immediate or basic. Given the choice, they usually still prefer me, but as quick students in the art of manipulation, they also understand they can get different things from me and from Sam.

I'm not naive enough to think that we have it all figured out. Time has become incredibly precious, and how we choose to allocate that time is an ever-present source of tension. We are probably condemned to repeat the same argument about Sam's Tuesday-night basketball games until he is physically incapable of playing. I'm not sure how many times we will have this conversation, or a version thereof:

Sam: What would you think if I went out with Mark on Wednesday?
Rachel: Are you asking me or telling me?

Sam: Neither, really. I'm making sure that it works. I mean, are you busy that night, or am I forgetting something that's already planned?

Rachel: Wednesday's not the best. Isn't there some other night that will work?

Sam: Not really. What's the big deal?

Rachel: It's not a big deal. It just means that it's me, on my own, all week. Tuesday night you have basketball, Thursday night is your course, and now Wednesday night.

Sam: So what? Can you suggest an alternative? I mean, are you basically saying that you have an issue with me doing anything any day of the week aside from my set commitments?

Rachel: What if I suddenly announced that I was taking off for three nights in a row?

Sam: I would say, "Great, go." We just have to work it out. You *have* gone away for that long before. And I'm not suddenly announcing that I'm going out. I'm arranging it right now.

Rachel: You always pick the worst times to bring these things up.

Sam: When would there be a good time? Should we have a set time called, "Sam pisses Rachel off time?" How about every Thursday at 9:30? Look, there is never a good time. Why does this shit have to be so heavy? Why can't we talk about these things without you getting so upset?

Rachel: I'm not upset. Okay, maybe a little. It bothers me that you don't take me into account when you're making plans.

Sam: Rachel, that's not true. I do take you into consideration. But I don't think it's unreasonable if, every now and then, I do something with some of my friends without you. I think the issue is that you don't really like spending time with both girls on your own.

Rachel: That's not fair. I'm not saying you shouldn't have time with your friends. That has nothing to do with it. In terms of the girls, yes, I sometimes find it hard putting both of them to bed at the same time, but that doesn't mean that I don't like spending time with them.

Sam: I won't go out until after dinner. I can bathe them.

Rachel: That's very generous of you.

Sam: Why are you being so nasty?

Rachel: Why are you being so obtuse?

Sam: Okay, seeing as I'm so obtuse, maybe you can explain to me what the big deal is?

Rachel: I wish you would stop saying that. I guess what I want is, when Mark asks you about Wednesday, for you to think, Oh, that might make things difficult for Rachel, and then for you to say to Mark, "Wednesday doesn't work." I want you to be able to put those things together without me having to go through all this. It makes me feel pathetic to have to spell it out for you.

Sam: Good fucking Lord. So Wednesday doesn't work. Okay. What does work? Do you see why I'm so fucking confused? Is it my fault I'm so fucking stupid? By the way, you look really hot.

Rachel: You are really annoying.

Sam: Okay, fine, I won't go. I'll call Mark and tell him I can't make it. Happy?

Rachel: No, because now I am supposed to feel guilty because I won't let you out to play.

Sam: I can never win with you. I thought you didn't want me to go. So now I'm not going. Isn't that what you wanted? What do you want?

Rachel: I don't know any more.

PART FOUR

Devotion

THE EASY WAY

SUSAN OLDING

Here's how it happens. I'm at the park, surrounded by other mothers, all of us pushing our pre-schoolers on the swings or watching them swarm around the sand pile. One woman is pregnant and another asks when she's due.

"Last week of August. But earlier than that, if I have any say. My mom's coming to help, and she can only stay until the first week of September."

A whoop of laughter. "Nice try. You'll be late. You were late last time."

The pregnant one rubs her belly and hums. From above, the rustle of leaves and the scrabble of squirrels leaping from branch to branch. Our voices rise and fall in a comfortable rhythm, interrupted by occasional shouts from the children or pleas for a snack. Eventually, talk turns to labour. Whose was longest, hardest, who had an epidural or an episiotomy, how long it took the scar from that C-section to heal. Somebody leaves to make sure her son gets his nap at the necessary hour. Someone else looks for a quiet bench where she can nurse. Cradling her baby, she offers her breast and his crying stops. The two of them sit locked in a trance of semi-erotic torpor, temporarily lost to the rest of us, gone to a private world.

As long as we're comparing developmental milestones or talking about the best places to find shoes for toddler feet, I'm a full participant in the conversation. But when the subject turns to pregnancy and labour, I'm quiet. At the mention of morning sickness, I distract myself with the thought of a spicy sauce I'll make for the evening's pasta and the Chardonnay cooling in our fridge. At a glimpse of stretch marks, I look away. I stare through and past the others, seeking a place to fix my gaze, any place but the Madonna and child beneath the maples. Mostly my silence goes unnoticed. I'm happy to keep it that way. But every once in a while, one of the park mothers will ask a question that forces me to out myself. A question like "Who's your obstetrician?" Or "Ever consider a home birth?" Then, taking a step back, fingers fanned in a gesture meant to deny special knowledge—a gesture that feels like abdication—I answer. "I'm no expert."

"Oh. Right. I forgot." My questioner's face brightens. Released momentarily from the mental fog induced by parenting two kids, both in diapers, she adds, "You did it the easy way."

IT MUST HAVE been easy for my partner, Mark, to produce that sperm sample—shut but not locked (there was no lock) into a dingy hospital supply room, interrupted—"Oh! Excuse me!"—by a nurse in search of an extra bedpan. I know it got easy for me to inject myself with Pergonal. After a couple of cycles, I was such a pro that I could take it with me when we went to a dinner party, do it in the powder room and be back before our hosts had finished pouring the wine.

I'm my mother's first child. I was born when she was thirty-three; my brother was born when she was forty. It never occurred to me that I wouldn't be able to conceive in my mid-thirties. It didn't occur to any of the residents I saw at the Family Medicine Clinic either. I'd tell them how long we'd been trying; they'd ask a few questions about my cycles, shrug and inform me there wasn't any reason

to worry. I wanted to believe them. Life was busy an
Mark's older kids, a teaching job, volunteer work, friendsh
writing. So it *was* easy—easy to delude myself that my reg   ʀ¹ᶜ-
dictable periods bespoke a tickety-boo reproductive system rather
than the tolling of my biological clock. But after a couple of years, it
became obvious even to me that I wasn't going to get pregnant in the
usual way. We started investigations. Ultrasounds, biopsies, blood
draws, more ultrasounds, more blood draws, sperm samples, surgery, and one ovarian cancer scare later, it turned out that those nice
young residents had been right—there was nothing seriously wrong.
Sure, they'd found a fibroid and some endometriosis, but nothing
that should have stopped me from conceiving. Ours was a case of
"unexplained" infertility. Easy-bake-no-bun-in-the-oven.

The gynecologist recommended intrauterine insemination.
They'd pump me with hormones, get me to release extra eggs and
double or triple our chances every cycle. I responded exactly the
way I was supposed to, but when the doctor assured me that my
eggs were like those of a "much younger woman," I wasn't sure if I
should feel flattered or insulted. Mark, for his part, made quantities
of excellent sperm. Strangely, since he is a decade and a half older
than me, no one implied that it might be stale-dated. Early mornings
on insemination days, we'd pass the precious liquid through a sliding door at the hospital. Later, purified and intensified, it would
enter me through the ministrations of one of several doctors who
prowled the ward. Some were gentler and more capable than others. After my injection, I'd wait for half an hour, knees akimbo
under a thin blue sheet. Gazing at the ice on Lake Ontario, I'd wonder when it might begin to crack, hoping for an omen.

ONCE I WAS A couple of days late. That's the closest we got.
When the clinic closed for the summer, we decided to stop. We
knew it wasn't going to work. We knew we didn't want to go on to

IVF or the fancier and costlier technologies. Some people engage in what are aptly called the "fertility wars" for a decade or more, spending sums that rival the defence budgets of small developing nations. But our approach came closer to old-fashioned trench warfare. A long period of waiting and watching followed by a short and desperate volley, then a retreat on one front and a surprise advance on another.

Our decision to adopt was instant and mutual. You might even call it easy. Walking back from the hospital after that last insemination, we stopped, looked at each other and said, "Let's do it." The west wind tickled our necks. Our faces stretched into smiles. We hadn't been planning this. I was already a stepparent to Mark's older kids and he was already a parent. We'd wanted a child together and didn't think adoption could fulfill that dream. And then, at precisely the same moment, we understood that it could. Our child would not be biologically related to us, but she'd be no less the child of our love for that. As a couple, as a family, we'd always prized what made us atypical. Multi-generational, multi-national, multi-ethnic, multi-lingual—Mark and his older kids and I followed different religious traditions, favoured different aesthetics, subscribed to different politics. Adding to our family through an inter-country adoption seemed like the deepest possible expression of our values.

CALLING THE SOCIAL worker was a cinch. She was the only one in our city's phone directory licensed to perform adoption home studies. Plump and panting with the exertion of climbing six steps to our front door, she collapsed onto our couch and presented us with a stack of questionnaires designed to test our fitness to parent. *Some people believe that adoptive parents are desperate for a child. What is your level of desperation? Did your parents agree on discipline? Who handled most of it? What tactics did they use? How do you handle conflict? What about you is difficult to relate to?* Our answers took months to compile and made a mountain. Then came health checks, police checks, financial checks, immunizations, passport renewals, visas, and multiple letters of reference for each of us from family, friends and co-workers. Meanwhile, chins and grey pincurls wobbling, Jennie mounted yet another set of stairs to the prospective nursery, wheezing out warnings about childproofing as she went. We counted ourselves lucky; at least she hadn't run a white-gloved finger across our mantel. Satisfied at last that two teachers who had already been raising children together for the better part of a decade would make responsible parents, she condensed her findings into a report and mailed it to the provincial government, where a recent hireling, flexing puny muscles, wanted to know why Mark hadn't worked harder to save his first marriage. Hadn't worked harder? Twenty years of family therapy, individual therapy, couples therapy and an attempt at reconciliation hadn't been enough? Even Jennie thought this was going too far. By then, we'd been trying for five years to have a baby. It was six months since we'd begun the adoption process, and we knew we had at least a year of waiting ahead of us.

We took out a loan to pay for the adoption. We got married to qualify, although until then we'd been comfortably and consciously unwed. Like most parents-to-be, we studied child development, but unlike most, we broke from Dr. Spock and Penelope Leach to brush up on Chinese history. We listened to and countered objections from friends who considered inter-country adoption immoral. We educated ourselves about potential challenges the newest member of our family might face, challenges to do with adoption itself, with loss of culture, with minority status. We even decorated that nursery and put together a crib. ABC, easy as one, two, three.

Really. It was. After the uncertainty, the grief and the loss of control we'd felt over infertility, adoption offered a clear process with a known result. We'd complete our paperwork, send it to our agency, wait for a phone call, and when the call finally came, we'd cram formula, bottles, blankets, rattles, baby clothes, weeks' worth of diapers, gifts, orphanage donations, and a *Rough Guide to China* into two small suitcases and fly to Beijing and from there to another as-yet-unknown Chinese city, where a stranger would introduce us—sleep deprived, jet-lagged and disoriented—to the equally travel-weary and disoriented baby who would become our daughter. We'd stamp our fingers and her feet in red ink to formalize our relationship, strap her into a Snugli, and for the next two weeks cart her in the forty-degree heat to the principal tourist sites of her native land, a land whose language and customs and currency would be alien to us—though surely less alien than we—big-nosed, cheese-stinking, nonsense-talking *wai guo ren*, foreigners—would seem to her. At last, touring over and acquaintanceship established, we'd board a plane for a thirteen-hour trans-Pacific flight, usher our baby through customs, fill out another stack of forms to make her a Canadian citizen, fly another five hours, take her home, and love her. What could be easier than that?

FRIENDS HAVE DESCRIBED their first ultrasounds to me. I've seen the images. Tiny amphibians, swimming in their amniotic seas, fists like sailor's knots or fingers splayed like starfish. "It's the first time he seemed real," one friend mused, "even though he looked like an extraterrestrial."

What's eerie about these photos is how early they're available. On the outside, you don't even show. On the inside, a *being*, complete with head, shoulders, knees and toes—and here is proof. Adoptive parents wait longer for this confirmation. We got ours—called the "referral photo"—only six weeks before we travelled to meet our daughter. In the picture, she was three months old. She did not look like an extraterrestrial. She looked like a porcelain doll or a starlet, if you ignored the chrome bars of the crib in the background. Orphanage staff had laid her on a red blanket, bundled in the palest yellow from which her baby fists barely emerged, her right arm aimed toward the viewer in a wave. Or maybe a punch. She was tiny, delicate featured, with expressive feet, a sad mouth and a direct, even accusing, stare. We thought she was the most beautiful baby we'd ever seen.

Meeting her was a shock. She seemed so different from that picture. She was seven months older, big, slack-faced. Photos taken on our adoption day show her engagement with the world, her curiosity, the intelligence that Mark and I were too frightened to take in at the time, but they fail to reveal what aroused our fear. Unlike most of the other babies adopted in our travel group, Maia didn't cry. I was not fool enough to read this as a positive sign. In my arms, those first few moments, she may have reached to explore, but anxiety fuelled her exploration. She heard everything, watched everything, her plump cheeks drawn in an expression of soundless worry. Later, in our hotel room, she sat for hours making that strange face and when the effort of maintaining her vigilance became too great, she lost all muscle tone and slumped toward the carpet, a cooked noodle. Even then, she fought sleep. She plucked at her own skin, scratched her ears raw in an effort to keep alert. When she finally dropped off, she screamed every hour or two and made a noise like a rake across cement. I stared at her, trying to figure out the source of the sound. "She only has two teeth," I said to Mark. Until then I had not known that a person could grind her jawbones.

How could I mother this child?

A few days into her life with us, Maia awoke with a laugh and pulled herself up on her crib rail. *Look at me*, she seemed to say. *Look at who I really am!* Not the terrified creature we'd known until then, but a vibrant, curious, determined, and talkative toddler. Yet throughout her first year with us, while sitting in her high chair after a meal or watching the dance of green leaves beyond a window, she would sometimes fall uncharacteristically silent and her body would begin to shake, a small current passing through her so she trembled, seemingly in sympathy with the leaves outside, and then with greater agitation, like an electric toothbrush. Were these seizures? Traumatic flashbacks? There was so much I didn't know. Couldn't know.

"Couldn't you have kids of your own?" people used to ask me. Assuming, of course, that adoption, as a second choice, must be second-best. Our culture, like most others, begins in the procreational imperative. To adopt a child, especially one who cannot be passed off as "one's own" is to insist that family can be bound by invisible threads of love as surely as by chains of genes. To adopt a child is, intentionally or not, to threaten the foundations of patriarchy. People tend to get huffy when you do that.

Adoptive parents may come reluctantly to the revolution, but invariably we make good fighters for the cause. Like most, I bristled self-righteously at the suggestion that adoption was an inferior way to form a family. I promulgated "adoption positive" language. Say "birth mother" not "real mother" or "natural mother." Say "relinquished" or "placed for adoption," not "abandoned" or "given away" or "unwanted." Say "*was* adopted," not "*is* adopted." And never, never, never ask how much the baby cost! The unflattering truth is that I may have committed these and other adoption-unfriendly faux pas myself before I became part of what the social workers call "the adoption triad." It would be tough not to imbibe some of our culture's negative attitudes toward adoption.

And those who don't disparage adoption tend to idealize it. The first time someone joked that I'd done it "the easy way," I felt stung by the tactlessness of the remark. Later, I understood the comment as a backhanded way of welcoming me to the club. Although I had escaped the pains of childbirth, I did belong; I had gained admittance to the sticky confusions of parenthood itself. "Once you have her," friends said, "you'll feel exactly the same as any other mother."

They meant to support, to console, to reassure. And oh—how badly I wanted to believe them!

When it came to ideas about adoption, Mark and I weren't all that different from anybody else. Adoption had presented itself as a magical solution, a promise of "happily ever after." Now, we brought our baby home and found not our perfect fantasy child but a real person with needs and strengths and weaknesses of her own. And we faced a welter of unanticipated questions, a thicket of unexpected problems. Here, too, we were no different from most parents, but the extremity of our daughter's needs and their unfamiliarity walloped us, sent us reeling.

When you adopt, there is no way you can analogize Matthew's dyslexia to your uncle Sam's; no way you can compare Emma's stubborn streak to your own. So you tend to read every twitch and tantrum for darker messages. What if your child grows up to be the next Charles Manson? After all, *he* was adopted. And when you adopt a child who has been living in an institution, you pledge your life to someone who may be medically, nutritionally, and emotionally deprived, someone who has no concept of family, someone who may never have heard the word for mother in any language. Nobody talked or hummed to *this* baby in the womb. Or if they did, you don't want to know what they said.

Think adoption is easy? Push your preschooler on the swings while nearby another mother nurses, the infant making a pillow of her body. Then conjure your own child, locked in a noisy orphanage, a bottle propped against her lips but whisked away before she's finished drinking. See that mother changing her baby? Think of your own baby, strapped to a potty seat for hours at a time, scarred from the restraints. Remember the blank look in your daughter's eyes when you first met and the back of her head, flattened from ten months' pressure against a crib's thin mattress. Carry her everywhere; celebrate with sparkling wine the day she first learns how to grip with her legs and no longer feels like deadweight against your body. Rub her back through her night terrors, hold her as she rages, try not to wince when she hits or bites, leaving bruises on your arms. Try not to cry when she tells you her birth mother would be nicer to her. Wonder if you and she will ever enjoy the easy trust that develops when needs are properly met from the start. Easy peasy, lemon squeezy.

Media representations of celebrity adoptions—Sharon Stone and Mia Farrow and Madonna and Angelina Jolie collecting babies like extra pairs of shoes—may make adoptive motherhood look like the ultimate self-indulgence. But that's not how it really is, not even for them. Becoming a mother—any mother—means learning to see through your child's eyes, to feel with your child's heart. Becoming an adoptive mother means accepting from the start that your child's heart beats to another body's rhythm.

Imagine you're learning to dance. You begin without the warm-up and you miss the first few classes, so you and your new partner are clumsy. You tire easily, lose confidence, lurch and tread on one another's toes. Sometimes you even fall. The steps you're learning are different—more intricate than the ones that other dancers need to learn, so while your classmates dip and swing, you'll still be practising your basic moves. Sometimes you'll envy them, wishing you had it as easy; ironically, a few of them may envy you because you got to skip those dull introductory lessons. Never mind. Keep dancing. You'll need to improvise a lot of the choreography. After all, unlike most of the others, you're combining moves from more than one dance form and more than one tradition. But improvisation is freeing, and drawing on multiple sources adds texture and richness to your art. As you gain grace, you'll glow with pride at your own achievement. Because you're unusual, you may attract stares in public and the kind of attention that nobody wants. But in time, you'll move so fluidly that people will comment on how miraculously you're matched. By then, like most dancers, you'll have lost your self-consciousness, forgotten the pain and embarrassment of your first halting steps. By then, you'll wonder what gave your life meaning before you learned to dance.

FRIENDS OF MINE say that they find it hard to remember who they were before they became mothers. For me, that's easy. All I have to do is reread the letters of reference I got for our adoption. *Loving, honest, loyal, nurturing, respectful of others. Never shies from challenges. An avid reader, direct communicator, passionately curious, intellectually agile. Has a fine sense of the ridiculous.*

Speaking of ridiculous, who ever heard of an unflattering letter of reference?

But my friends were, if anything, more forthright than most. Along with the panegyrics, they permitted themselves a few little words like "impatient" and "intense." I recognize myself more easily today in those labels than in the glowing ones.

Mark says motherhood has made me both more and less patient. "You're more patient with your daughter," he says. "And less patient with the world."

So I am. Bored sometimes beyond reckoning, I can still play with her for hours. Ten minutes into a mildly predictable movie, I jump from our couch, saying I have better things to do than watch that crap. Nine times out of ten, I swallow my anger with her when I feel like exploding. Nine times out of ten, I speak my anger—or, more shamefully, shout it—if provoked by anyone else.

LATE AFTERNOON. The schoolyard is nearly deserted. It's just me and Maia, now six, and two older girls. Grade 2s. Maia has warned me about them. Catherine and Jennica. One, a Barbie-doll blond, and the other a tough-looking Asian. They like to "budge" in line— playground parlance for push themselves ahead—especially when adults aren't watching.

So I stand about five metres away and watch.

When it's Maia's turn on the rings, the other girls stare at me. They whisper. One jabs the other with her elbow. They stare again.

I can guess what's coming. It won't be the first time.

Finally, the dark-haired one, Jennica, calls out. "Are you her mother?"

Maia reaches for the rings. Her face, already taut with concentration, tightens a fraction more.

"Yes, I'm her mother."

Usually it ends here, but these kids are bold. More whispering, this time louder, and the blond girl giggles. "No. I mean, are you *really* her mother. Was she *born* from you?"

Maia grasps the bar, drops and swings. If you didn't know her, you might think she hadn't heard the question. But I know she heard, and I know she is hurting. Later, she'll tell me that the kids do this all the time—ask her why she looks different from me, ask about her *real* mom—and she hates it. It makes her feel singled out. "Like a freak." Later still, I'll make up a rhyme to remind her that difference signifies strength as well as weakness, and we'll laugh together as we chant: *I'm not a freak, I'm unique!* But now, something wild and wildly protective leaps up in me. I think about her first steps, her first English words, the way she takes my hand in her own small one when we walk across a busy street. I think of the way she looked at me, those first few days in China, with a gaze so penetrating and intent that I feel as if I haven't blinked since—nor will I, until I sense that she is ready to look away. And forgetting for a moment that these two girls are children, I want to shout at them, to shame them. No—I'll be honest. *Remembering* that they're children, I want to shame them. In my mind, I roar like the Red Queen. *Off with her head!* Or dredge up disdainful phrases from another era. *How dare you ask a personal question like that, young lady?*

But this is Vancouver, an affluent west-side neighbourhood where children are coddled and treated like dignitaries, and I'd probably be run off the block for talking that way. Besides, what example would it set for Maia? As she grows up and goes out into the world alone, she'll need to field these questions again and again—whether or not they're spoken aloud. Encountering strangers on the street or at the market, bringing home friends from high school, arriving from college with a new love, she won't have me to shelter her. She'll have to do the explaining. Already, she has had to ask her Mandarin teachers for homework instructions in English: *My mom can't read Chinese.* Soon, she'll be adding, *Did I mention that my parents are white?* And, *This is my brother. No, not my uncle. My brother. I know he's the same age as your dad, but my dad's older.* And in case that wasn't enough, *What do you mean you weren't expecting me to look the way I do when you heard my name? Yeah, I'm Chinese. But I'm also part Jewish!* This is her future, and I want to make sure she has the self-acceptance and confidence to negotiate these conversations with dignity and poise.

At the same time, I'm loath to lie.

Was she born from you?

On the windowsill of her bedroom, Maia keeps a fishbowl. In it swim five guppies, golden-brown striped, flecked with teal and red. Gifts from a friend. You'd have thought he'd offered her the world. She loves animals, but our landlady does not allow furry pets, so she bubbles with love for these bland, cold-blooded creatures, who seem, mysteriously, to have awakened her own maternal impulses. She watches them for hours, feeds them precisely measured doses, helps to clean their bowl every week, reminding me if I lose track of the days. One of these fish is pregnant. Maia has named it Susan. "I know *you* couldn't get pregnant, Mom, but Susan's the best name in the world for a mother."

Are you really . . .

Eight-year-old girls may be married to literal fact and to logic, but I dive for the heart's truth. Squaring my shoulders, I summon from my teaching days a voice of calm authority. "I'm her mother."

My answer, ambiguous to the two girls, is perfectly clear to Maia. "Forever and ever," she says. She stretches an arm for the next ring, clasps it and swings from side to side, trying to work up the momentum to skip one in the series—a long-time goal of hers, until now unmet.

Jennica raises an eyebrow. Catherine shrugs. They glance from Maia back to me again, chins mulishly lowered, faces skeptical. I stare back. Extending once more, Maia clutches, secures her grip, swings, and her face unfolds in a brilliant smile. She drops to the platform with a thud, feet spread apart, springy and grounded. "Mom! Mom! I did it!"

And something shifts. Jennica moves to let Maia go past, then reaches out to take her own place on the equipment. "Wow," she says. Her voice loses its prematurely cynical edge. She almost allows herself to smile. "Cool."

"Cool," repeats Catherine, flipping her golden hair.

A TALE OF TWO MOMMIES

RACHEL ROSE

It was the most chaste of times, it was the most promiscuous of times, it was the spring of hope, it was the winter of despair; we had everything going for us, we had insurmountable obstacles in our path—in short, we were a typical lesbian couple trying to reproduce. It was the year of Our Goddess one thousand nine hundred and ninety-eight, and we were so baby hungry that we had begun to make inappropriate inquiries of strange men at parties.

I was out of control. I couldn't attend a social event without checking out every male in the room and mentally fusing their features with mine and Isabelle's. It got so bad that I couldn't hold a normal conversation with a member of the opposite sex. I can't tell you how odd the situation was for us, but here's an analogy that might help. You know when you see someone attractive at a café and a brief fantasy flits across your mind? Well, forget any innocent daydreams of fumbling with strangers. Go directly to the ramifications of having said stranger's children, with the added kink of asexual reproduction. Then, discuss this fantasy in detail with your spouse, pointing out all possible genetic and social shortcomings, until, instead of finding him cute, you find yourself grateful for having narrowly avoided ruining your life. Do this multiple times a day for a year and see if you don't get a little neurotic too.

"HEY, WHAT about the FedEx man?" Isabelle asks as we prepare for yet another insemination attempt, having just thanked said delivery man, shut the door and hauled the liquid nitrogen tank to the bedroom. "We know he's a nice guy, good eyebrows, never says a word when he asks us to sign below 'Receipt: Human Semen,' always friendly. And the potbelly's probably not genetic."

"I am *not* fucking the FedEx man!"

"C'mon. It's fresh, more likely to work. He'd probably do you free. Just put on something low-cut. I'll take a walk."

"Forget it, Isabelle."

"Think of all the money we'd save!"

"Read my lips: no FedEx man."

THE TRUTH IS, we were desperate. We spent months talking our heads off about how to start our family, until we were both sick of the whole subject. That's what two women do together: we *process*. We go over the ramifications of the ramifications, the ethics of the ethics, the fears of the fears, until we have covered everything six times over, and then we begin again. We were, I say in our own defence, faster than many lesbians: we did not involve our therapists, meeting in conjunction with our couples' therapist, the potential donor's therapist, or our lawyers to rehash what we'd already hashed.

Everyone we knew had an opinion, knew a nice guy or was a nice guy and wanted to be in on scoring sperm for us. This was 1998—the Year of Inappropriate Donors. Old boyfriends of mine volunteered to "give us a hand," or the equivalent of "one for the road." Friends called to say they'd talked to younger brothers and would get in touch shortly with a deal for us. My sister graciously volunteered her husband without even asking him first, and he promptly made a very sweet visit to tell me he was ready and willing whenever we were. Even my parents got involved—*way* too involved. My mother was recruiting much older relatives for Isabelle, praising their sperm in ways that made me squirmy. And my father, bless his well-meaning wacko heart, called to tell me about a childhood friend of mine who would fit the bill perfectly. "He just got out of rehab. Nice kid, just never did anything with his life. Tall, green eyes, likes to read. And he could use the money." It got very odd, though we knew the intentions were loving. We were like Ancient Mariners, stuck afloat in a giant sea, with "Sperm, sperm everywhere, and not a drop to..."

When I had boyfriends, the goal had always been to stay as far away from pregnancy as I possibly could. Funny how context changes everything: how something that was once a slippery menace was now coveted, more precious than gold. I thought of all the wasted sperm, all the cold condoms I'd peeled off and tossed, and it made me both nostalgic and annoyed.

While my parents joined me in obsessive questing, Isabelle's parents kept their distance, both literally and geographically. They were still choosing to believe that we'd come to our senses, forget this crazy plan to breed and just start a literary salon, like normal gay people do in Paris. Alas, even for gay people we were weird.

Even then, I knew that would be part of the inheritance for any future children: weird parents. Most of the time, I figured our advantages as parents tipped the balance in our favour, even if our family would be unusual. Isabelle and I knew we loved children; we met doing volunteer child care in a housing project in Montreal. We had it made in terms of love and fun, books and affection and adventures. And we knew, from the time we got together, that we would have children of our own. Although we never felt the same as the normal families around us, having children always seemed like the sweetest part of family life, and we were sure we'd find a way to bring that sweetness home.

Of course, I don't find normal families particularly sacred. The Vatican recently called lesbians who bear children a sign of "the eclipse of God," but I have never answered to such a God, nor do I hold in high regard an institution that has subjugated women and children for centuries. I often wonder why some heterosexuals have made their life's work the persecution of people who love their own sex. Notice that the Vatican did not call the millions of girls who are "disappeared" through female infanticide, or the thousands of women murdered by their husbands within the sacred institution of marriage, an "eclipse of God." No: lesbians who want to participate in creating and raising the next generation are singled out for that condemnation.

IN THEORY, I liked the idea of a known donor, certainly more than Isabelle did. I liked the kids being able to ask their biological father the hard questions rather than saving them up for us. But I was also terrified of custody battles, having the scars from surviving those battles between my mother and father. Isabelle adamantly didn't want to have three parents in our family. We were living in Quebec, which had laws on the books at the time that said no matter what kind of legal contract was drawn up, if a biological father's identity was known, he had the right to joint custody. How could we face such a risk?

Also, without the patina of romantic love softening our visions, everyone we knew seemed flawed or risky. It got to be too much. We knew we'd love any kid that came to us. But when you have to choose, *how* do you choose? I know I wouldn't have chosen myself as an egg donor, not with that pesky alcoholism in the family, that bad knee, that severe bout of depression as a teen, that thigh cellulite. It became apparent that what we needed was less information, not more. We were drowning in possibilities and ramifications; trying to plot out relationships with men I'd dated and was no longer with because of irreconcilable differences, or men we liked but didn't love, or men we loved but didn't entirely trust.

If we'd had any money at that time, we would have gone straight to adoption. We had always planned on adopting at a future point, had always promised each other that we'd work for the welfare of vulnerable children. We knew three families on our street who'd adopted little girls from China and a close friend who'd adopted from India. But we couldn't even secure a credit card at that point, never mind the thousands and thousands of dollars needed for an adoption. We put that plan on hold, thinking (mistakenly, as it turns out) that we could grow our own for nearly nothing.

THE DAY I tested positive dawned grey and miserable. Isabelle was doing her rotation in internal medicine, which she hated, and I told her at breakfast I couldn't take much more of this. I was going back to bed and wouldn't get up again until I was pregnant. After all our previous resolve, we'd started eyeing young, virile men in the *dépanneur* again. From my quilted cocoon, I called my old boyfriend T. and asked if he'd still consider helping us. To my everlasting gratitude he said yes. I called the airport to make inquiries about a flight to where he lived. Then, still fretful, I called the American Association of Tissue Banks in Georgia and asked the woman who answered how she knew for sure that freezing sperm didn't just kill them off. I couldn't shake this fear that I'd been paying hundreds of dollars a month for dead spunk.

"Ma'am, it's not like frozen peas," she said. "We've had pregnancies result from a thawed sample after more than twenty years." I sighed, brushing away a few stray tears of pity. Why was everyone else pregnant but me? I thanked her and then I went and listlessly peed on a stick. In two minutes, my life was transformed.

I took a cab to the Jewish General Hospital and found Isabelle. We rushed into the bathroom and I triumphantly peed again. I felt like a magician as I watched both lines turn blue for the second time. We jumped up and down and held each other. We were going to be mothers! I was so overjoyed and so scared of what we had begun. But there is no going back. You fall in love, you want to share your love and then, holding hands, you stand on the edge of the cliff and jump.

AFTER GAINING fifty pounds and suffering through all sorts of complications, I had to be induced, and after twenty-four hours, with my fever creeping higher along with my baby's heart rate, I had a C-section. I saw my son's face for only a minute when he left for the intensive care nursery with Isabelle following. I was wheeled alone to recovery, where for some reason I was forgotten. There was a shift change. My mother and Isabelle were with Ben. My mouth was so dry that I felt myself to be dying. My belly was empty of child and my arms were empty too. I watched the minutes tick past, softly calling for help, but no one came. Finally I yelled. I rang the buzzer. I demanded they bring me to my baby, page my partner. I had turned into a leaking, suspicious animal; I no longer recognized myself.

Isabelle held him first, carried him first. I know she was a bit uncertain of her role as the non-biological mother in those first few weeks. I distinctly remember going to Café Santropol with two-week-old Ben snuggled into a baby carrier on her front. She ran into an old friend and showed him her son. "Wow, you look great!" he gushed. I was waddling behind, one hand protectively cupping my stitches, staring at my breasts, which suddenly stuck out like muskmelons, but I saw her smile and blush as she answered, "Thanks!"

Years later, when I had my daughter, Gabriele, it was much the same, though she spent more time in the neonatal intensive care unit than Ben. I remember those middle-of-the-night shuffles down the hall to the elevator, holding my hand across the stitches of my belly where my uterus had been lifted out like a Christmas ham, cut and stuffed back in. I walked until I reached that wing, where we had to scrub for two minutes before we were allowed to enter and make our way among the babies with their skin raw as cranberry jelly. I remember finding my big full-term daughter, heels bruised and arms red from needle sticks, being monitored because of her blood-type incompatibility. Her eyes were swollen in sleep. I remember how I asked them to call me when she wanted to nurse and they decided to give her a bottle instead, how every cell in my body craved to have her in my arms, where she belonged. Isabelle was at home, mostly, with Ben, and I was in the hospital trying to cope, turning my head away as they stabbed and poked, milked her heels and prodded the veins in her hands for blood.

GABRIELE'S CONCEPTION was unique, and we are among only a few hundred in the world who have done what we've done. The thing was, Isabelle couldn't get pregnant, and nobody could tell us why. It was probably just a fluke of statistics. Frozen sperm is puny stuff, and our supply was finite and expensive. After a year of trying, she decided to go straight to IVF. She was only thirty years old, and every test she'd had was perfect. She made more than a dozen "grade A" embryos, but each time they put them back, none of them stayed. It was such a sad time. We had our little boy, our darling Ben, but we also had this vision of how it would be for us, a child from each of our bodies, and then two adopted children. It was hard to let that vision go.

Eventually, Isabelle stopped trying, stopped the injections and the hormones and the vaginal suppositories that coloured her whole world a woolly grey. She said she was finished. I would try again. But there were still six of her embryos left. We decided to put two of them into me and see what happened.

I got pregnant the first try. What it was like for her to pick up her biological baby from my body I cannot tell you. What it was like for me was a mixture of wonder and pure love. I loved carrying our baby and knowing it came from her, even as I nourished it. I loved that we had succeeded in making at least part of our dream a reality.

PEOPLE ARE CURIOUS about how we are different from mom-and-pop families, a question I find hard to answer. With boyfriends, there is a certain approval, a certain lack of watchfulness that makes life very easy. Everyone is glad for you because you are doing what you are supposed to do. That, however, has never seemed reason enough to do anything. We don't usually get approval from strangers we meet—we get questions, demands for information, puzzled looks and critical commentary.

Although I get tired of the questions, I also would not wish to be straight. The bonus, for me, is that Isabelle and I have a closeness that many straight mothers I know envy. I know straight couples who feel divided when their children appear. The mothers feel burdened and mistrustful; the men feel neglected and mistrusted. They often retreat to their expected roles and stay disconnected. If I feel guarded in public, not entirely understood or accepted, I feel more than compensated by the quality of understanding and connectedness I share with Isabelle at home. Some women have social acceptance but loneliness in their marriage. I have the reverse, social disapproval but deep satisfaction in my life with Isabelle. That is a common thread I've seen in many gay and lesbian families.

I've heard mothers rage at motherhood, at their children's constant needs, at their own sacrifice of autonomy, career, sleep, at the loneliness in their marriages. In my experience, it is rare that a lesbian mother regrets her chosen motherhood. I can complain with the best of them, especially about the quicksand of the first year in which I felt myself to be drowning, my identity like a lead apron over my shoulders, pulling me down. But I can't imagine my life empty of their presence. I have never once regretted them.

Perhaps simply by following our hearts, we have finally found a way to create a new and powerfully egalitarian model for the family. Perhaps this is why I've never seen a lesbian mother express the same depths of frustration about mothering as some of the heterosexual moms I know. Perhaps when mothering is separated from the gender inequality between men and women, and the implicit denial of self that society expects only of mothers, it can become something more powerfully satisfying than anyone envisioned.

Perhaps, but I doubt it. Perhaps my vision is just a sentimental load of crap. There are so many variations in the dance between parents and children, so many ways in which things can go wrong, or can unexpectedly correct themselves. And the dance itself is larger than we are, nearly infinite in its ability to expand or change its steps according to circumstance.

All parents make compromises. We are so often genuinely unsure of the right path. A lot of my former confidence has been transformed into an anxious hopefulness for my family and the other families, straight and gay, that I adore—that we will find enough love, enough luck, that we will muddle through with a modicum of grace, that our children will flourish somehow. Ordinary wishes indeed for a revolutionary.

Looking back nearly a decade now to the time when we began our quest, I am more certain of what nobody, straight or gay, can know until after they've tested it out: I chose the right person to have children with. And I say this with great relief and gratitude. But being on the cutting edge sucks sometimes, especially when you are choosing to put yourself and your children out there. Even before we had them, we knew we would make them forever different, and for all our talk about not finding the status quo something worth imitating, we knew that this would be a burden they did not choose. It came down to this: they could have life. They could have two mommies who loved the holy crap out of them, but they'd be permanent members of a family everyone else thought of as odd. They would, no matter what, have a lot of explaining to do for choices that were beyond their control.

And here, from the other side of the parenting vortex, I finally find myself ordinary after all: I line up for music classes, buy Rice Krispies in bulk, have deep conversations with strangers about stain removers and circus camp, language acquisition and playdates. Though I couldn't have articulated it when we began, my revolution is all about the right to be ordinary and different at the same time.

OKAY, SO ISABELLE'S a bit more of a suck than I am. Okay, so she gives them more chocolate and chips than I would. But I love the way she parents. I love the confirmation I see every day when she and Ben do his French homework, when she fills the pool up for Gabriele and her friends to splash in. I love her through them and them through her.

Both the kids preferred me as babies, because I had the functional tits. Isabelle had to be a patient, loving, exciting mommy, the one who sang songs and told stories and kissed boo-boos. All I had to do was whip out a titty. It wasn't fair that Isabelle couldn't comfort them easily, but neither was it fair that I had to sit up in the middle of the night with a screaming six-month-old with the stomach flu who wanted nothing in the world but to nurse, even though she puked it up all over me every seven minutes. And did I mention the saggy boobs? We quickly learned two things: we are an excellent team, and it's not about what we want any more, and never will be again. It's about what they need. I love that she sees that too, and that we do whatever it takes for them.

I used to think, forgive me, that marriage and monogamy were to be avoided at all costs. I thought it went like this: you got tired of dating, so you resigned yourself to one person, then entered a steady period of declining expectations, libido, sex appeal, and increasing wrinkles, resignation, and debt. But marriage is not like rolling down a slope into a cemetery. It's like crossing the Pacific in a sea kayak. There are storms, passion, periods of deadly slackening, dry heat, becalming; there are icebergs and huge waves.

A school of silver minnows swims up the broad river of my hips, another across my stomach. I am changed completely. The stretch marks used to be red, fierce, as though I had been licked, tattooed by fire. Now the flames are going out, silvered to ash, but I will carry forever these marks where my skin was torn. And Isabelle is the only one in the world who has loved my body through this transformation. How could anyone else touch me with such knowledge? How could I trust any other hands?

It's easier to describe the hardships involved in parenting than the joys, because the sentiment inspired by their sweetness is all out of proportion to the actual incidents that bring it on. We just get such a kick out of them! Simply watching them learn how to use language is reason enough to have a child. I love the memory of Ben shocking the other parents in Vancouver, right after we left Montreal, when I took him to a family drop-in centre and watched him point to a seal and yell, "Fok! Fok!" as mothers and nannies looked up in horror. (Seal in French is *phoque*.) When Ben, aged two, smiles at me and asks gently, "Mama, why does your breath smell like dog food?" When Gaby, at the same age three years later, makes up a song just for me:

> I love my mom, my tiny mom!
> When I dump it, she wipes it up!
> My tiny mom!

And most of all, when I come home from a rare late night out and find them all three asleep in our big bed, I am run over by the bulldozer of sentimentality. I am crushed. Everything I love most is in that bed. I am living the most joyous years of my life, and I'm lucky enough to be aware of the joy even in the midst of the daily business.

I realize that it's nearly impossible to write about family life without sounding either smugly sentimental or deeply anxious and shocked at the turn one's life has taken, and it's certainly more interesting to read about the latter. Though I've had my share of anxieties, I now fall firmly into the smugly sentimental brigade.

As oppressed people go, we have it pretty good. We don't live in Moscow, Mongolia or Montana. We live in a country where we can legally marry, a city where there is protection from anti-gay harassment in the schools, and a neighbourhood with a tolerant artistic hippie tradition. In our neighbourhood, we get the sense people actually like hanging out with us because we aren't mainstream, which may explain why I haven't gotten to watch season two of *The L Word*—all our straight friends keep borrowing it!

Paradoxically, though I fear future obstacles, I believe that each potential difficulty our children face could also be a potential strength. If our son and daughter learn to be comfortable with difference, that's a gift. If they learn the art of verbal self-defence from an early age, more power to them. If they have a sense of what life is like on the margins, if they become sensitized to injustice as children, I won't regret it. If they learn to value personal achievement and humanistic values over ethnic, linguistic or geographic ties, all the better. Though I would never wish them pain, neither would I wish them complacency. I want them to be uncomfortable enough in the world—where millions of children just as beloved as they are die of diarrhea, malaria, AIDS and hunger—that they will feel a great need to act. Where does empathy come from if not from a sense of not entirely belonging? I have this crazy optimism that we can give them this, while still protecting them enough that they grow up whole, secure in themselves.

This is not why we had them, though—as some political project, as walking, talking proof of the equality of our love. We wanted them in that desperate, irrational way that any couple who has been longing for a baby will understand. We wanted the weight of them in our arms, the caramel smell of their breath. We wanted to watch their lives unfold, to participate in the beginning of a journey that would extend beyond us. And despite what felt like insurmountable obstacles, we succeeded. Without the FedEx man.

EVEN NOW, WE still have four embryos on ice and we can't quite decide what to do with them. I can't help feeling a desire to thaw them, let them spring free, let them develop into whoever they are. I know, I *know*, I sound like a militant pro-lifer—which I'm not, except that I can love the life before it has become a full life. Things get complicated when you conceive your children out of body. They are there, just sitting in six-celled suspended animation, as Gabriele once did for all those dark months, waiting for a womb.

As Dickens writes in *A Tale of Two Cities*, "A wonderful fact to reflect upon, that every human creature is constituted to be that profound secret and mystery to every other." Dickens's Jarvis Lorry has the distinct feeling that he is recalling someone to life; I too think of our four embryos, waiting in suspended animation in their storage tank.

> "Buried how long?"
> "Almost eighteen years."
> "I hope you care to live?"
> "I can't say."
> (*A Tale of Two Cities*, chapter 3)

Will they care to live, even if life brings with it a sense of being different, bewilderment about biological connections, fatherlessness, an absence? We tell ourselves that our love will give them the tools they need to develop a sense of self. Whether or not they decide to meet their donor, we hope with all our hearts that we chose well, that he is a good man, that they will be able to make sense of it all, to find their way through. They are so lively, so curious, loving, stubborn and much too smart. They are so clearly *meant to be here*. They delight in the physical world: the lapful of puppies at their grandma's house, the smell of new cedar in their granddad's shop, salt on their lips as they hold my shoulders at Jericho and swim into the sea. Our children give this dusty, tragic world a little more shine than it would have had without them. They are not the eclipse: they are the light.

NO INTERRUPTIONS

CARRIE-ANNE MOSS

It was day one of my forty-day seclusion. Day one of my new life as a mother. Day one of my son's life. And there we were snuggled and huddled in our big bed, skin to skin, mouth to nipple, breath to breath. Pure bliss. Over the next forty days I would spend almost all my waking and my few sleeping hours in that bed, in that bedroom and in the room next door. My husband and I had decided to create this sanctuary for our family because we believed it was the most sacred event of our lives—becoming a family. We wanted to honour this time and allow it to gently take place without interruptions from the outside world.

I remember the way the light poured in through the curtains at sunset, the way it refracted off the blue walls, the way the house seemed alive with colour, as if all my senses had just woken up. I remember the way time slowed down and I was always surprised it was only four o'clock.

In those days, I took care of the baby and my husband took care of me. We had hired a woman to come by in the mornings to do laundry, cook us delicious meals and rub my feet. In the evenings, I would bring the baby downstairs, and my husband and I would watch *Everybody Loves Raymond*. I wanted to laugh. Motherhood had made me feel so vulnerable and I wanted relief. I think we watched every single episode.

In the thirty-five years before sequestering myself in my house for those forty biblical days, I'd never sat still. I'd gone from busy Hollywood actress to earth mother in just a few days. It was a shocking transition, but one that I was ready for, desperate for. I believed having a baby would be a rest. I know that sounds funny because it isn't really "restful" if you account for the sleepless nights, caring for sick babies, and all the other constant demands of motherhood.

But I knew that motherhood, for me, would be my time to be home and hang out. Before I had a baby, I was never home. I was always travelling and living in hotels. I got pregnant two months after wrapping up production on *The Matrix 3*. My baby gave me a reason to say no to everyone and everything. Finally.

I'd been working since I was a teenager, at first at restaurants, then as an actress. I was ready to surrender, and it came as a huge relief. My movies gave me the financial freedom to take time off and be with my babies.

I've always wanted babies. I babysat when I was eleven and taught kids to tie their shoes and write their names. I'm surprised some days that I don't have eleven kids and that it took me so long to have my first child. In my fantasies, I was the bohemian mom in the peasant dress with no makeup. And sometimes I am that woman. But I am also a tornado with baby on hip, phone in hand, jacket flinging across the room.

My forty-day seclusion with my firstborn seems faraway now. But when I close my eyes, I remember the hours spent in my rocking chair, rocking my way into motherhood. I remember thinking, as I rocked my baby, that there are millions of other mothers around the world doing exactly the same thing. I remember getting up in the middle of the night and having a strange and euphoric energy. I thought, Hey, this is supposed to be irritating, but I chose to do it with joy because I knew it would go by quickly.

In my seclusion, I spent day after day after day with tea in hand, baby at the breast, in our own unique rhythm. The bed was our world. I cut off any connection to news or current events. I had a few visitors, but though their occasional presence relieved the isolation and loneliness, the experience was often draining.

My baby would fall asleep. A friend would ring the doorbell. The dogs would bark and suddenly I was stressed: about waking the baby, entertaining my friend, engaging in adult conversation. Once, when I was nursing my baby, a well-meaning friend asked, "Aren't you nursing too much?"

What? I thought to myself, my confidence eroding. After hearing this one too many times, I actually attempted to nurse less. The baby would start crying. Then I would start crying. I wouldn't offer the breast because, well, we all felt he couldn't possibly need to eat again. I called the doctor, my nerves frazzled by the noise. I talked to the nurse, and she said, "Offer the breast."

"But everyone says I'm nursing too much," I tell her, sobbing.

"Offer the breast," she gently encourages.

So I do, and like magic he soothes. The words of a nurse are the most important words I hear in those early days: don't listen to others, listen to your baby. And the lessons begin.

Around week two, I decided to go for a walk around the block. Alone. I was feeling anxious about being away from my baby, and when I saw a gorgeous woman walking down the street pushing a baby carriage, I wanted to scream, I have a baby too!

Instead, I waved at her. She stopped.

"I just had a baby," I blurted out.

Her baby turned her face to me and I saw she had Down's syndrome. Then I saw the mother, so alive and so excited about being a mom.

"That's great," she said.

I remember walking home thinking this girl was a gift. She was a reminder to cherish my beautiful baby boy and never take motherhood for granted.

Week three. I was tired. So tired. I was walking a friend to the door to say goodbye wearing only a nursing bra, my big baby tummy sticking out, holding my baby on my hip. When I opened the door, I saw the paparazzi camped out on my lawn. They took a picture of me crying, holding my baby.

I hadn't realized they knew where I lived. I was upset, shaken, furious that my baby would never be safe. My husband went out to talk to them, and they said that if I would just pose for a picture, they would go away. We didn't believe them.

I didn't leave the house after that. I don't think they knew what was going on. So in a sense, if I hadn't had a self-imposed forty-day seclusion, I would have had to do it anyway.

Now, I'm often followed by the paparazzi. I won't go to certain parks with my kids because I know they'll be there. I'm used to it at this point. I know how to deal with it. But in those first few months of my first baby's life, it was terrifying. I felt as though at any minute they were going to kidnap my baby.

A wise friend once told me that it would be hard to stay balanced as a mother, that I would have "to find my moments inside my family." That is what those forty days were all about. That is what I still strive for. As I write this, I am in my parked car, with baby number two asleep in his seat, and I'm "finding my moment."

With the passage of time, I'm a lot more relaxed. My life as a mother is so different from what it was like in those first forty days. Now, I never stop moving. I'm either making something to eat or wiping something off the floor or doing dishes or laundry or driving my son to preschool or trying to put the baby to sleep for his nap or going to the park or giving them a bath. Most nights, we watch a show together as a family and then climb into our big bed exhausted, all of us together.

This is where it all ends—where it all started. In my bed, with my husband and my two boys under my wings, cuddled in, warm and safe in the world.

SPILLED MILK

DEBLEKHA GUIN

It's a typical island potluck, and a handful of new moms are hovering over a culinary mishmash, discussing what our lives have become. We move to the living room to nurse our wee ones by the glow of a crackling fire. The detritus of the host's previous life is all around us: the DJ gear, the stacks of vinyl placed where their ten-month-old can't reach it. But there's also evidence of their new reality: piles of laundry, baby books, baby toys, the general chaos of baby things.

Once we settle in, it doesn't take long before our conversation turns to sleeping arrangements. "I love that I can love somebody with such expansiveness," I say. "So much so that I'm willing to sleep in the awkward space between a sprawling baby, a teddy bear and the lap edition of *Good Night Moon*. And mostly I do it gladly. But if I don't reclaim some of the bed's real estate in the near future, I'm afraid I'll be making a bed I don't want to lie in—one where my personal space will be cramped for years to come."

"Yeah," laughs the easygoing host. "On most nights, Richie and I get bumped down to the mattress on the floor and Caleb ends up with our bed to himself."

"It was musical beds in our home for years," adds the mother of two elementary school tots. "My sweetie and I started in our bed together, but Cyrus inevitably ended up in bed with me and Wreford joined Simone in hers."

"I finally got Christopher out of our bed," says another mom. "And I'd begun to night wean him when he came down with the stomach flu. Now he's back in our bed and nursing all night long. Who knows when I'll have the energy to go through the trauma of cutting him off again?"

"Don't worry, you'll get caught up on your sleep when they're two or three," pipes up a veteran mom. "And then you'll lose it again when they're teenagers."

This flurry of anecdotes is followed by a distinct lull as each of us silently contemplates the implications of the small sacrifices we make and the mixed feelings they evoke. There are hints of resentment in some of the stories these mothers tell, but there is also an unmistakable chord of self-sacrificing pride. Ah, the contradictory emotional brew that is motherhood.

For two years, since the birth of my daughter, I have struggled to reconcile sacrifice and self-respect. For two years, I've been fumbling along in my attempts to learn the art of balanced giving. And for me, breastfeeding has been the centre of this struggle.

I live on a small island off the coast of British Columbia where many young people (of all social and political persuasions) are managing to raise families despite the inflated land costs that come with being in a recreational zone for wealthy urbanites and retirees. To call the island "child-friendly" would be an understatement. It is a place that boasts an abundance of both public and private spaces where kids are not only welcomed but looked out for and consistently nurtured. It's a place where "free-range kids" can genuinely thrive and where "children without borders" can blissfully run amok.

Ella's father and I have attempted to structure our lives so that each of us gets to enjoy time with Ella and time alone (which hasn't left much room for time for each other, but that's another story).

Aside from yoga and fit-ball class, my "alone" time is spent working out of the house three days a week. When I'm with Ella, her father gets the time and space to pursue his interests, and I do my best to park my other agendas (a challenge for a recovering workaholic like me) and let Ella's interests lead the way. Sometimes the road is smoother, sometimes rougher, but generally, we've arranged our lives to achieve what we hope is a parental middle path.

Before I had a baby, my sense of this middle path involved setting reasonable limits on what I thought I'd be willing to give, or more accurately, give *up*. Like many women on the brink of motherhood, sleep and a degree of physical autonomy were the two things I was most afraid of losing over the long haul.

In an effort to protect my body in advance, I developed some pretty specific ideas about breastfeeding. "If they're old enough to ask for it," I often joked, "they're too old to get it." For some reason, I became attached to the arbitrary figure of eighteen months as the perfectly "moderate" amount of time one should breastfeed. It was a symbolic way of asserting my desire to give beyond the state-sanctioned year of maternity leave while guarding against the prospect of becoming an ever-depleted vessel of giving. Of all the things about which I could have drawn a pre-emptive line in the sand, why this?

One contributing factor was a moment at a kids' party, years before, when the child of a very close friend screamed, "I want my boobies!" from the other side of a crowded room. It left a lasting and disturbing impression. Whatever else happens, I thought, I'm going to stop breastfeeding before my child can put a sentence like that together, let alone bellow it with such an air of possessive entitlement.

I remember counselling that same friend when she struggled with the decision about whether it was time to wean her daughter. "Look," I said with the clarity and bluntness that can only be mustered by someone who has never nursed or navigated the rocky terrain that is weaning. "If you're starting to resent it, your milk is probably already sour, so I wouldn't sweat cutting her off."

So this is what it feels like to eat your words. My daughter, Ella, is now twenty-one months old, and I've only recently begun coaxing her to consider access to my breasts as more of a privilege than a right. And I'm asking myself why I am experiencing such a disconnect between my prenatal expectations and my current reality.

For one thing, I wasn't prepared for the primal pleasure I get from the ability to actually produce food to sustain another human being. Amid the whirlwind of trying to fulfill the most basic work and home responsibilities, nursing also forces Ella and me to slow down and snuggle quietly. The depth and uniqueness of the connection nursing fosters is often so profound that I can hardly imagine our relationship without it.

Then again, there are times when Ella nurses with such all-consuming gusto that it feels as if I'm literally being devoured. There are also times when she goes straight for my breasts without a moment's pause to look into my eyes or do anything else to acknowledge my status as more than a food source. Not exactly my ideal version of closeness.

To my surprise, the clash between my reverence for and bitterness toward our nursing rituals prompted the introduction of manners into our relationship. Before having a child, I never really understood mothers who would constantly be at their kids to say "please" and "thank you." From where I stood then, making superficial and token gestures of gratitude mandatory only inhibited real appreciation (I still think this can be the case). Worse, I thought most demands for "please" and "thank you" revealed a need for recognition that I frankly considered to be pathetic. I guess I can add this to my humbling series of pre/postnatal reversals.

I realize that saying "please" and "thank you" doesn't guarantee authentic appreciation, but I'm amazed at how those simple words (yes, words of recognition) can make me feel more "pleased" about giving. It's really a symbolic and pragmatic way to establish some autonomy and preserve a tiny but necessary thread of self-respect.

I'll never forget the first time I told Ella to "ask nicely" before I'd let her nurse. She flashed me a look of total indignation before trying to lift up my shirt. The tug-of-war was on. I held down my shirt with unwavering commitment. She refused to ask and continued to wrestle with my shirt. I persisted, as if my very survival depended on it. She did the same. Finally, she scrunched her face into a question mark, pointed at my breasts and asserted with diminishing confidence "Ella's."

Ah, the crux of the matter. "No," I replied, at once offended and relieved for the chance to clear up this misunderstanding. "They are not Ella's. They are Mama's. Mama sometimes shares with Ella." She wasn't impressed, but desperate for "nummie nums," she ultimately acquiesced.

She doesn't always ask politely before going for it, and I don't always demand that she do so, but asserting my right to refuse and delay access has made me enjoy nursing more and—for better and worse—extended the lifespan of our nursing relationship.

The initiation of these protocols is obviously about my need to establish some autonomy and receive some recognition, but it's also about Ella's long-term well-being. Given that most of her waking hours are spent asking for things, it's imperative that she start to learn that the fulfillment of her needs demands effort and sometimes sacrifice from others, and that it's important to acknowledge and, ideally, to appreciate those who give on her behalf. I realize it's developmentally impossible for her to actually *get* gratitude at this stage in the game, but I figure it can't hurt to start planting the seeds.

I suppose attempting to walk a parental middle path means being as mindful about how our children do the taking as how we, as parents, do the giving. When life is in balance, giving is easy and the give-and-take of it unfolds organically. The challenge for me is identifying when things aren't in balance early enough. And here we return to the seminal act of giving and the constant lesson that is breastfeeding.

Ella and I were recently in the midst of recovering from a long and conflict-ridden night weaning process. The taxing nature of weeks of being woken up by ear-piercing pleas for num-nums and heartfelt cries of sorrow and loss was exacerbated by the fact that I was severely sleep deprived when we set out on this voyage. Though it wasn't conscious, on some deep emotional level, the nighttime power struggle in which we were engaged made me start to see Ella as something of an adversary, an opportunistic being I needed to protect myself from and guard against. Not surprisingly this skewed and bleary-eyed perspective tainted a lot of our daily interactions. During that bumpy period (and for a while afterwards), almost every act of giving felt more like an act of giving in, like a gesture of submission, like one step closer to a hostile takeover.

Given the rather extreme spirit of these sentiments, you might wonder why I didn't start night-weaning earlier. Mostly I wanted to compensate for the time I'd missed with Ella (my work week had escalated from three days to five at that point). And I was operating under the mistaken belief that I could handle the loss of sleep required to carry on our all-night feeding/cuddling sessions.

I'm embarrassed to admit it, but it also had a lot of to do with business, laziness and fear of the unknown. I was so up to my eyeballs with domestic and work-based commitments that it was a struggle just to maintain the status quo. Just trying to imagine what life might look like without breastfeeding sent me into a tizzy— never mind actually attempting to execute such a paradigm shift. However obviously unsustainable, it felt like more work to change gears than it did to "keep on keeping on."

The volatile dynamic of this Catch-22 scenario became most pronounced during the parental fishbowl/pressure cooker that is "play dupe" as Ella so insightfully calls it. Ella was starting to make a habit of grabbing toys and pushing other kids—relatively normal toddler behaviour, but none of the other children at the play group were doing it. This was met with raised eyebrows and a range of subtle and not-so-subtle comments that suggested she was starting to be regarded as something of a "problem child." In my sleep-deprived and ultra-sensitive state, it became all about me, and how embarrassed and inept her antics made me feel. Partially out of a desire to appear like a more "in-control" parent, I adopted a cop-like persona during the dreaded play group gatherings. The more I policed her, the more she'd act out. The more she acted out, the more I'd engage in pre-emptive interventions that were invariably based on expecting the worst whenever she made a move toward another child.

It was a truly vicious cycle, and it started with my inability to see how indulging Ella's all-night feeding habits, an apparent testament to my love, was turning into the opposite. With the luxury of hindsight and a comparatively well-rested point of view, I can see the damage that was done by my tendency to overgive to the point of exhaustion and resentment; how it established parental practices that swung between the extremes of excessive lenience and abrupt restriction—the opposite of the middle path I so aspired to.

Despite being a second-generation feminist, I still tend to admire and often measure myself against mothers who seem to have bottomless pits of patience and a bounty of emotional resources to share with their children; mothers who appear to have seamlessly shed their formal selves and can fully dedicate every ounce of their energy to the myriad tasks of being a parent. And when my arrogant martyr complex is in full swing, the first thoughts that go through my head when Ella acts up are about myself. What am I doing wrong? What am I not providing her with or giving her enough of? What is my work outside the home really costing her?

At the same time, I know it wouldn't be healthy, for Ella or for me, if I emulated the family dynamic in Shel Silverstein's famous children's story *The Giving Tree*, where the metaphorical mother-tree is ultimately reduced to a stump by her voraciously needy and ungrateful child.

I suspect the mixed feelings I've had about what I've been willing and able to give (in the realm of breastfeeding and otherwise) have at least something to do with the mixed messages given to modern moms. We're supposed to graciously provide for our children while simultaneously maintaining fully actualized and independent lives. We're supposed to be smart enough to see the pitfalls of playing the role of the all-sacrificing mother and yet able to play the role to perfection at the same time.

It's way too much ground for one person to cover. And after two years of trying my damnedest, I'm finally willing to admit that I have to downsize my expectations. It comes back to striking a balance and trying to navigate that middle path. Not just in theory, but in practice. For me, that means cultivating a clearer sense of what my capacity actually is and trying not to give beyond it. Mostly I am content to give and give and give to my daughter. Most of this giving inspires a rewarding and spiritually gratifying feedback loop. But I need to be honest about when this isn't the case.

One of the downsides of having an apparently bottomless pit of energy, mixed with a heavy dose of Taurian determination, is my inability to see the end of my rope until I've already reached it. I often overgive, to the point of either exhaustion or resentment, whether it's with Ella, my partner or work. These are my personal issues, but they are tendencies that have been socially sanctioned for women for hundreds of years. It's bred deep in my bones, but it's a pattern I don't want Ella to inherit through her mother's milk.

The upside of realizing that I've been spreading myself too thin is that I'm being forced to take stock and institute some changes. Despite all my angst, neither Ella nor I is quite ready to declare a complete moratorium on breastfeeding. But I am definitely ready to moderate the "feeding frenzy," and I've already started to impose pretty strict limits on nursing times and locations. Baby steps, yes, but steps in the right direction.

I don't doubt there will still be days when I resent Ella's physical dependence on me. And there will also be days when I relish the fact that she sees my body as a safe and comforting haven. I guess I'm still a bit torn.

Perhaps it's unrealistic to think that the art of balanced giving can ever be fully mastered or to expect that attaining some measure of balance will cause all mixed feelings to cease. And maybe balanced giving is an impermanent art—one that needs to be learned and relearned with each stage of a child's growth.

Then again, I may just continue to indulge my angst and find that I'm still breastfeeding Ella when she graduates from high school. On some days, that doesn't seem like such a stretch.

SLOW SURRENDER
CHANTAL KREVIAZUK

The night before my first baby was born, we had a raging party. I had already done way too much that day: I hiked, I swam, I cooked food for dozens of guests. By the end of the night, people were doing shots, and I thought, the one night we have a party, I'm going to go into labour. By 2 a.m., people were passed out all over my house, even sleeping in the baby's nursery. The kitchen was a disaster, the sink clogged with broken glass.

In full nesting mode, I found a plunger to clear the kitchen sink. As soon as I pushed it down, my water broke. I couldn't drive myself to the hospital, and my husband, Raine, was in no shape to drive. I had to call a friend who hadn't been at the party to come get us. When we got to the hospital, the contractions were coming really fast. After my epidural, the nurses told me I'd have about three hours before the baby was born.

So I got on the phone. I called my mom, my mother-in-law and my mixer. Avril Lavigne was finishing her album. I had worked on it with her, and she was living with us at the time. In between contractions (which I could still feel despite the epidural), I talked to the mixer about what still needed to be done. After I hung up, a half-hour after getting the epidural, I told the nurse I had to push. She told me I just had to go to the bathroom. I begged her to look. She

238

did, and she finally let me push. One push and Rowan's head was out. Second push and there was his tiny, beautiful body.

Sixteen months later, I was back in the hospital giving birth to my second son. Lucca Jon came out in one push. We had tried to schedule his arrival around a music session, but it didn't work out that way. Right after the birth, we went home to a recording session.

I didn't think, even the second time around, that I needed a pause. It wasn't until two weeks later that I realized I was going to have to slow down. Surrender came slowly, and then there I was— my ambition slipping away and a great, surging love for my boys taking over my life.

I've always been "a career person." I thought my work would be even more important to me after I became a mom. There would be clear black and white lines between our house and our home studio. Black and white lines between Chantal the mom and Chantal the musician. But those black and white lines are very grey, and most days they are stained with tears and heartache. Leaving the boys to cross to the other side of the house, where we have our studio, can break me apart.

I once had a beautiful cousin who died suddenly at the age of thirty-six, just a few years before I had Rowan. She was like the sister I never had. She left behind her two- and four-year-old girls and a loving, awesome husband. After Rowan was born, when things were tough, I thought of her. When Rowan was puking or having explosive diarrhea, or screaming and peeing all over me at the same moment, I would think of her up in heaven laughing at me. And when Rowan would make sounds for all the animals I named while we lay in bed at night, I would think of her and miss her and feel sad and blessed at the same time.

Every Thursday, Rowan and I have a special ritual. We go to a parent-toddler class in a building at the top of a hill. You have to park your car at the base of the hill and do the eight-minute walk up with your child. It is a magical eight minutes. We listen to the birds, look for squirrels, see if the ducks have come by the creek for a visit, look to see if any flowers are in bloom. Sometimes we sing. . Sometimes we say nothing at all. Most of the time, Rowan, halfway up the hill, says, "Uggie, uggie?" which is his own unique way of asking to be carried.

After we finish our class, the teacher gives Rowan a sticker on his belly button and we make our way down the hill and hop into the car. We head to an eatery at a little mall for French toast and latkes. There is a toy store steps from the restaurant, and we pick up a new toy on the way home.

One day—May 4, 2006, the birthday of my late, beloved cousin—I was in a rush. I had to work at one-thirty, and by the time we finished eating, got a toy, and picked up a gift for a friend's new baby, I was running quite late. Rowan was dilly-dallying, wanting to look at his new miniature animals. I told him we'd get them in two seconds when we got to the car.

"Mommy, I need my ostrich now!" I love the way he says ost-wich, and in that moment, I could understand how badly he wanted his toy. I understood that he didn't know what "We'll be at the car in two seconds" meant. For all he knew, it could be a lifetime from now.

Without thinking, I dropped my bags and sat down on the concrete with Ro. We dug through the toy bag until we found his ostrich. Then I got up and began packing again. Suddenly a woman came over to us. "I just want you to know that I've been watching you with your child. It was so beautiful to see you stop before a tantrum started and get down on the ground and get what he was asking for."

I was shocked. In my job as a musician, I am always complimented. Sometimes, although I am grateful, I wonder why people compliment me for doing what comes so naturally and easily, for something that already comes with so many hyperbolized rewards. Mothers, however, rarely get compliments, regardless of how richly they might be deserved.

The woman continued, "I want you to know how much I've learned from watching you. I will take that into the rest of my day and into my own journey as a mother."

In *my* journey as a mother, I have watched my two worlds collide: my music and my babies. And I'm surprised at how they reinforce each other. I've never felt so creative in my life. My latest album, *Ghost Stories*, is my least ambitious, yet it's my favourite. One of the songs on it, "All I Can Do," is about my sons.

It's all I can do to love my children with my heart and soul. Motherhood has made everything in my life feel more authentic. It's made my music better. It's made me feel as if I've landed and can really be myself.

> All I can do is love you to pieces
> Give you a shoulder to cry when you need it
> When the day is long and the night is coming down on you
> All I can do
> All I can do
> All I can do...
>
> What a lovely day to shape your dreams
> And you don't even have to sleep
> You can make it what you want to be
> You can fly away
> You can change your name
> Have a happy face
> It could be so real
>
> Ohhhh

All I can do is love you to pieces
Give you a shoulder to cry when you need it
When the day is long and the night is coming down on you
All I can do
All I can do
All I can do
It's all that I can do.

THE PERFECT CHILD

ESTÉE KLAR-WOLFOND

It was a perfect year, sort of.
I dreamt of the perfect child and then there he was, my Adam, sitting in his playpen, wearing the bib Grandma made with a big number 1 sewn on the front. He turned one in April. At his party, I hung balloons from the balustrade and baked three different cakes for our guests. Grandpa was busy taking photos. And Adam was pulling himself up and peering over the gate to watch a DVD of one of his favourite movies—*The Sound of Music.*

"Wow, he really likes that movie," said cousin Rhonda. Everyone watched Adam, the celebrated boy, in awe—his attention so focused on Maria singing alone in the hills. "I should buy him tickets to the musical," she said, half-joking. "I've never seen a child so intense."

Just a month earlier, Adam read a title, *Gotham*, from the bookshelf that sat next to his playpen. He would stare at it for the longest time. "Gawthum," he finally whispered under his breath. I was tidying up the living room and stopped dead in my tracks. We were already in awe that he knew all of his letters and numbers, but *reading*? Was he actually reading that book of Shakespeare he picked up at eleven months of age, his tiny hand turning each page carefully, deliberately? He was trying to make his little body into the shapes of the letters and

243

numbers on tiles I had bought for the floor. Henry pulled the pieces out like a puzzle and would ask Adam what letter or number it was.

"It's amazing," he said. "None of my other four children could ever do this." I swallowed silent gulps of air, thinking that my first, long-awaited child would have special gifts. I envisioned a musician, a mathematician, private school, maybe Harvard—and me, the proud mother, wearing a hat and pencil skirt during graduation.

I pulled out the birthday cake with one candle and gathered our family and friends in the dining room. I hoisted Adam out of his playpen so we could sing "Happy Birthday." But as soon as the lights went out, Adam began to cry. I cajoled him, turning my body so he could face the candle, but he turned his head away and tried to wriggle from my arms.

"I think there's something wrong," said Henry, after the party. Adam was now delightedly playing with the stark shadows cast on the living room floor by the four o'clock sun. The guests had gone and a mound of presents lay beside his playpen.

"There's nothing wrong with him," I insisted. "C'mon, Adam, let's open this present." I resented it when Henry compared Adam to his other children.

"He doesn't run up to me the way my other kids did. He doesn't roll the ball back to me. I'm telling you, there's something—"

"I've been to the doctor," I interrupted. "He says nothing is wrong, that Adam is just a little anxious." I tried to entice Adam with his first birthday present, stretching my arm out. "Flor, do you think anything is wrong with Adam? You've seen kids before." Adam played with his fingers, watching their shadows on the floor, ignoring the present.

"No!" replied Flor. "He is a sweetie pie." Flor, our Filipino nanny, tried many times to console Adam under the fluttering leaves of our hundred-year-old maple tree. She had been the nanny to Henry's other four children.

Henry reminds me about our first date and all the things we talked about, all the plans we made for our future together. I wanted at least one child, a family of my own. I was an only child from a long line of only children, and I needed a family. Henry would only have one more child. We would get married, travel, then build a house. I would convert to Judaism. Our fragile balloon glasses held our red wine. The restaurant kept us and our dreams warm in the dark winter evening.

I became a stepmother slowly. I don't think there is any other way to become a stepmother. Unlike a biological mother, I had to work at getting to know my stepchildren, letting them expand without interruption, even though I was very much an interruption in their lives. Many days I felt sorry for them, with my intrusive presence, trying to figure out when to fade into the background. They filled me with guilt: I wasn't supposed to be there. I was an encumbrance. I was supposed to leave because they wanted their parents to get back together, as all children would. As an only child, I didn't have my own family and couldn't fit into this one. I had no real place, and I felt isolated and angry.

Henry always used to say, "They're your children too." But he was wrong. They are my family, but not my children. Adam's birth became the bridge by which we all became closer. They became his brothers and sisters.

WHEN I HEARD Adam's voice for the first time, it was a full cry after a long wait. He had swallowed meconium, and his entrance into the world was silent. He was brought to me swathed in blue hospital flannel, his moist almond eyes darting around the room. "You've got my nose," I joked, weeping. Meeting your child for the first time is like meeting a part of yourself and seeing your future.

"Michael, Helen," said Henry enthusiastically over the telephone to my parents at nearly four in the morning. "You have a grandson." Adam was now crying hard in the background—the healthy, *I'm alive!* sound of new life. I pictured my father with tears of joy, an expansion of our short family line of only children.

At five in the morning, we were wheeled down a long hall to our room, the bright lights hurtling above us as Adam continued to cry. "Shh, shh, little one," I tried to comfort him. "It's okay." He was assaulted, it seemed, but I was elated. He didn't stop crying until we brought him home.

Bringing Adam into the house for the first time was like returning after a long absence. Everything seemed strangely new and awkward. His little body twitched every now and again in his car seat. I went upstairs to bathe while Henry watched him, with some relief at being by myself again. But I felt pulled downstairs. There was now someone always there, needing me. I didn't know what to call this feeling at first, but I know it now, four years later. It is fear. Fear that if you leave for a moment, nothing will ever be the same. Fear of letting go. Fear of letting your child out into the dangerous world. Fear takes a grip at birth and never lets go. I took a quick shower to return to him faster.

I wanted Henry to take the week off work to stay home with us. I was having trouble getting Adam to sleep. It was taking three to four hours to get him in his bassinet. Then, I'd crawl out of his room ever so slowly on my hands and knees. He was sensitive to every slight creaking sound of our old house. After an hour, he usually awoke again, and I was back in his room, doing the same thing over and over.

Henry took only three days off, and he was clearly impatient staying home. I sat in the rocking chair in the early morning, all messy and rumpled, dark circles under my eyes. Henry stood in the doorway, smelling of cologne and wearing his pin-striped suit and crisp white shirt.

"I'm going to work," he said.

I couldn't go to work any more. My clothes that no longer fit hung in the dark closet, and a feeling of being chained to the child suckling at my breast swept over me. It was a complicated joy, mixed with happiness, love and resentment.

"I thought we agreed you'd take a week off work?" I said, upset with him.

"I gotta get back." His eyes were defiant. I felt that Adam and I had become a burden. Tears welled in my eyes. I look back and see how men develop into fathers more slowly. This wasn't Henry's first child. It was his fifth and my first. For me, the universe had changed, and I expected the earth to stop spinning along with us. I expected Henry to be elated and to coo over every sound, every twitch, along with me. For Henry, it was status quo. He left in the early grey of the morning and closed the front door. Adam and I sat together, our new rocking chair creaking softly.

As the air warmed a little more and spring turned into summer, Adam and I took walks together, but at some point he always began to cry. There were hours when he wouldn't stop crying, and we all thought he was colicky. The grandmothers came by to try and soothe him. Once, Henry told me to go for a walk around the block while he tried calming Adam down. When I returned, he was still screaming, his face all red and sweaty. My brother-in-law took him outside for some fresh air; friends tried bobbing him up and down. Flor succeeded sometimes, holding him under the maple tree so he could watch the leaves move in the breeze. Adam's cries began to feel like alarms, pressing all my buttons. Instead of a calm child I could take anywhere, he was difficult. I couldn't take him anywhere without wails and distress. Once I parked the car on the side of the street and hopped into the back to nurse him, because he was crying so hard that I thought he would choke to death. I became the anxious mother.

Some months passed, and Adam became a little more comfortable in the world. His crying abated. I did what other mothers did.

I enrolled in Mommy and Me classes. I tugged and pulled him to join the group: shake this rattle, roll this ball. I was an enthusiastic mother, reluctant to let go of my expectations, thinking that his seeming lack of interest would soon pass.

Other children happily ran up to the Itsy Bitsy Spider when it was coming down from the ceiling during circle time, while Adam seemed oblivious. They would clap their hands on cue, while Adam wriggled out of my arms to run back and forth. Other kids would begin sorting colours, or putting puzzle pieces in, while Adam preferred to take each puzzle piece out and throw it on the floor. Instead of playing with me, he wandered around the room, unable to focus on anything without my prodding. My favourite time was when the lights went out and the class leader shone a flashlight on the rotating disco ball to "Twinkle, Twinkle, Little Star." It was Adam's first favourite song and the only time he would sit calmly in my arms, mesmerized by the mirror's magical reflections.

At home, he enjoyed Baby Einstein videos and learned every letter, number, shape and colour—a stark contrast to the Mommy and Me classes. He could focus and recite the words, and later jumped up and down after doing so. The outside world seemed difficult for Adam, yet he had this profound ability. One day I tested it. I wrote down some words he'd never seen before. He was sixteen months old. We were alone at the dining table, and he was sitting in his high chair, eating chopped tomatoes.

"Whale," he said effortlessly. *Oh my God!* I thought. *I can't believe this.* I was excited.

"Horse," he said perfectly.

"Snake, cat, dog, elephant…"

How can he know this? Especially the word "whale"? I knew that Adam was different from the other children. I knew he was smart and sensitive.

"I think Adam is autistic." I was sitting in the salon chair getting my hair dyed when Henry called my cellphone. "I just had a conversation with someone whose child is autistic. It sounds just like Adam."

"He's not autistic!" I said a little too loudly, sending the salon into silence. "He's not sitting in the corner rocking himself back and forth!"

"I'm telling you, I think he is."

At home, we began to argue in front of Adam, who cried in response to our anxious voices. "Look at this." Henry handed me a printout of an Internet article. I read the words: *lack of eye contact, repetitive movements of the hands such as finger flicking, lack of imaginative play, fascination with movement, in most cases an associated diagnosis of mental retardation, may be abnormalities in the development in cognitive skills, language skills and overall intellectual level are the strongest factors related to ultimate prognosis, only a small percentage of individuals with the disorder go on as adults to live and work independently.*

I shook as I read it.

"No, no, no. It can't be true. It can't be." I pounded on Henry's chest. "I can't lose my son." Today, I can't read the *Diagnostic Statistical Manual of Mental Disorders* and not become depressed and somewhat fearful. It is not an empowering book. Fear now took on an entirely new meaning.

We quickly had Adam diagnosed. He underwent a dozen tests, assessing his ability to respond, his cognitive ability, his hearing, his diet. I wanted him so much to perform, but I could see that he couldn't do many of the things that were asked of him. Yet when it came to identifying words, numbers, shapes, and colours, he amazed the psychometrists, their eyebrows rising in interest.

"He's hyperlexic," said the psychologist to Henry and me, slouching in our winter coats on the leather couch. "Statistics show that those who are autistic with hyperlexia have a better chance."

She offered me a lifeline, although I was already determined that Adam would succeed. The psychologist told us Adam was a high-functioning autistic. Another psychologist told us he was moderately autistic. His scores always seemed to differ.

Suddenly we began to hear of so many people we knew who had autistic children. Where had they been and why didn't I know more about this? Should I have listened to my father-in-law who handed me an article from *The New York Times* a few months ago about the danger of vaccinations? Was Adam's autism all my fault?

Henry and I listened intently to everyone—other parents, literature, doctors. We tried special diets and hired consultants and therapists for weeks, then months. Adam, my perfect child, was seen now as far from perfect. All of a sudden, family faces were awash with concern. Friends stared at him in pitiful silence. Other family members were afraid to go near him. Others still thought it was all a joke and Henry and I were taking this far too seriously.

"All children get anxious," said many people we came across over time. I struggled to define autism for myself, let alone a group of people who had never before come close to the word, let alone to an autistic person. It is still difficult for me to describe Adam as a delightful, intelligent child who has special needs. Autism is like that. It's a paradox: something present and something missing, an ability and a disability. To others, Adam was either fine or he wasn't.

Henry and I went south of the border to meet "experts" who might help us. We flew in consultants in verbal and applied behavioural therapy to offer us advice. Adam would sit in the living room as these strangers came in and peered from behind their glasses, asking me questions about his birth and infancy. Their expert postures, "uh-huh" responses, the scratching of their pens on disposable lined paper were irritating. Adam's way of responding to things became a kind of predetermined pathology, and before he turned two he was expected to sit at a table for forty hours a week in traditional applied behavioural therapy. His behaviour was considered "inappropriate" and the goal was to make him "indistinguishable from his peers."

"Look at me!" the therapists yelled, aggressively turning his face to meet theirs. He would respond with loud cries. I had had enough.

"This isn't right," I said to Henry. "They're making learning unpleasant. He's not even two." I hit the books. I collected a library of hundreds of books written by therapists, psychologists, psychiatrists. The books that changed our lives were the ones written by autistic people, some who couldn't talk, but who could write about their profound autistic experiences. I began to look at art created by autistic people, and as a curator of art I found answers more poignant than science could reveal. I found understanding, comprehension, empathy, emotion, passion, desire. I found the paradox of being and the value of human difference. It was a far cry from reading endless scientific theories and data from non-autistic scientists who believed that autistic people lacked imagination and empathy. I found humanity in autism, where science dehumanized it. Art is a warmer, more comforting language. I decided to curate exhibitions about it, and people came in droves.

I LOOK OUT to our new backyard. We moved here a year ago, to a new house to accommodate a growing family, the one Henry and I spoke of on our first date. Our beloved maple tree is gone. Now, there's a new garden with many trees and flowers, and Adam is playing with Flor under the sprinkler, running around happily, his naked body unencumbered, still adorable and innocent. He still loves to flick the water with his fingers and watch it move in the air.

I have tried to define autism for several years now, watching Adam with delight. He's always surprising me. We are far from the days when we viewed autism as an illness to be cured. Far from believing that autism defines someone who prefers to be alone, rocking himself back and forth, hitting his head against a wall. At first I thought his diagnosis was an unbearable injustice, that my only child was not going to be able to keep me company or return my love. Now I know better.

I decided I would work with the therapists myself, forming my own team, adopting my own philosophy filled with faith given to me by other autistic people, and by family values. Henry's trust in my decisions gave me strength to keep going despite the many doubtful moments we had. Over time, I decided that no one would enter our house who couldn't work within this positive framework. Adam was going to have fun.

Adam is perfect. This is what autism has taught me. It is the world that isn't. Adam can learn. It is the teachers who often can't learn from autism. Autism is part of his world, his version of "normal." There is no other normal but the normal we create for ourselves. I am going to offer him joy—the joy of relating to others, the joy of learning, the joy of being Adam. It is up to him, and perhaps his destiny, to determine the rest. I say this with trepidation, knowing the world is unkind. I will always have fear.

Adam follows me, his tiny feet slapping against our limestone floor. He still has many programs and needs to learn. But now he seems to really enjoy learning new things. He's four, and I am the centre of his universe. Wherever I go, he follows like my shadow—to the kitchen, up the stairs, to my office, the bathroom. He is my loyal little loverboy. I am taking all I can get before he grows up. There were people who said that he could never be affectionate, never understand emotion or be social. I call them all naysayers.

"Mom, Mom, Mom," he mumbles after me, his *m's* melding together. I am delighted when he calls my name.

"Yes, Adam? What do you want?" He pauses and I can see him anxiously trying to find the word.

"Wawipop!" he finally exclaims, pulling me toward the cupboard and reaching upward.

"Okay, but just one," I say. Adam has been reaching for a lot of lollipops lately.

He smiles, fixated on the bin. I let him pick out his favourite colour—purple. He chooses carefully and hands it to me.

"Now what?" I ask, trying to prompt him for more language.

"Open it," he says softly, sweetly.

I open it and he grabs it, rolling it around in his mouth.

PART FIVE

Redemption

TESTING FAITH

MARY LYNK

Desire to Be a Mother

All my life I wanted to be a mother. So much that I feared it would never happen.

I used to carry a quotation around with me—*Keep the faith. It's easily lost*—but as I neared forty, one of my greatest desires was slipping away. I'm not saying becoming a mother makes you a better person or that it's for everyone. I'm just saying having a life's dream slip away is tough. I was losing *the faith*.

MEN

Part of the problem was my relationship with men, or lack thereof.

I never fell easily. I had passionate relationships. I loved some bad boys, but I was not in love with them. I loved some good boys, but I was not in love with them either.

I did have one special relationship. He was a wonderful man. But after six years and one wedding dress purchase, we decided to part ways. It wasn't meant to be. Eleven months after our breakup, he married someone else and immediately had one kid, then another. He was happy. And I was happy for him.

So, at thirty-two, I was single again and would be for a long time.

Late at night, if I was alone, I could reach for the phone. I had male friends to comfort me, but for the most part I preferred being on my own. I cherished my independence but ached with loneliness. I wanted to be *in love* not just *love*. Damn the poets and their sly way of painting that most complicated of emotions. Mr. Cohen, you have a lot to answer for! (And I notice that you've been mainly a bachelor.)

FINDING THE LOVE OF MY LIFE

Six months before turning forty, six months from being part of that questionable statistic that claims I'd more likely be hit by lightning than get married, I met the love of my life.

God, he's great. He's kind, handsome, smart, artistic, funny, sensitive, strong and socially aware. A bit of a hermit, but, hey, I don't mind taking my extroverted self out on my own.

When I met Sandy, I realized that something I was always holding out for, but deep down didn't really believe in, was true. The mad reciprocal love that the poets write about does exist. Mr. Cohen, I apologize. (Note to self: keep the faith.)

Sandy and I were "in love" with each other. We'd never felt like this with anyone else. It was perfect.

Well, almost.

Sandy told me, very early on and very strongly, that he didn't want any more kids. He already had a teenager. While he and his son's mother had never lived together, he took his fatherly duties very seriously and helped raise his child, whom he loves very much. He was also almost fifty and after many sacrifices was finally finding the time to devote to his sculpture.

I begged him to give it time. He said no. I asked again. *Maybe we could talk about it in six months?* At my tearful insistence, he reluctantly agreed. But told me not to be hopeful.

Well, maybe you can't have it all. I had found my soulmate. How many people get that in their life? Some dreams stay dreams. I had Sandy, but no kids. And he was the only man I had truly ever wanted to be with.

My best friend, Joann, assured me Sandy would change his mind. I didn't believe her.

So I accepted my lot, which was surprising for a single-minded person like me. He was worth the sacrifice. Anyway, less than two months into our relationship, and two weeks before we were to move in together, another more serious obstacle was hurtling toward me.

BREAST CANCER

On September 11, 2001, I had my own confrontation with death. First thing in the morning, I had a biopsy on my right breast.

After the procedure, my dad picked me up from the hospital and took me to my parents' house for the day. When I opened the door, I heard my mom sobbing on the phone. She was talking to her best friend's husband. Their son, Bruce, aged forty-one, had just died unexpectedly from pancreatitis.

Facing my own mortality, and then the breathtaking sadness of a young man's death, I decided to go lie down in the den and distract myself with television. That's when I saw the second plane crash into the World Trade Center. What the hell was happening with the world, Bruce's world, my world? What was wrong with my world would be explained with a phone call a few days later. I had cancer.

AFTERMATH OF THE CANCER AND MY RELATIONSHIP

The cancer wasn't so bad. It runs in the family, so it wasn't totally unexpected. My mother had a mastectomy when she was just thirty-three and I was three months old. A few months later, my aunt, then thirty-two, also had a mastectomy. But they are still alive and in their late seventies, so I was full of hope.

The doctors reached in and took a chunk from the side of my right breast. It was, they said, "intermediate grade," but "contained."

I could have gone for more radical treatment—radiation or even mastectomy, but I was advised a simple lumpectomy would probably suffice.

However, the surgery and recovery meant I had even less time left to conceive a child. Still, what did it matter if Sandy wasn't up for it?

At this point, I had truly given up on the notion of having kids. Then one night a few months after my operation, Sandy brought up the topic. We were splitting a bottle of wine, musing about life, and out of the blue he started talking about children.

I asked him to change the subject. I told him it was too painful to talk about kids because I knew that he didn't want any more.

And what happened next? Sandy spilled that he could think of nothing better than to have a child with me. (Sorry, Joann. And thanks for keeping the faith.)

For him, I had given up one of my greatest dreams—motherhood. But here he was saying how deeply he wanted us to have a child. I couldn't believe it. Love does change everything.

So just before my fortieth birthday and his fiftieth, we started to try. But yet another obstacle was stepping up to the plate.

INFERTILITY

Sandy and I tried. God, we tried. I never thought sex could be monotonous. Never thought it would be a chore.

But nothing happened. Perhaps Mother Nature was telling us we'd missed the boat. I was starting to lose faith again. Maybe we'd fallen in love too late in life to become parents together. You can't have everything, Mary.

In a last-ditch effort, we ended up in a fertility clinic. What a depressing place—not the decor, but the mood. Such a sombre waiting room. Such unhappy, worried couples. So many smart, professional women of a certain age—just like me.

We went through all the indignities. Sandy hated depositing into that little cup for all those tests. So many mornings I would be running down hospital hallways, crumpled brown bag in hand, trying to get his sperm to the clinic on time. Or taking fertility drugs until I thought my ovaries would burst into machine-gun fire, spewing eggs everywhere.

Finally, we decided to take a more drastic and hugely expensive step—in vitro fertilization.

But, wait, a new obstacle.

THE C-WORD: PART 2

Man, oh, man. Two years after my first bout, in the middle of trying to get pregnant, damned if the breast cancer didn't come back.

It's weird, but that second phone call from the doctor taught me that sometimes death isn't the worst news.

My first thought wasn't about the possibility of dying. My first thought was, What if this means I won't be able to have a child? Even if the cancer didn't kill me this time, would it prevent me from conceiving?

In the raw moment of diagnosis, I found out that cancer is not as scary a word as infertility. Death is inevitable; motherhood is not.

The maternity ward was replaced by the cancer ward. Again, the doctors reached in and took another, much larger, chunk of my right breast.

This time I would need a prosthetic to make up for the difference between my right breast, now getting smaller with every visit to the surgeon, and my full left breast. This time I had to endure six weeks of radiation. Every day I would go. I was usually the youngest in the waiting room. I'd get zapped. Then I'd get progressively more tired. And I couldn't help wondering, as my forty-second birthday was approaching, if time was running out for becoming a mother.

IN VITRO FERTILIZATION

After some time for recovery, then eight months of intensive work to pay for the costly procedure, I began the taxing process of in vitro.

A Toronto fertility clinic had rejected me as a client. They said I was too old, and they would only treat me if I used donor eggs from a younger woman. The fertility clinic in my hometown of Halifax was more welcoming—creaky eggs and all.

Now, instead of a radiation clinic every day, I was making daily trips to the fertility clinic. But this time I was one of the oldest in the waiting room. I also noticed a disquieting difference between the two experiences. In the radiation clinic's waiting room, if people didn't talk, they would at least give a compassionate smile to one another. More often than not, strangers would tell you their deepest secrets. But here in the fertility clinic's waiting room, people were so cold and solemn. They were ever so careful not to make eye contact, not to talk—as if we were all at an STD clinic instead of trying to have babies.

Finally, a year after my second biopsy—the same date, October 14, again in the morning—the world righted itself. This time a piece of life, not death, was removed from my body. Twenty-one eggs in all—an impressive number, yet few bursting with vitality, having been stuck in the dusty corners of a forty-two-and-a-half-year-old woman.

It still humbles me to think that death and life were so profound on the same day one year apart.

After three days, only three of the twenty-one fertilized eggs had survived in the Petri dish. Quickly, they were put back inside me. One egg was graded A plus, the other B plus, and the other C.

I did everything by the book. In fact, if I was supposed to lie still for a day, I did it for a week. I took my medications at the very same time every day. I tried not to be stressed. No coffee. No alcohol. Just trying to make my womb as inviting as possible. At the same time,

I didn't have high expectations. I expected it probably wouldn't work. It was too painful to be hopeful.

After a week I rose from the couch and the soap-opera world of Victor and Nicky Newman and returned to the real world. You have to wait sixteen days to hear if you're pregnant or not. What an emotional roller coaster! If this didn't work, I was going to carry on with life. Shelling out more than $8,000 isn't easy. Also, who knew if it would work on the second try, when I was even older.

For the following few weeks I wouldn't allow myself to think about *what if* I was pregnant—except for one time. I was watching a rented movie with Sandy. It was dull, so my mind wandered into that dangerous territory. Only for a brief second did I go there—just to think about *what if* it was a girl, *what* would her name be, *should* it reflect my mother's Lebanese heritage, *maybe I should* call her Laila after my aunt. Done. It was over in a flash. I returned my attention to the TV, and at that exact moment, the main female character introduced herself to Colin Farrell and Al Pacino, saying, "Hi, I'm Laila." Freaked me right out.

SIXTEEN DAYS PASS

Sixteen days pass and no bloody word. Seventeen days. Eighteen days. I forget what the hold-up was. I just remember it was hell waiting.

Finally, on day nineteen at work, my cellphone rang. It was the clinic. What followed was the most difficult few milliseconds after hello I've ever experienced.

Then it happened. She said, "Congratulations." I was forty-two and I was pregnant. I felt so grateful to everything and everyone. I was so happy.

THE PREGNANCY

The pregnancy was a bit of a trial. I bled heavily with bad cramps once and feared I was going to lose the baby. I took it easy for a while and things calmed down. Then I was told I had a one-in-thirteen chance of having a Down's syndrome child. I had to wait four weeks to find out that everything was okay genetically. Then my baby was underweight. So I had to have an ultrasound every two weeks for my entire pregnancy.

In the final month something inexplicable happened that confounded even my veteran obstetrician. He said he wouldn't have believed it if he hadn't taken the earlier measurements. My baby went from being extremely underweight to normal weight. Again, given time, the world righted itself.

AND THEN...

At forty-three, I gave birth to a perfectly healthy and happy baby girl. I fed her solely with my good breast, my left breast, for six months. And I am still breastfeeding. It's huge. I went from a D cup to an F cup. I call it "the breast that ate Manhattan." I stuff the smaller right breast with my prosthetic and three now tattered shoulder pads to make up for the size difference. Sometimes the shoulder pads slip up and peek out my top. It appears as though I'm trying to look like Dolly Parton, the cheap way. I don't bother to tell strangers it's because I had breast cancer. I'm too happy with the one good breast and the one amazing child.

The bond between my daughter and me has made me, I think, a better person. I can't help looking at strangers—an old woman, homeless man, anyone—and think most were once held in their mother's arms and loved as I love my daughter. Whatever has passed, they still deserve that love. She has also brought my mother and me closer. Motherhood and breast cancer are so intertwined in my family. When I was born, my mother was too ill with cancer to look after me for the first few months. The loss of that bonding time had repercussions on our later relationship. But our mutual love for this child seems to have healed wounds. Again, I am grateful.

Life is beyond bliss. Sure, I'm exhausted, broke and wear the same thing too often. But I love my little girl so much. She looks a lot like her dad—fair skin, blue eyes. With my dark ethnic features, I look more like the nanny. But she knows who her mom is.

I am now forty-four years old. My child is eleven months old—an absolute joy. A beauty named Laila. Actually, I didn't name her. She named herself when my faith was most tested. I guess I never did completely lose faith. I always kept a little on the side.

WE ARE HOLY

HARMONY RICE

I'm sitting in front of a computer
at a small university by the ocean in Nuuk. Nuuk is a beautiful sea-
side town in Greenland with red, yellow, and green buildings with
purple and pink trim. There are whales swimming by and a mountain range in most directions. There are dogs on leashes. Where I
live, we don't have whales swimming by or dogs on leashes. It's nice
here in Greenland, but it's not home. It's not like being home with
my five-year-old daughter and holding her in my arms. In our place.
My daughter is my home. And I need to go home to her.

My home is actually similar to this town in some ways. We live
on an island in a bay, surrounded by water. Our community has the
same kinds of social, health, and welfare issues. Nuuk is predomi-
nantly made up of Greenlandic Inuit people, who share similarities
to the Inuit in Canada. I'm here with twenty other indigenous people from around the world studying self-determination and the
rights of our people. Every time I turn around, there is something
else about this place that reminds me of home.

But unlike home, Nuuk celebrates its industry, education, natural resources and Arctic food systems. It is a self-governing sovereign
nation on its way to becoming an indigenous state. Like the ones
back home, the people here have brown skin of all shades. Here in

Nuuk, I actually blend in and resemble the Inuit. But when I speak to people in English, they say, "Where do you come from?"

"I come from Canada," I tell them.

"Oh, you're an Inuk from Canada," they say.

"No, I'm Anishnabe from Canada, from around Georgian Bay."

Then the locals shrug and say, "Well, you look Inuit."

Here in Nuuk, I see young mothers pushing baby carriages and their beautiful babies remind me of my own daughter, so cute and brown and bright. I miss her terribly. I almost have to look away just to hold back the tears. But sometimes I'm shocked because the mothers look so young. That too reminds me of home. Back home, they claim the rate of teenage pregnancy on our rez has decreased. But the fact remains the same: there are still more First Nations youth having babies and becoming mothers than finishing high school.

Government bureaucrats might see this is a sign of poverty or serious socio-economic conditions. For our mothers, grandmothers and aunts, it's a harbinger of sorrow. I think there is something more important about native motherhood to note.

In our communities, a grandmother, aunt, or cousin will always support the mother and raise the children with her. On my rez, which is home to about seven large families, we have always raised and supported each other's children. That is what I envision for my own children—a sense of being raised and nurtured by the whole community.

When I managed to finish high school and then college before getting pregnant and having a child, I became an anomaly. I thought I should be proud of my difference. I was blazing with opportunities and places to be. Then people began to ask, "So when are you going to have kids?" I had it all planned: finish school, start a great career and then, when I was thirty, I'd get married, get a house, have a baby. I thought the timing was all up to me. "When I'm thirty," I would say. My grandmothers and aunties would look at each other sheepishly and say, "Good for you."

And then it happened. I suddenly felt tingly and swelled up like a sponge. Then there was the pregnancy test and my inner voice saying, No. No way. I'm not ready for this. I'm not thirty. I have my whole life ahead of me. I didn't know about the guy. He didn't know about me. It was the worst possible timing.

And then it was over. R.E.M. played in the background. The sun was shining and there were pictures of fish on the walls. I went home to bury what I had done. And I never, ever talked about it again. I was ashamed of myself.

I didn't want to be judged. I didn't want to be judged by my community, by the women, by my friends or cousins. I didn't want to be judged by my family. I didn't want to be judged by my future daughter. And most importantly, I didn't want to be judged by the spirit world and all of creation as someone who would stop life from happening.

My family raised me to believe I was a special girl. A good girl. A pretty girl. A girl rich with culture and love, raised with language, ceremonies, connection to land. I could run through the bush for hours barefoot without ever looking back or getting lost. Elders, cousins, and aunties were always around at the ceremonies, eating blueberry scones and laughing loud.

I could picture the day I would be a mother, and my daughter would enjoy the wealth of love from the community. I could picture my daughter running barefoot in the sweetgrass: a bright girl with round brown eyes and a wonderful smile, a kind spirit with so much hope for the world.

I come from a line of strong women—strong in personality and responsibility but small in stature. They are Anishnabe women from Wasauksing with Pottawotomi ancestry that takes us all the way back to Wisconsin, Michigan, Missouri, and Kansas.

When my grandmother passed away a few months after my abortion, I thought, God, what have I done? What did I take away from her? From our lives? I thought I still had years and years with my grandmother and had looked forward to the day she would become a great-grandmother to my children.

The guilt came on like a wave. And it grew and grew as the days of mourning went by. My grandmother had raised me and taken care of me. She had been proud of me and wished for the day she would see my first child. I had an opportunity to share new life with my grandmother and I blew it. I went and destroyed everything. Did nothing my grandmothers and mothers taught me about motherhood actually sink in? I was confused by all I had learned about women and motherhood. I was frustrated with the Creator and with myself. My guilt and sadness consumed me.

So I left home. I had to leave the memories and go far, far away. I went to South Dakota and hid out working in a restaurant serving coffee for $2 an hour while my boyfriend worked as a reporter by day and served up tacos by night. We would come home to a small motel room in our little uniforms and watch MTV. It was the complete opposite of the life we had been living back home. My boyfriend's grandmother passed away within a month of my grandmother. We were numb. We were empty. And together we cried at night into the starched white sheets. In those Black Hills, our lives were a blur.

Then, after months of desperate living in South Dakota, at the lowest point in my life, a light came to me. It was like a new day and it lifted our spirits. We went home to my community and to my family.

Nine months later, she came. The kind spirit I had dreamed of. It was a difficult labour, but after it was over, a healthy baby girl looked back at me with big, beautiful brown eyes. She could see right through me. Being held up by the nurses, she could see beyond everything I'd been through. She could see the good person I was and the dreams that I had. She seemed to know everything about me.

On our first night together, we just talked and talked. She hummed and hummed. It was as if she couldn't wait to tell me everything about her time inside me, growing love and a heart and a mind. She couldn't wait to say how excited she was and what it felt like to be in her body on her own in the world now.

This was the moment that changed me forever.

We looked into each other's eyes. And she believed in me. And I believed in her. And I believed in myself. That I could be her mother. That I could give her everything. That I could be a good woman, a great woman. A strong Anishnaabekwe. That she would be the same. That I could provide the safe, warm shelter that she would need. And she forgave me, and I took it to mean the Creator forgave me. I hadn't destroyed all my learning and understanding, after all. Life was life. And we just hummed and hummed. And the world finally made sense.

For the first time in my life, I saw myself as a proud, strong, and young Anishnabe mother. I knew what my daughter meant when she cried. I knew how to touch her and how to hold her. I came away from my little girl's birth ready to take on the world. Head-first. It was like being willing to fight a war, just me against a million others, knowing that I was going to win. I had so much energy. I wanted to make the world so much better.

In the days following her birth, I started to feel a sense of urgency. There was trouble in the world and I wanted to play my part. I started to believe that I had something very important to contribute—a role, a world view, a voice, an indigenous woman's perspective. I wanted to ensure that my little girl would never experience racism or poverty or war. I wanted her to always know the animals, the trees, and the flowers. I was ready to put myself on the front lines to defend her place in the world.

Today, as I sit here far away from my daughter, with an ocean between us, I must admit that my life at home feels like a dream. From way out here in Greenland, I can think of so many things to be thankful for and things I want to change. But it's lonely. My dreams are vivid and meaningful. My late great-grandmother and grandmother have been visiting me.

In one dream, I'm running from a war zone and a car door swings open. I look inside the car and my grandmother, great-grandmother and all the other grandmothers from my community are sitting in the back seat. They look worried and ask me, anxiously, to drive them to safety. I jump in the car and drive. When I awoke from the dream, I felt as though they had offered support for my visit here, as though they believed in what I was doing.

I want to be a good example for my daughter, just as my mother has been for me. My mother taught me about our connection to land, to culture and to history. Even as a small child, I knew about the Indian Act, the residential school system and the massacre at Wounded Knee. As young as five, I would imagine people marching across the prairies thousands strong, for Annie Mae Aquash or the AIM protests, humming Buffy Sainte-Marie's tune "Universal Soldier."

Even through my loneliness and aching for my faraway daughter, I know I am learning something here across the ocean: about motherhood, my daughter, how important she is to me and our relationship to the world.

With all the ice and water in Greenland and the hot sun beaming down, it is easy to see the reflection of the Creator bouncing off the glare of the ice and into our eyes. It is holy here and we, I know now, are holy.

Our survival is necessary. We need Anishnaabekwe raising their babies to be strong people in the world. Raising them to know their history, to get an education, to understand their connection to the land and their ancestors. I was fortunate enough to get this, and I aim to provide the same for my child—the good and the bad. My child is my power. And our collective future.

In Greenland on this summer trip away from home, I am learning about the survival of family, of a people, a culture, a society, a natural world and the way we remember it. I am committed to this natural world and to a place for my child in it. It's so beautiful to see the water, the ice, the waves, the trees. This is my identity.

The world and I are the Creators. The world and all women in it are the Creators. We make mistakes and we gain understanding and love. I forgive myself for the abortion. And I give that experience love. I give the energy that came to me, the spirit that visited me, love. That spirit is still with me now, teaching me about life. I'm so grateful. This time away has offered healing.

My daughter healed me. Seeing the glaciers and icebergs has given me new ways of looking at the world. It is constantly changing. And we change with it. The shadows of the trees have their own language, the waves and ripples in the water too.

I am an Anishnaabekwe mother.

My mother is strong.

My grandmother was strong.

My great-grandmother was strong.

My ancestors were strong.

I am strong in the world.

And my child is stronger than me.

COMPARING NOTES:
A CONVERSATION
BETWEEN MOTHER
AND DAUGHTER
JOY KOGAWA AND
DEIDRE KOGAWA-CANUTE

Hi, Dee. It's dark outside, 4:01
a.m. I just awoke from a dream. Obviously I'm not going to phone
you at this hour. Thanks heavens for email. We were late, you and
I. It's not an uncommon dream theme for me. Late, late, like the
white rabbit in Alice's Wonderland, needing to get here, get there.
The need to get you to safety.

*That's interesting, Mom, because I have those hurry-up dreams too.
What's the rush, I ask myself. Why are we so frantic? Where do we have to
go? Why are we so worried all the time? We're tearing our hair out down
through the generations, getting balder as we go.*

My mother's hair was pretty thin by the time she was ninety.
But she was the ultimate in calm on the outside. Inside, I think there
was a volcano of worry. Maybe all mothers worry. When you were
a baby in Grand Forks, I used to worry that the hill beside our house
would fall on you.

*And did it fall? But speaking of dreams, I had one the other night
about Grandma. I was returning home from somewhere, and I was greeted*

273

by her sitting up on a small, hard, tiny bed—the one that was in the Coaldale house. She pointed her finger at me and said in a voice that sounded like thunder from God, "Be yourself!"

What a riveting dream! What do you make of it?

Well, I'm not sure. Was she telling me to be more authentic? More self-respectful of my decision to be a full-time mother? Was she telling me to remain my nice self?

I think you're a sensitive person who likes to put people at ease. It's part of your charm to be nice. I like being with you in social situations because you're so skilled at the pleasantries, which I so am not.

The feminine niceness act is highly overrated in my books—the need to "appear" pleasant. We try so hard to be calm and pleasant as mothers. But what mother truly feels cheerful and tranquil in the midst of a two-year-old's tantrum, while wiping up a pitcher of orange juice and hearing glass breaking in the background? Our daily lives are a huge litmus test of acid versus alkaline moods.

In the midst of all this, I don't have time for the big question Grandma may be asking in my dream. Who am I? Right now, I've got to get going and pick up the kids. Matthew has his first kick-boxing class at four, Anne has ballet, a quick supper and then I have to get Matthew to his guitar lesson at six. A few years ago, I thought looking after babies was exhausting, but I didn't even imagine how demanding and rigidly scheduled life would get. Someone could have told me to enjoy the baby-filled free hours. Now, with my twenty-first-century school-age kids, it's one thing after another after another.

Rush, rush. Do we even have time for this conversation? When you were little, people weren't so busy and harried—both parents these days are carrying full-time jobs, burdened by mortgages, struggling to pay the rent, perpetually buying stuff. Kids too, as you say, rushing around—off to school, off to lessons.

I guess I'm being nostalgic, but I do know the great release and freedom there is in having less stuff. Less is more, as they say, and it's true. Annie Dillard has something to tell us about the freedom there is in having less. She says that the life of sensation is a life of greed in which we grasp for more and more. But in the life of the spirit, we require less and less. I love her phrase "Time is ample and its passage sweet."

Maybe when you're older and without young children, you can live with less and less, but kids need stuff. They have such a fierce need to belong, and they're constantly bombarded by glitzy ads pressuring them to buy and buy. On top of that, parents are pressured to provide homes in safe family neighbourhoods in good school districts, which often means huge mortgages, not to mention all those extracurricular activities. It feels like a merry-go-round of endless striving. It does make you wonder. Dad once said that as people get richer, they don't necessarily become more content. They just get more and more socially competitive.

Yes, I'm sure that's the way it is. We're like the fisherman's wife, grasping for bigger houses and the sun, the moon and the stars. A voice inside screams, Stop! We know in our bones that greed doesn't work.

I think our job as mothers is to pass on our values. Kids learn from their parents and our society that they need "stuff" to belong—better neighbourhoods, bigger houses, more toys. I think what they really need is courage to buck the trend. My question would be, Is it more freeing or less freeing to have more stuff? If we're leaner in our living, I think we're keener in our hearts. If we'd turn aside from our obsession with "stuff," we'd discover we had more time for each other, be less harried and "late, late." We'd find our spirits lifting, spreading their wings. We'd be better mothers. I'm sure of it. Calmer. More deeply content.

Well, I agree that change begins at home. And I know, as a mother, that that's my responsibility. Maybe that's why I've chosen motherhood as my calling. Staying at home with my kids full-time is my choice. That's where I belong. Whatever I think about, whatever I do is about mother-

hood. It has become all that I am. And right now I've got to get going again.
Back to the kids.

The term "working mom" is certainly redundant. What mom is not working? I didn't have any choice in my day but to stay home. And I turned to writing when you were a baby partly because it was something I could do at home.

It's interesting that all three of us—you, me and my mother— gave birth to two babies, a boy first, then a girl. Three generations of that particular configuration. And then we went through our traumas. My mother went through the internment of Japanese Canadians in the 1940s, the destruction of the community, the loss of everything. I went through a divorce and you've just lost your beautiful house and community in Hawaii. We each lived in such different times. During my early adult years, jobs weren't scarce at all. But I bore the scars of the economic and racial traumas of my childhood and much of that became the work of the pen for me.

It must have been crazy for your mother during the uprooting of Japanese Canadians—and being so hated by society.

I remember that phrase, *"Kodomo no tame.* For the sake of the children..." When I was seven and eight, living in the internment centre in Slocan, I remember thinking that my mother was, without a doubt, the best mother in the world. She was attentive. She played games and told stories. But then after Slocan, we were moved to dreadful poverty in southern Alberta. That was after the war and during the "dispersal policy" when the government, after confiscating our farms and fishing boats and homes, wanted to make sure we could never be a community again. As the newspapers said, we were "a stench in the nostrils of the people of Canada." Some families never recovered. Many Niseis turned the hatred that was directed toward us into self-hatred, into rejection of their parents.

My mother had once been such an elegant woman who loved beautiful things and clothes. It broke her in many ways. One of my friends told me that when I wrote *Obasan*, I made her into two peo-ple—one was the idealized young mother in Vancouver and the other was the silent, suffering, stoical woman that my mother became. During my adolescence I was embarrassed by her. Talk about the need to belong! She began to look like a bag lady in my eyes, with her unfashionable clothes. And she was so sad and melan-choly. I didn't want to be around her. It wasn't until I'd written *Obasan* and realized some of what she'd had to go through that I began to be more understanding. My sweet, gentle mother. I just ache for her now.

I have an uncanny feeling, Dee, when I consider my life as a young child, then your life as a young child and now your kids' lives, that certain patterns are being repeated. In each of our lives, there was a big upheaval in early childhood, loss and loneliness, a father not there, a longing to go home. Do we in some way conspire to repeat our lives down through the generations? Maybe like the char-acter in the movie *Groundhog Day*, who repeats the same day over and over, trying to get it right, families are trying, through the gen-erations, to somehow fix the suffering in the past by revisiting the same emotional disasters, trying, hoping to get things right this time.

So, what you're saying is that when you were a child, your family's world was turned upside down. Are you saying that when I was the same age and when you and Dad were going through your divorce that you were somehow revisiting the big upheaval in your life and passing it on to me?

What happened to you as a child was completely beyond your parents' control. But you and Dad were in charge of your lives when you split up. I swore that if I ever got married and had kids I would never break up my family. I have to say I still don't fully understand what you were going through to subject us kids to a divorce. My kids are being wounded because of economic insecurity. And they are not alone. There are thousands of kids today going through forced dislocation because parents, through no fault of their own, are losing their jobs and then their homes.

You lost your paradise. So did I. Tim lost his job. My kids' bucolic life in Maui, where children played together freely outside every day, is now a distant memory. Here in this urban setting in Vancouver, the kids stay inside after school, venturing out only to attend their many planned activities, chaperoned by weary moms. I miss my life in Maui. I regret the loss of community. Every day, I fight these feelings of regret.

It's true that all three of us—you, me and Grandma—were all young when our safe little worlds collapsed, and none of us was able to go back to the homes we lost. And now it's happening to your kids. I hope you and Tim will be able to find the spiritual resources to protect your children and their inner lives.

Kodomo no tame.

When I was on my own as a young mother, I was overprotective. At least my friends tell me I was. I rescued too much. So while I was overindulgent as a mother, I was distracted and absent as a writer, needing time alone to think. You tell me that when I sent you out to play, you experienced that as rejection, whereas I experienced the opposite in my childhood. When my mother kept me at home, I desperately wanted to go out to play. No doubt when she was a child, she had desperately wanted to be kept at home. Are we stuck, like broken records?

I know that we're both perfectionists and want to be the best mother, the perfect mother. But every minute, I'm full of doubt and uncertainty. After living in the nurturing tropical lifestyle of Hawaii for twenty-two years, I found the move back to Canada a bit of a culture shock. But there were so many upheavals—the untimely death of Tim's sister and the illness of his parents, and on top of all that, Tim's job loss. Did we make the right decision to come to Canada? Was basing our decision heavily on money and educational opportunities for the children the right thing to do? Should the children and I have stayed in Hawaii to be with Tim and his parents? Every day I ask myself these questions, and every day I have different answers. Had we stayed in Maui, we would have struggled financially with a huge mortgage. I was also anxious about my son's future high school options and knew he wouldn't be in an academically challenging environment. But looking back, I feel I should've considered the emotional environment more seriously and the effects of uprooting them from the community.

Then again, I always felt I should raise the children in Canada. The social and political fabric are more in line with my own thinking, not to mention that you and Dad are both here. But Tim and I were always uneasy about how the move here would affect his career. And that's why he decided to stay in Oahu doing contract work.

This is clearly not an ideal situation. But Tim is very supportive of the move here because he feels that being on Oahu is not a realistic option with our limited financial reserves. Hawaii is just too expensive. Housing prices are out of sight.

We have all faced doubts over our many decisions. How do we ever know what might have been, had we decided something else? Life is often a maelstrom, and we find ourselves doing things we regret in spite of our best intentions.

For what it's worth—not that you're asking—I wonder whether you're doing everything possible to be together as a family. Are you being driven to repeat your parents' mistakes? Although you say the kids understand the situation, the sadness of daily missing their dad is the one thing you said you would avoid at all costs. So why is that going on?

I, like you, tried to be different from my mother. And my mother tried to be different from her mother. My mother's parents separated, and my mother was put in an orphanage for some time when she was four years old. That was a huge disaster for her that she never overcame. She said she wet her bed until she was in high school, and I remember how tender and kind she was to me if I ever wet my bed. She was so sad most of her life. When I was divorced, I recall how despairing she was, and she said, "All the effort of my life, it's all drifting downstream. It's all being lost." I was surprised by that remark. At some level, because she was so controlling and had such a need to own me, I felt I had gone through the divorce for her sake. I remember a dream I had at the time, and wrote a poem with these lines:

> Night Mother,
> I have murdered the world for you
> And brought bloodied babies for your feasting
> Why are you still so thin?

So many of our urges and impulses come from unconscious directives. I find myself wondering whether the fact that my mother's parents separated had something to do with the fact that I too went through a separation.

You're suggesting that my present separation from Tim for economic reasons has parallels to your separation from Dad? Are you suggesting it is having the same kinds of devastating emotional effects on my children that your and Dad's separation had on me?

I don't know. I'm just wondering. I know that as a family and intergenerationally, we're all so entwined in one another's lives. It's probably more complex than we can understand. I certainly don't want to be critical of you. Help! I don't want to be, but I know my comments are often taken to be critical. I remember one time I was being critical of my mother for not schooling me in the proper etiquette, for not sending me to charm school. I knew I had hurt her, and she said quietly, "I did my best." I know she did. We're all caught in the wind currents of our lives, but aren't we all trying to do our best?

I think all mothers try very hard to do their best. I was at the library yesterday looking for a book about raising girls. Anne is going through so much turmoil inside with the changes we've been through, so I wanted to understand and try to provide the most stabilizing force around her. I found an interesting passage in Girls Will Be Girls: Raising Confident and Courageous Daughters, by JoAnn Deak, that was not so much about Anne and me but about the relationship you and I have, perhaps. The writer said that girls these days, unlike previous generations, are being brought up by mothers who are successful in the public sphere. And so they're having to choose whether to measure up to their mothers' high standards. And sometimes they try really hard, or sometimes they just give up.

I know that I'm a daughter of a successful mother. But I don't think I was ever trying to be you. In fact, I have in many ways decided to follow a totally different road from yours—one for me that is as important as yours is for you. Just because I'm the daughter of a successful woman in the eyes of the world should not mean I'm not measuring up or that I'm copping out. On the contrary, I think at this stage of my life as a woman, I'm focusing on life's greatest challenge—motherhood. That said, I do concede my feelings may change as the children move on with their lives.

I also realize that many women today don't have the option to stay home with their kids. Tim and I were fortunate that selling our home in Hawaii enabled us to have a mortgage-free townhouse here in Canada. Many women have to join the workforce because they have to keep up those mortgage payments and rental payments and in some sense have less choice than women had years ago.

Then there are the mothers who choose to work outside the home even though they don't need the money. In an age when our value as productive members of society is directly related to our ability to generate income, it's no surprise that most mothers feel compelled to work. For those who do care for their kids at home, there is always that sense of social inferiority. We rush off to make business cards for anything that hints at autonomy. Yes, I am a mother, but I am also a professional dog-sitter! Or, yes, I operate a small catering company! Yes, I know I have my children at home with me, but I am also writing a novel! Yes, I, too, can be distracted from my family obligations. I, too, can be out in the world!

Do you remember the movie *Turning Point?* One woman chose the world's accolades. One chose the accolades of family and motherhood. Each chose whatever was most significant to her. And at the end of the movie, it was hard to say which was really better, except that I felt the woman who got the world's accolades was more bereft than the other woman.

Perhaps Grandma's command "Be yourself!" is her way of assuring me I don't need to be you. That being a mother at home is truly the right choice at this stage of my life. And everything else is a distraction that can be considered for another time. So I tell myself Grandma is telling me to stay the course on motherhood, to not be influenced by my mother's adventures on life's stage.

Aha! But the dream is your dream, so Grandma's voice is your own voice. For me, I think "Be yourself" refers to our values and our essential inner beings. And if we're thinking about Grandma, she was such a truthful person. She hated small talk and gossip and the hypocrisy of flattery. She called it *ojozu.* She told me every person's life has its tragedies. And her choice when the big tragedies of life hit her was to go deeply inward. She was so good, as a wife, as a mother, as a helper to people in need. But so un-fun. And such a lecturer. As an adolescent, I just wanted a lighter mother. I know this is what you want too. Screech!

Never mind, Mom. We're both just doing the best we can. And I know your mother would appreciate this. What appears as tedious meal preparations, shopping, cleaning, and all the other little chores to maintain a home are, in sum, the core of my life and the core of my family's well-being. As in the theory about the whole being more than the sum of all its parts. But what about you? Who are you?

I have often thought of myself as primarily a person who trusts. Or at least aspires to trust. I'm sure this will sound heavy to you, but do you remember the story of poor old Job, afflicted with all kinds of distress? He said, "Though He slay me, yet will I trust in Him."

I'm trying to realize what that meant. I want to live in this real world, awful though it is, and yet trust that there's enough love in it, no matter what. I guess all this talk makes me like my mother. Quite un-fun. I mean, if the love and trust were in fact being lived, I wouldn't have to talk about it, right? I mean, the freedom would shine right through me, instead of all this opaque talk.

When I think of you as a little girl, I remember a bright, charming child who loved the spotlight. You were happy in it. What do you think that little girl would say to you now?

She would probably say, "Lighten up!"

I have to say, whenever I hear ye olde biblical quotes, I immediately blank out. Time to cut my toenails. I think the real me is someone who tried to stay away from heaviness, no matter how often it was thrown at me, which was very often (she said bitterly). I think I developed a way of coping through humour, although one would never know it by reading these emails. And I remember as a little girl dreaming that one day, I would be able to be a mother, preferably one who stayed home. I would cook colourful meals in a tidy home with beautiful, brainy children, many hypoallergenic pets and a doting husband. I think, to a certain extent, my dream came true. But the rage and rancour side effects were not in the brochure.

Oh, well. Here we are, being who we are (who else could we be?). And there's your dream of Grandma. I think it's telling us that, for one thing, the world's accolades mean nothing without a healthy inner life. In a certain Zen practice, people are asked to meditate on who we were before our parents were born. We have to realize our identities are clouds drifting by against an unchanging sky. I believe that when we are doing the right thing, we're on a path of peace—a deep blue peace.

I wish I had known Grandma better. But I imagine that I can see her reflected in you, just as I imagine that who you are is in some way reflected in me. We are all powerfully connected, and we have bucked the trends of our times. You entered the public sphere when women were expected to remain in the private sphere. I choose the private life when all around me women are running toward the public life.

Do you remember when you were fifteen and in the middle of a rage, I wrote this poem?

Bird Poem

> when deidre was so angry she
> could only droop with it after
> hitting the wall so hard she said
> her hand was broken and i
> could hardly remember that much
> helplessness and rage
>
> i am prepared for many forms of farewell, but this? a
> bandaged wing, a wild bird
> my fifteen-year-old high school girl
>
> i wait without push or pull
> through rage and flight and
> unexpected landings
> as did my mother with her
> long-distance night praying
> her cage of arms
> a net and nest

I can't remember what was making you so angry—were we having an argument? Was I lecturing, as I tend to do? Sigh. I imagine that most mothers and their adolescent kids go through these painful times. But there are so many other good memories for us to draw on—picnics, camping, Christmases, birthday parties, games, playing piano together, picking blueberries.

What was enraging me at that point was having to endure the insanity of a broken family with another broken family foisted upon us, with you and your boyfriend breaking up all the time. It really messed me up when your boyfriend's kids came to live with us.

I do so regret that terrible time for you. What kind of a mother puts her children through so much—moving you from your relatively stable life in Saskatoon to poverty in Vancouver, then back to Saskatoon and then to the suburbs in Ottawa and following that, the experimental living that you hated in the commune at Pestalozzi College. I was so self-concerned and so needy, going from your father to another man and then eventually one other. I could argue that the sixties were crazy times, but I'm shocked when I look back at my unawareness of how all that instability would affect you and Gordon. I have so much admiration for your steady hand at the helm in your life. It's amazing that our relationship has survived all the turbulence.

Well, from one frail mother to another, let us continue along our fragile journey, one vertebra at a time.

TRADING MOTHERHOOD FOR DOLLARS

CRISANTA SAMPANG

*After many years of serious under-*achieving, I found redemption at the age of twenty-one.

I saw it in the eyes of my two-year-old daughter as she looked up at me, face shining with pure devotion, as if I were Imelda Marcos and an angel from heaven rolled into one, the only person in this world whose kiss could make all her boo-boos disappear and the bedtime "momos" retreat into their caves. Suddenly, all thoughts of sleepless nights and ten thousand diaper changes faded into the mist. I picked her up and held in my arms this miniature version of myself, this extension of my ego, fulfiller of my unachieved dreams, the future doctor or lawyer I'd always wanted to be and never became. She snuggled against me and said in her little baby voice, "Lub you, Mommy." At that very moment, I swore to myself I would never let her down.

When I did, much later, I did it unknowingly.

There are very few things in this world that are irreplaceable. One of them is a mother's presence in her children's life. It's a lesson I've had to learn twice now, first as a nine-year-old going to school in the city and living away from my parents, then as a mother when I left my three daughters and went to work as a domestic in Singapore and later in Canada.

When I was nine, I would gladly have forgone studying in the city for the chance to stay with my parents on the farm. I would have been happy to grow up barely literate, get married to a sugar cane farm worker, have six to nine children, lose my teeth one by one, live out my life in that narrow rural world, poor but close to my mother.

I grew up in Pagulingin, a small farming village in the Philippines where school only went up to Grade 4. My parents believed I would benefit from higher education, so they sent me to board with relatives in Lipa, a city thirty minutes away from our village by jeepney. They didn't tell me they were doing this because they loved me. They assumed I already knew. I went, but I held it against my mother for the next eighteen years. I grew up thinking my parents gave me away. I became an angry teenager. I dropped out of college at eighteen, and by nineteen I was married and pregnant. I only forgave my parents years later, after I left my children in my mother's care.

Motivated by an impoverished childhood, I was determined never to let my daughters experience any poverty. I went away so that I could raise them the way I wanted to. Alone in another country, separated from my little ones, I understood the lengths a mother will go to ensure the welfare of her children.

I'll never forget the second time I left my daughters. I had spent a month's holiday with them and, very reluctantly, I was going back to Singapore. On departure day, I hired a jeepney and the whole family came to the airport to see me off. When it was time to leave, we walked together from the parking lot to the immigration gates. I kissed everyone and said goodbye, then walked slowly away without looking back. I heard Maricel start to cry. Maricar and Catherine joined in. My mother called out a blessing. I walked on, faster and faster, farther and farther away from them, my heart beating as if it would explode inside my chest. I thought I would pass out. But I did not stop. Because if I stopped, if I looked back, I knew I would never leave; and I needed to go. My dreams for my little ones were only half-fulfilled.

Today, my grown-up daughters tell me they understand why I had to leave. Yet, given a choice, they would have picked poverty and the pleasure of welcoming me home every night after weeding a sugar cane field over dollar remittances. They would've exchanged a truckload of imported goodies and a month's allowance for a week of my presence. My youngest daughter, Catherine, first expressed it when she wrote me, at age eight: "You don't have to buy me a Barbie doll, just come home now!"

I wasn't listening properly then. All I heard was the insistent voice of my plans for their future: *I am doing this because I want you all to go to a good school and have a good education. I want you to have everything money can buy. Hang in there. I'll come home soon.* As it turned out, despite spending all my holidays with them, I never really came home for twenty-two years.

I HADN'T BEEN married long when I decided to leave my husband, a young businessman who loved beer and imported whisky. Drinking is a habit I hate almost pathologically. I'd seen my male relatives drink themselves under the table as I was growing up, and I wasn't about to condone the same performance from the father of my children. After witnessing another of his all-night drinking sessions with his buddies, I packed my bags and went with my daughters to live with my mother.

I was twenty-seven, jobless, and had three kids to feed. After things settled down I looked for a job, any job, but found nothing. I tried applying for work in a factory and was told I was too short. I had no office skills. I'd never worked on a farm. I didn't know anybody influential who could help me get employed anywhere else. So, later that year, I took the only option available to me. Following the waves of Filipinos going out of the country to find employment abroad, I left my home to work as a maid in Singapore. Like thousands of other mothers who left for the Middle East, Hong Kong and Singapore, I left my children in the care of others. We traded motherhood for dollars.

But the family members left behind benefit financially: they will be able to build their own house, start their own small business, send the children to a better school. For this, I willingly lived through tired days and sleepless nights in a foreign country, all by myself, while tallying up every day the kisses and cuddles and hugs and birthdays and Christmases I'd be missing.

My daughters belonged to a subculture of students in their school—children whose mothers had gone away to work in another country. Many of these kids looked neglected. Their school uniforms weren't ironed or properly laundered; sometimes they'd attend classes with mismatched socks. These same kids wondered, according to my first-born, Maricel, why she and her sisters appeared normal, if their own mother wasn't around. Grandma, she told the others, looked after them. I felt buoyed by such stories. In my mind, their being with Grandma was just as good as being under my own care.

I worked for three and a half years in Singapore. After that, I went on to Canada, once again as a domestic. The country's Live-In Caregiver program allows a qualified foreign domestic to sponsor her family into the country after working continuously for two years. Like many Filipina mothers before me, I hoped to take advantage of the plan. But after two years, I changed my mind. I watched other women work sixteen hours a day to finance their families' sponsorship applications, then continue working the same number of hours to provide for them after arrival, even when there were fathers to help out. I was a single parent. I got very frightened about raising my daughters without adequate supervision. After a long and painful consideration, I decided to let them grow up in the Philippines, raised by Grandma and an army of relatives.

Much later, I regretted that decision. In fact, I'd been mistaken in a lot of ways. I had believed that Maricel, my eldest, was coping better than her sisters. She was very independent. She had taken the role of big sister seriously. She graduated from university with a degree in communications and went on to work full-time for a computer assembly company. Everything seemed fine until recently, when she received a job offer from Vancouver and started getting her papers ready. Then, with no warning, Maricel told me she was pregnant and planning to marry a man fifteen years older than herself. What's more, she intended to leave her baby to work in Vancouver as she had initially planned.

After so many years, the shock of this turn of events gave me the courage to confront what I'd always been afraid to face. I asked my middle daughter, Maricar, about my absence in her life. After much prodding and some crying, she told me that despite their grandmother's presence, she felt there was a hole in her life, an indescribable void, that couldn't be filled by my regular visits home or long-distance telephone calls or a regular and generous allowance.

Maricar dropped out of school during her first year in engineering and got married early. She succeeded in filling up the emptiness in her life by raising her own family. Today, she is a very protective mother of three small children. She doesn't let her kids out of her sight for more than thirty minutes. Once, Maricar's mother-in-law invited Francis, the oldest boy, to spend a weekend with her back in the village. Maricar refused to let him go. When I asked her why, she said, "I grew up away from you and I know how it felt, not having a mother around. I will never let my children feel the same way, ever."

I suspect Maricar is trying to compensate for my absence in her childhood. Maricel is repeating my history. These discoveries make me feel very sad and extremely guilty.

My youngest daughter stopped studying in her third year of computers to work in Singapore. That's where she met Robert, a young sailor from Tacoma, Washington. Tacoma is only a three-hour drive from Vancouver, where I live. They got married within a year. I asked her sisters whether Catherine married Robert because living in Tacoma would bring her closer to me. They assured me that Catherine was in love and very happy with the man she married.

"Proof?" I asked.

"Catherine cried every day after Robert got on his ship and sailed away," I was told, "until the day she left to join him in Tacoma."

That's at least one load off my mind.

Through the years, I've met other absentee mothers in Vancouver and Singapore, all of whom feel guilty and are trying to soften their absence with presents—the latest iPod, cellphones, Game Boys, PlayStations, all the brand-name denim jeans the kids want—a practice that spawns materialistic and brand-conscious children. My own daughters would settle for nothing less than a genuine pair of Levi's 501s, something far removed from my child-hood, when my mother made my dresses out of cotton hog-feed sacks, which actually came in many designs and a variety of lovely colours. Yet none of those expensive things are replacement enough. Every long-distance mother knows this deep inside.

Sociologists confirm my experiences. Research I've read on the phenomenon of women's migration shows that kids of mothers like me feel different, unloved and angry, despite being left under the care of devoted relatives. Many of them display tendencies toward materialism, bad school performance, or drug addiction.

I've done my best to avoid these pitfalls. I went home every year. I regularly remind my daughters that they were there and I was here not because I abandoned them but because I wanted them to enjoy things I never had as a child. That I loved them and that one day we would all be together again. I believed that if they weren't told my reasons, they would form their own conclusions, perhaps the wrong ones.

Because I stayed away for too long, my children chose their own paths. I'm still alone in Vancouver. I'm still caught in the same time warp that my friends, other mothers, have successfully left behind. My kids have never grown up in my mind. At forty-eight, I'm still frantically trying to make up for lost time. Whenever I visit my daughters, despite their husbands, kids, and other people being around, they become my little girls again. I'm a young mother again, and they revert to their childhood habits. We cuddle a lot. I cook for them. We go shopping together. I buy them presents. Then I leave to pursue my own life once again, and we're back to replaying the same drama at the Manila International Airport.

Afterwards, their husbands jokingly tell me they've had to deal with their wives' "Mommy hangovers" for days. This wasn't what I'd hoped for when I left them in 1984. I may have changed the course of our lives, but not in the way I wanted. I console myself with the fact that I did not fail too badly. None of them turned to drugs or ran away from home. They've grown up relatively normal and happy with their choices. They say they have forgiven me for going away because they know I was only trying to do my best for them.

And I will keep doing so. On a recent trip home, I gathered my brood together for three weeks. One day, I watched with overwhelming grandmotherly joy as my three older grandchildren—Francis, who is eight, Charles, seven, and Patricia, three, all happy, well-adjusted, and secure in their mother's presence—learned to work together on a computer I bought for them. This is how a family should be, I thought.

And as I cuddled my latest grandbaby, Maricel's two-month-old Margaret Sydney, I reiterated everything I vowed to myself as a twenty-one-year-old parent: I'll do my very best to give you everything, I promise. And then I add another thought—another promise—one I wish I'd made in my own life as a mother. I'll make sure your mom never leaves you.

THE AMAZING ADVENTURES OF POTTY HEAD

CHANDRA MAYOR

When I was in university, I became fascinated with the notion of the hero's quest. Setting off from the known and familiar, carrying only a small parcel of necessities slung over your shoulder, you would meet companions and guides and have mythic adventures along the way. At the end of the quest you would finally confront yourself in the mirror, where all the dark and messy bits and pieces that you thought you'd cast off along the way would stare back at you, and you would know that the experience had transformed you forever. The story was everywhere I looked—in Greek myths, *Star Wars,* and the VHS copy of *The Lion King* that I watched endlessly with my three-year-old daughter, Julika.

How mythic, I thought, as I trudged back and forth to the University of Winnipeg with its crumbling sandstone facade, lugging Julika and all my books behind me in a green wagon, catching up on the required reading with an open book in front of me as I walked. I read about the hero's quest, wrote about the hero's quest and even, on one memorable occasion, dressed up as a dragon and showed video clips of *Northern Exposure* to illustrate my thesis.

The problem was, in all of this mist and mystique and grandeur, there was no place for me. I was twenty-three years old, living in subsidized housing on Furby, right where the margins of a very respectable neighbourhood dissolve into sketchiness and late-night street fights and broken glass. I would regularly stand with the badly dressed clusters of welfare moms. We would watch our kids play on the blue structure out front, endlessly plotting how to get out of the building and into a real apartment somewhere else. I had a predilection for vintage ball gowns and seventies bridesmaids' dresses, which made me an outcast among welfare-housing out-casts, sitting alone on the playground mom-bench. I alternated between student loans and social assistance, rolling pennies to buy milk and carefully plotting my once-a-month outing to the dyke bar. I dropped Julika off at daycare and went to class. I picked her up again and came home. I made baked Spam with strawberry jam for dinner. ("It's like a glaze, really," I told people.) And I surreptitiously studied while watching *Aladdin* for the 863rd time, acting out Shakespearean scenes with Julika's Polly Pockets and her stuffed and scarred white bat. I descended to cajoling, pleading, and finally brib-ing to get her to go to sleep so that I could write papers. I stayed up late into the night, writing, staring at the blinking pumpkin lights we'd nailed along the window (even though it was March). I was aimless, struggling, and drifting through my day-to-day life. I did my best to be a good mom, a good student, a good citizen, but lived with the sinking feeling that I wasn't really cutting it at any of the three. I patched the ragged edges together and made do. It wasn't very mythic of me. I longed to live at the centre of my own story. I loved my daughter fiercely and rabidly, but I longed for motherhood to be something other than another thing I tried and almost suc-ceeded at. I longed for rites of passage, revelation, transformation.

I fully expected Julika's birth to be a seminal moment. I thought I would set forth into the valley of darkness and pain, accompanied by my mother and my doctor (and whatever other vaguely medically related personnel felt like wandering by and checking out the dilation of my cervix as I lay panting in bed). I fully expected I would connect mystically with millennia of women. All through my pregnancy I kept meeting women who assured me that the second she was born, my life would change. That I would become someone new. That the memory of the pain would melt away like wet sugar, leaving only an intensity of love and new meaning and purpose in my life. I fully expected angels to sing at the moment of her birth, choirs of rainbows to inhabit my vision, and a profound thrumming of the Divine to fill my body. I'd read feminist theorists positing that the feminine version of the hero's quest inevitably involves the uterus and its magical sending forth of the child through the red tunnel. In this hormonally induced melding of feminist thought and suburban-urban myth, I expected to Become.

What a load of crap. Sixteen hours into labour, I opted for the epidural. *Screw the millennia of women*, I thought. *I'm going to die.* Eight hours after that, as she was finally crowning (after, of course, the numbing effects of the epidural had seeped away, leaving me effectively paralyzed but finely attuned to every screaming nerve ending in the lower half of my body), I made weird animal noises in my throat that I'd never before considered humans capable of. Three minutes after that, the doctor placed this tiny, slimy, wailing thing on my chest. I waited for the angels. I really did. I waited for my Transformation. But all I felt was as limp and wrung out as a dishcloth, terrified and confused and totally at a loss as to what I should do. I waited for the pain to wash away, but all I felt was the doctor cheerfully stitching me up. All I wanted was sleep.

In the next few days I named her, loved her, felt my own breath catch in my throat in fear every time she paused for hers. I could no longer imagine my life without her. But I still felt like the same old me, except more exhausted and terrified than usual. I learned to breastfeed and change diapers. I lived through colic and spontaneous vomiting (hers) and weeping and the complete disappearance of intellectual ability (mine). I felt tired and full of love and stretched past my limits, but untransformed. I felt like a sham, a fraud. I felt like a mother, but not the way the books and the rapturous women in the grocery store said mothers should feel. I drudged through my life moment by moment, and yet felt I was living in a dream. I was certain that there must be a larger pattern, a larger mythic weave, but I couldn't find it. I longed for Joseph Campbell to make a posthumous visit to my messy apartment, linking up the tiny motifs of my life into a grand narrative, a story that resonated through time and the known universe. I wanted someone to show me where I stood in my own story.

Three years later found me sitting on my old blue beat-up couch in my subsidized apartment on a Thursday afternoon without classes, flipping through a gender studies text and watching Julika hunt through her bin of toys looking for something new and fun to play with. What she found was a pink potty seat, an obnoxious, bright, bubblegum-coloured ring, festooned with Looney Tunes characters. It was a gift from an ex-girlfriend who in those far-off days was optimistic (or naive) enough about my long-term commitment capabilities to think we would be together in Julika's potty-training years. Julika was pretty much potty trained now, and she'd never really used the thing, but I'd hauled it around from apartment to apartment, packing and unpacking and promptly forgetting about it. She found it stuffed in the back of the crafts closet, hauled it out, rolled it around for a while and then inspiration struck—she stuck it on her head like a bright pink corona, Bugs Bunny and Daffy Duck gleefully cavorting around her head.

I couldn't help laughing, which of course delighted her and encouraged her to do the Potty Seat Crown Dance around the living room, bobbing her head as if she was in a Punch and Judy floor show. It was a mutually satisfying and delightful diversion from Judith Butler and her impenetrable texts of performative ontological gender problems, but then disaster struck: she tried to pull the potty seat off her head. It wouldn't budge. A look of panic crossed her small face. Her eyes welled with tears. Still laughing, I grabbed the edges of the potty seat and pulled. Nothing. I pulled again. No movement, not even a wiggle. I began to feel the flutterings of my own panic. I sat her down on the couch, gripped the horrid thing with both hands, and pulled straight up until she yelped and lifted a little off the cushion. Nada.

"Off, Mommy—I want it off!" she yelled, looking up at me, her mom, her saviour, with big teary eyes. I looked down at the top of her head, and Bugs Bunny now looked decidedly menacing. As her mother, I was clearly the one who had to fix this, to fix everything wrong with her life—and the nice thing about three-year-olds is that even a general screw-up like me can usually accomplish that, most life problems of toddlers being fairly rectifiable. But this was beyond me. I tried a few more times, pushing down on one side and pulling on the other, then reversing, and only succeeding in wedging it ever more firmly onto her head. She was wailing in earnest now, and I felt like joining her. I wildly considered margarine, Vaseline and soaking her head in cold water. But those things worked for stubborn rings on swollen fingers. I wasn't confident about their restorative powers on potty seats stuck on toddler heads. Aware of the tragicomic dimension of the whole situation, yet unable to figure anything out, I decided to call in the big guns— I phoned my mother.

At that time, my mother was recently divorced and newly discovering life's many and various delights. This is the sanest way I can phrase it. She'd stumbled upon the realization that every woman's life improves with the addition of a Latin lover (or two or three or thereabouts), and spent most nights hanging out at the local Latino bar with her girlfriends, happily salsa-ing the night away with any sundry married Salvadorean former death squad leader who happened her way. She scoured the back of bridal stores and thrift shops for anything short and sequined and on sale—the shorter and shinier the better. She didn't drink, but she could tango the night away on sheer exhilaration. She was simultaneously a very practical woman with a no-nonsense streak and a falling-down house. So she did what any self-respecting woman would do in the same situation: she had a Duo-Tang of men with their names, numbers and skills. Not those kinds of skills. I mean plumbing, drywall, carpentry, and accounting. It was this tome of wisdom that she pulled out when, in desperation, I dialled her number.

"Mom? Oh my God, I have a problem."

"What? What's that noise?"

"That's Juli. That's the problem. She has a potty seat stuck on her head and I can't get it off."

"She has a what?" (Pause for hysterical laughter.) "Can't you pull it off?"

"No, Mom, that's why I'm calling. I can't pull it off. I can't pry it off. It's, like, stuck. Forever."

I was aware of the note of hysteria in my voice but unable to help myself. How could I send her to daycare with a potty seat on her head? How would I explain that? How would I ever send her to school? How would she make friends? How would I ever face the other mothers at the playground? They already thought I was a nutcase. My child would be a freak. A pink potty-seat freak. All her life it would be, "Hey, potty head!"

"It won't come off? At all?"

"No, Mom. That's what I'm saying."

"Well. Oh my. Hang on." I could hear pages turning, and I knew she was looking in her Duo-Tang.

"Oh God, Mom, put the book away."

"What? Listen, Jorge works as a caretaker in the Sinclair building. I bet he has a hacksaw. I could call him."

"Christ, Mother. No hacksaws!"

"Or what about Francisco? He's a construction worker. I bet he
has something. Like a giant hammer. Maybe we could pry it off."

"Oh. My. God. No. No, no, no. None of your freak-o men and
their destruct-o tools! Just come over!"

"All right then. Relax, already. I'll be right over."

I hung up the phone. Julika was still sitting, haloed, in a corner
of the couch, crying. I wasn't sure whether to cry myself or laugh
hysterically. I had a complicated relationship with my mother. (I
know, they're all complicated, but really.) Of course I loved her
fiercely, and you couldn't help being slightly awed by the sheer force
of her personality. But given my stay-at-home-with-the-kid-and-
study life compared with her painting-the-town-with-a-large-
sequined-and-Spanish-brush life, I sometimes wondered which of
us was mothering whom. Her relationships were more screwed up
than mine, and that was saying something. She'd been June Cleaver-
about-to-crack in my childhood, but as a grandmother she was
flamboyant and unreliable and full of love and, well, operatic. A
Wagnerian Valkyrie in heels and lipstick. In fact, the whole situation
began to strike me as operatic. Julika was certainly providing a high-
octave soundtrack rivalling anything by Puccini. Everything had
that intensified and surreal quality of operatic stage scenes. I just
couldn't decide if it was high tragedy or low comedy—the potty
seat aspect lent itself to Chaucerian comedy, but the wailing and
despondency put me in mind of *La Bohème*.

Dimly, in the back of my preoccupied mind, I was starting to
sense a grand archetypal narrative emerging, and I was not
impressed. This was definitely not what I'd had in mind, and I had a
very bad, foreboding kind of feeling.

And then the door burst open, and with that simple act, my opera became burlesque. My mother stood triumphantly in my doorway (damn myself for giving her a front door key), resplendent in turquoise and fuchsia. Standing behind her, at least seven feet tall each, were three firefighters in full fire regalia. Julika stopped crying as her eyes widened to take up her whole face. "What the fuck?" I managed to gasp before I could help myself.

"Well, I was on my way over," my mother trumpeted, "and I found these nice young men downstairs at a fire in the basement. The fire was over, so I said"—here she swung her arm in a wide arc—"'Come on up, boys!'"

"They were at a fire? And you just...waylaid them?" I squeaked.

"Kitchen fire, ma'am," said the lead fireman. "It's out now. What seems to be the problem?"

I pointed at Julika. "It won't come off. It's totally, completely stuck."

My mother, preening on her imaginary white steed, waved him over. The other two hung out in the doorway, surveying the messy fire hazard that was my home. Fireman number one walked to Julika and surveyed her head. She stared in equal parts fear and wonderment at his huge fire-retardant coat, his yellow helmet, and giant boots. And in the most anticlimactic moment of all, he reached out to the potty seat, turned it about an inch to the left and popped it right off her head. No hacksaw. No fire axe. Just pop, and it was off. He handed it to me as I stared stupidly at him from the couch. Then he nodded to my mother (who magnanimously made way for him in the doorway) and left with his two cohorts. My mother grinned, trilled, "You're welcome!" waved and departed behind them. Juli and I were left on the blue couch, me holding the wretched potty seat in my hands, Julika still wide-eyed staring at the door. Unsure what else to do, I hugged Julika, put the offending pink ring on top of the fridge and called my current girlfriend at work, narrating the whole sorry debacle for her while she laughed hysterically.

I had not a shred of insight into the whole mess to offer, not that day, not that week, not later that month. Eventually it just became a funny story to tell people, a story about my crazy mother and my ridiculous life, one of many similar stories that I collected like beads and strung together however I could. And it eventually occurred to me that that's all the hero's quest really is—stories strung together by someone to provide a frame for the ridiculous, the impossible, the ordinary. This is not an epiphany or a moral. It's just an observation from someone with a crazy, ordinary life and a crazy, ordinary kid and a penchant for narrative.

I can clearly see now, of course, the high (and low) comedy of the whole situation. I can also see the undertone of despair and self-doubt that made it melodrama. I can see that in her own way, my mother really did save the day. I can also see that she played it out in her own narrative structure—Julika (and probably me) as a kitten in a tree, rescued by a real-life cliché, the big strong fireman. I can see that perhaps if she'd just come over and been the calm one, she might have figured out that the opening in the ring was oval and not round, and that twisting it just a little in a common-sense sort of way would pop it off. Or if I hadn't been my mother's daughter, I might have figured that out on my own. If that had been what really happened, I'd be missing one great story from my repertoire. It all depends on perspective.

But back to the hero's journey I longed for in the first paragraph: I can see now that my heroine's fabled bundle of possessions is the sturdy old green wagon I use to haul Juli and my books and the paraphernalia of my life around. I can see everyone—the other playground moms, the firemen, my own mom—as my companions and teachers. I can remember distinctly the valleys of darkness I wandered through, doubting my whole existence. Making it through every day was a mythic adventure, really. And every time I looked at Julika, I faced my own image in the cave. And her own fierce self looking back at me. Nothing's as simple as the narratives in books. Nothing's clear when you're stuck in the middle of something. Juli and I transformed each other, surely and inevitably, every day, every night, making games and mistakes and grand opera of every moment.

I'm no longer afraid of pink potty seats. (I'm still a little afraid of my mother, though she's since moved on from her Latin stage.) I no longer feel like a fraud or a sham. I just don't. I cut myself more slack, and give myself permission to be a heroine every time I make it through a day, transformed but still the same.

WIRED AT THE HEART
CHRISTY ANN CONLIN

May you take heart and deeply listen to all of the life lessons you will be given by your life's greatest teacher, Silas Conlin-Morse.

—Spider and Jeanne Robinson

When Silas was born I received this good wish from two science fiction writers, Spider and Jeanne Robinson. Spider and Jeanne are an anachronism. They've never left the sixties. They embody all that was good about the hippie era, a time that is endlessly fascinating to me. But those years are, indeed, lost in time—a period that was not mine, one that came before me. They are the last holdouts, continuing to believe in love and peace and harmony, in things like baby as grand teacher. In the blur and fatigue of those early days it was hard to imagine learning anything from Silas except how to survive on no sleep. This precept of *baby as teacher* seemed quaint. But it was prophetic: Silas, now eight months old, has indeed become my greatest teacher. And as I look back, it should be no surprise that Silas's biggest offering so far has been my new appreciation for my own previously unfathomable mother, for the very concept of motherhood.

I was forty when I gave birth to Silas. By that time, I had really come to terms with the fact that I wouldn't have a biological child of my own. I'd never met anyone with whom I had wanted to have a child and I didn't want to do it on my own. My conclusion came as something of a shock. Time had passed so quickly. I was suddenly in my mid-thirties with a full and interesting life, but a life without a family of my own. It was bewildering. I had always assumed I'd have children, but I was never in a hurry.

I spent my high school summers as a nanny to five children, and rather than turning me off having kids, it inspired me. It was a home full of wonder and happiness. The parents had a very close bond, and having children seemed to enhance and deepen their relationship. Their home was a warm and creative place that truly imprinted on me the value of family and the profound joy of raising children with someone you love.

But what was also imprinted on me was the massive commitment family and partnership took. Having a child was forever, and nothing is forever when you are a teenager. It didn't compute. I decided that would be for much later in my life. First, I'd go after my career dreams. Baby and family would come in their own time.

I was a teenager growing up in the country, and what I wanted more than anything was to see and know the big wide world. This desire took me out of rural Nova Scotia on a whirlwind of living that would last for years. I moved to Europe by myself when I was seventeen, then spent the next eighteen years as a tumbleweed. I was a bon vivant, always looking for adventure, moving on when I began to tire of present circumstances. I went through men like a box of chocolates.

And so the years passed. At thirty-four, I found myself in Northern Ireland, about to publish my first novel. One night over wine, a friend told me my fertility was starting to plummet. I was horrified. Educated as I was (or thought I was) about women's health, I hadn't known this. It sent me into several months of darkness. It was time to start thinking about having a baby. The problem was that there was still no one with whom I wanted to have a child. I had to let go of my dream.

Feeling old and tired from so many empty relationships, I decided I would settle into a life of happy spinsterdom and celibacy in the place where I was born. I planned to move back permanently, after all those years, to rural Nova Scotia to finish my second novel. I made a few phone calls and my retreat was set up. I arrived in my spinstermo-bile with a laptop, boxes of books, clothing, and china cups. Shortly after I arrived, one grey day in April, my mother asked me to sell daf-fodils for the Canadian Cancer Society. A man I'd known years earlier came to buy some for his two daughters from a previous relationship. James and I had picked strawberries together as kids. I remembered him as gentle and kind, and I was struck by this as he stood shyly buy-ing flowers from me, his daughters by his side.

The rest of our story is predictable: we fell in love and decided to have a child together. And then I was pregnant. At fourteen weeks, we found out the pregnancy wasn't viable. I was devastated. Looking back now, I see myself crumpled in a ball, bleeding and weeping on the bed, a cold December wind blowing in from the north, goosebumps on my legs, not caring enough to even pull the sheet up, to shut the window. I remember lying in James's arms, howling that I wanted my baby back inside me.

Six blurry weeks later, I was pregnant with our son, Silas. I showed the pregnancy test to James, who at first thought it was an ear thermometer I'd bought for his youngest daughter. It seemed unreal that after such a sad Christmas, this could be happening. I went through the first trimester holding my breath, worried that things would go wrong. It was one thing to have James and his daughters in my life. It was altogether different to have a child of my own. My longing for the journey of pregnancy and motherhood, a journey that I had almost missed, was deeper in me than even my longing to write.

I REMEMBER THE first time Silas discovered he could splash. He was sitting in his tub, beating his arms up and down like little wings, beads of water flying up in the air. His laughter was magical. He smiled with his whole face, as babies do. He had a look of genuine delight in his eyes, an enormous grin as he watched his hands hit the water. The pure bliss on his face moved me to tears. Becoming a stepparent is a unique experience in mothering, but it's very, very different. My stepdaughters already have a mother and a father. They are connected to me, but separate.

With Silas, there's no separation. He is truly the love of my life. We've been together since his very beginning. He has humbled me and filled me with delight. He's brought a much-needed simplicity to my life. I find myself able to forgive, to understand others in a way I never did before. From the moment he was conceived, Silas launched me on a journey toward my own heart and soul, a journey that for all the telling I could never know without experiencing motherhood myself.

There are many things I didn't know about pregnancy, childbirth, and motherhood. Like the gorgeous mane of hair you get when you're pregnant because your hormones stop the shedding process. Like how much hair you shed after the baby is born—so much that you're convinced you'll be bald before he turns one year old. I didn't know I wouldn't have a clue how to "push" the baby out. "Push where there's pressure," the doctors told me. Well, there was pressure *everywhere*. I didn't know I would sweat so profusely for the first few weeks after the baby was born, soaking the sheets night after night as my body rid itself of fluid.

No one told me how crazy you can become in the first few months, when your body chemistry is changing, when your entire life has been altered from the moment the baby was born and nothing will ever, ever be the same again. People don't talk about these things, perhaps because they don't want to scare you. Perhaps they don't tell you because these things fall away so quickly after the baby arrives that those who would tell no longer remember. And if they do tell you these details before you have had a child, they have no meaning and no context. These are truths you must seek and know alone, in the quiet late-night hours when you are rocking the baby, breathing in the tender newborn scent.

They don't tell you how you'll feel immediately after birth when the baby's dark eyes search for you, how those eyes lock on to yours with a gaze that says *I claim you. I belong to you and you to me.* No one tells you how you will feel when baby smiles for the first time, laughs for the first time. How you feel when baby reaches out a soft tiny hand and strokes your cheek, curls itty-bitty fingers around yours in an instinctive grip that is startling and moving. No one tells you these things because, until you experience them, you cannot understand the profound and intense shiver of exquisite joy your soul will feel. The intimacy is shocking, the rapture pure.

What they do tell you is that when you have kids you'll finally appreciate all your mother has done for you. It's a cliché I got quite tired of hearing in my pregnancy. I already appreciated my mother and the sacrifices she made. I couldn't see how this lesson would apply to me because I'd already learned it. And learning it didn't make things easier between us. We had a stormy relationship before Silas was born. I always felt my mother was telling me what to do. She didn't listen to me. She diminished and rarely acknowledged my individuality and my personal experiences.

When I was pregnant the first time, the ultrasound at fourteen weeks showed no heartbeat. I had to have a D and C right away. We had told very few people about the pregnancy, but because I would be in the hospital for the surgery, we decided to tell my mother, in confidence. When we returned from the hospital, my mother was waiting for us. I was high on Demerol and feeling very sad. After my mother left, there was a knock at the door. It was our landlady. She stared at me and said I looked terrible. I just nodded. She stood there awkwardly and then said, "Are you okay? Your mother told me to come over to say hi. I didn't know you were sick."

We realized she had no idea what had happened. We filled her in and she very kindly left us alone. I was upset that my mother had done this at a time when I so clearly needed and wanted to be alone. So, pregnant a second time, and so soon after the last experience, I cringed at the thought of being a new mother and having to constantly keep my own mother at bay. It seemed simpler to do things on my own.

I'D HAD A twenty-nine-hour labour. In my exhausted state, I didn't notice how neurotic I'd become. I'd been taken over by my instincts. I was like an animal, caring and tending to this tiny creature, wary and cautious as a cat, moving my newborn kitten if I felt the slightest threat. As soon as Silas was in my arms, I was overcome with love for him. And suddenly there seemed dangers everywhere.

We'd had a few complications after the birth, so I had to spend an exhausting extra week in the hospital. The obstetrics unit intersected with the medical unit, and the last few nights before we were discharged, I lay in bed listening to the endless screams of a woman with Alzheimer's. *Help me, help me, why won't you help me.* It went on for hours. It was a painful start to life as a new mother. I was desperate for home, the house we live in on the apple farm on the South Mountain with its breathtaking view of the Annapolis Valley. It was harvest time, and I wanted to sit by the fire looking out at the orchards with Silas in my arms. But I was stuck in the hospital with my hormones raging.

I was so tired that I felt ill. More than anything, I was acutely aware of the responsibility for this new and tiny life. I'd hold the baby close to me through the long night. While the demented woman screamed, I whispered to tiny Silas that his daddy and I would look after him, protect him and guide him—we would crawl to the end of the earth and back again for him. There was no sacrifice too big. We would keep him safe always.

They say being a bit neurotic goes with being an artist. A writer once said that the difference between a crazy person and writers is that writers are supposed to be in control of the voices in their heads. Well, now I had voices in my head calling, *Beware, beware the dangers that lurk.* I'd always possessed boundless energy. I was full of verve and vim, piss and vinegar. But now I was a mother suffering from sleep deprivation and homesickness. I was pumped up on hormones, elation, adrenalin, and neuroses—wired.

In those stressful hospital nights, as I brushed my lips over the baby's soft hair and skin, I felt so incapable, so unworthy of my son. James had to go back to work after just a few days, and I cried from the loneliness. He was on long shifts, and I was by myself in the hospital with our newborn. An actual human being was completely dependent on me for everything. In all my travels and adventures, I had never experienced anything like this. My life's achievements seemed instantly insignificant. All my travels were dull in comparison. My commitment to the baby was instantaneous and primal.

SILAS WAS ALMOST nine pounds at birth with perfect Apgar scores, but he was still a tiny human being with a soft skull and weak neck, an inability to do anything but cry, poop, pee, and suck. He was swaddled in vulnerability. Now that he was out of my womb, I was terrified I'd drop him. My fears: he would drown in the tub. He'd snap in two when I was changing him. He would suffocate in his cradle. I'd roll on him if he was in our bed. He'd die from SIDS. I wouldn't be able to produce enough milk and he'd starve. I'd produce too much milk and he'd drown. He'd freeze to death at night. I'd end up overdressing him and he'd go into a heat coma. I wouldn't buckle his car seat properly. His sisters would cuddle him and would accidentally poke their fingers through the soft spot on his head. I would sleep through his cries and leave his tiny needs unattended, thus ensuring him years of psychotherapy *if* he even managed to survive his childhood. It went on, ad infinitum.

So picture me in the shower. The kind of shower a new mother dreams of—luxurious and long, soothing and steamy, leisurely soaping up with healing lavender shower gel. Letting the hair conditioner soak in, slowly rinsing all the conditioner out. Picture me humming. See the baby monitor on the vanity, the baby monitor that was so kindly giving me this sumptuous shower. Silas, a newborn, dozes in his cradle. Our baby monitor is state of the art. With this great technology, every precious sigh, smack, and cry comes to me even through the sound of the cascading water. This technology allows me a bit of freedom and peace of mind in a time where I am consumed to the heart and core of my being with the needs of my newborn baby.

So I turn off the water and step from the shower, relaxed and clean. I stiffen. My heart pounds and my hands shake. What I heard in the shower was *not* the gentle breathing of my baby but the sound of a freaking chainsaw that the oh-so-sensitive freaking baby monitor had picked up and the freaking cascading water had muted.

See me run naked up the stairs to the nursery convinced that Silas is about to be massacred. As I run, I realize the chainsaw is obviously not upstairs, but then I worry he's suffocated while I was selfishly indulging in a long shower. Lurching into the room, I find the baby lying quietly in his crib, chewing his fingers. He is listening to the saw outside his window where our landlord is cutting down a birch tree. He coos. He likes the drone. My heart melts and aches at the same time. I collapse on the bed, tears in my eyes, laughing from relief, weeping from fear, consumed by a neurosis so extreme that I have no idea how I'm going to make it to my son's first birthday.

My mother calls and I mistakenly tell her about the baby monitor. She suggests I get rid of it. I'm horrified. It's essential, I tell her. It would be like getting rid of the bottle warmer. She points out I'm breastfeeding, not bottle-feeding.

"Well, that's not the point," I tell her.

"Back in my day," she says, "we didn't have such things. We heard you if you cried and we came. We would have been institutionalized if we listened to every single breath."

My eyes are crossing and I'm panting mad. I wipe the drool from my lips. My mother is clearly out of her mind. Can't she see that? All the gadgets we have make mothering easier than she can ever imagine. I plan to embrace them all. Never mind that I almost popped my breast off with the pump the first time I tried to use it. While I rant and rave, my mother quietly offers to come over and hold the baby in her arms while I shower. She would be happy to do it, she says, for as long as I need.

DURING THE FIRST three months with a first baby, you realize that you are hard-wired to this tiny creature. Biologically wired. Wired at the heart. You are physiologically attuned to each other. Your instincts are operating on high, instincts you never knew you had. Your hearing is ultra-sensitive. You swear you have a sixth sense—you can perceive the baby's slightest movement and sound when you are in another room. You can hear his heartbeat without touching him. You smell his gorgeous newborn baby scent from two metres away with your eyes shut. When you hold him in the dark it is as though you are still joined, just as you were in the womb. It's disconcerting at first, these elevated instincts, this desire to protect and provide. It's like being possessed.

So, enter my mother. After my shower fiasco, I'm finally so tired and anxious that I can't bear it, and I begin to ask my mother for help. It's then I realize how much space she has given me. When

James is working night shifts my mother comes and gives the girls supper, baths, and stories and tucks them into bed while I rock the fussy baby.

My mother doesn't come unannounced. She is sensitive to my anxious state in a way I never expected she could be. She always asks what I need. She brings surprise treats, things she knows I love. She brings presents for the girls, so they will feel special too. She does the laundry. She puts flowers on the kitchen table. She changes the sheets on our bed and opens the window so the crisp autumn wind will freshen the room. She brings me fresh lavender and parsley and ginger tea. She brings chicken pot pie and strawberry jam she has made from the berries she picked on that hot day last June when the smell of pink roses inhabited the air. She brings red apples and places them in a green glass bowl on the kitchen table.

When I cry that I'm not worthy of the baby, she strokes my forehead as she did when I was a child and tells me I'm a splendid mother. She tells me I'm doing so well, looking after a newborn and two small stepdaughters. That soon the baby will smile and laugh and I will know a magic I can't imagine. She tells me that some people say fairies sing when babies laugh. I smile up at her through my tears, and she kisses me on the top of my head, soothes me with tender songs, lullabies that I will sing to my son:

> Sleep my child and peace attend thee,
> All through the night
> Guardian angels God will send thee,
> All through the night
> Soft the drowsy hours are creeping
> Hill and vale in slumber sleeping,
> I my loving vigil keeping
> All through the night.

Whenever I call my mother she comes immediately. Her devotion to me, her only daughter, is profound and unending. I see her as I never have before, a woman who let many of her dreams go to raise me and my two brothers. I understand instantaneously and on a profound emotional level her compromises and sacrifices. I see the dreams she released to the wind as she turned and took our hands, moving forward with us. The wind was always at her back, but she never turned from us.

From my perch on the sofa I look down at my wee baby and know that he, Baby Silas as his sisters call him, has opened this new window for me. I peer through it to a time in my own childhood. In rural Nova Scotia, when I was a child, there were some hard times for my family. My parents were unemployed, and we lived in a tiny cottage on the Bay of Fundy. My parents did not know what the future held for them. Things were uncertain. We had no television and no running hot water. I remember the Bay of Fundy turning grey and green, the huge white sky overhead, foamy waves pounding the black rocky shore.

I see my parents bathing us in the sink with water heated on the wood stove. I see them bundling us in blankets warmed by the fire, listening over the wind off the bay for our cries from the bedroom should we wake and need comfort. I remember my father's keeping the fire going so we would be warm, my mother's making hot chocolate for us and telling us stories by the fire or walking us up the dirt road to get the school bus. I remember all these things as I nurse my baby on the sofa while my mother washes my dishes in the sink and my father puts wood on the fire. My meat-and-potatoes father who now brings me soya nuts and introduces himself to our doula as my mother's partner.

The screenplay writer Robert McKee says we experience joy only in the same amount we are willing (and able) to experience sorrow, that they are inextricably linked—it's the great irony of love.

Sometimes now when I am sitting in the garden with the baby and he is enraptured by a butterfly or the wind in the ferns, I think of a friend who gave a baby up for adoption when she was seventeen. She said shortly after the baby was gone she realized that creating another human being was the most profound thing she would ever do. There was nothing else that would equal it. She then dove into a five-year drunk, emerging finally to go on and become very successful. I think, however, that she still considers the birth of her daughter the most significant act of her life and what the birth taught her the most significant lesson. I never truly understood this until I had my son. His birth gave me a compassion for her experience that I'd never had before.

The baby is the great equalizer—he blesses us with forgiveness and understanding, patience and acceptance and boundless love. In the few short months of Silas's life, he has resolved years of issues faster and cheaper than any kind of therapy ever could have. I look back now, at the sad ending to the first pregnancy, and realize that my mother had felt helpless leaving us that night as I lay depressed and drugged on the couch. She had sent in my landlady, a long-time family friend, as a desperate and somewhat reckless gesture of compassion. The baby has also helped give my mother an understanding of me as an individual. She sees me on the mothering journey now and graciously lets me find my own way.

I now know why people say having a baby makes you appreciate your mother in a way that nothing else can, how truths lurking inside clichés leap into the light. Silas is a blessing that came to me when I least expected it. He has brought a richness to my life that I never knew before. The restlessness that always stirred within me has settled. And now I listen carefully to the lessons of my baby, for there is a deep wisdom at work here, one that is mysterious and wide and unending. And I take heart that he is here on this earth with me, with us.

EDITOR'S ACKNOWLEDGEMENTS

First, to all the wonderful women I enlisted for this book who were all so willing to share their secrets, skills, and time for a dime. Why they were so willing remains a mystery. Let me just say I am forever grateful, and besotted with all of you.

To my soul sister, Carol Shaben, with whom the seeds of a book on motherhood began. Thank you for all that conversation and all that love. You are an inspiration.

To my agent, Hilary McMahon, for her faith in my idea and for her ability, at eight months' pregnant, to get me a deal in two short weeks.

To Linda Pruessen at Key Porter for finding my old proposal and bringing it back to life. And for her skill in managing my neurotic tendencies.

To my own mother, of course, and to her mother, my late grandmother, my earliest and strongest role models in unconditional love and devotion.

To my sister, the second mother to my children, for always being there, even from afar. I couldn't have done "this whole motherhood thing" without you.

To my beautiful husband, who has taught me so much and loved me even in my ugliest moments (birth would be one of those).

To my beautiful children, who put up with one distracted mama for two solid years. Sorry for neglecting and ignoring you while I "just had to get something out of my head." Thank you for the transformation, and for all the lessons, big and small.

ABOUT THE AUTHORS

THE EDITOR

CORI HOWARD is an award-winning journalist who has worked in newspapers, magazines, television, and radio. Her work has taken her around the world—to Costa Rica, Mexico, Brazil, Burma. She has written for *The San Francisco Chronicle*, *The Globe and Mail*, *The Independent*, *Condé Nast Traveller*, *Maclean's*, *Chatelaine*, and *Canadian Geographic*. She spent three years as a reporter for the *National Post*. Then she had her first baby and started to write mostly about motherhood. She continues to write, about motherhood and other things, for magazines and newspapers in Canada and abroad. She lives in Vancouver with her husband, Htu Htu, and their children, Ty and Jaza.

THE CONTRIBUTORS

LISA BENDALL is a freelance writer whose work has appeared in *Reader's Digest*, *Canadian Living*, *Homemakers*, and *The Globe and Mail*, among others. For over a decade, she was managing editor of *Abilities*, Canada's lifestyle magazine for people with disabilities. She left *Abilities* in 2005 so she could spend more time at home, where she juggles full-time writing with scouring the bathtub. Her first book, *After Disability: A Guide to Getting on with Life*, was published in 2006 by Key Porter Books. Lisa is also an award-winning fiction writer. She took top prize in *Seventeen* magazine's fiction contest and was a finalist in the Writers' Union of Canada Short Prose Competition. She lives in Toronto with her husband, Ian Parker, and their daughter, Emily.

RANDI CHAPNIK MYERS shares with her husband, Rob, three insanely beautiful children: Seth, born in 1996, Rachel, born in 1998, and Aaron, born in 2002. A journal keeper since she learned to print, she followed her mother into law, detoured into a stint as full-time mom, and finally ended up a freelance writer, often writing about what she lives most fiercely: motherhood. Her work has appeared in *Today's Parent*, *The Globe and Mail*, *Saturday Night*, *MoneySense*, *Chatelaine*, and *Toronto Life*.

CHRISTY ANN CONLIN's bestselling and critically acclaimed first novel, *Heave*, was nominated for the Books in Canada / Amazon First Novel Award and was a Globe and Mail Best Book of 2002. Her short fiction has appeared in numerous journals and anthologies including *Best Canadian Stories 04*. She has an MFA in creative writing from the University of British Columbia and apprenticed as a storyteller in Northern Ireland. Her second novel, *Listening for the Island*, will be published by Doubleday. She lives in Nova Scotia with her family.

LEANNE DELAP is a Canadian journalist who fell into the fashion beat. She figures people looked at her and went, "You're tall and skinny, so you must understand that stuff!" At her first job at *Toronto Life* (where she was hired to work in the food section because the late food editor Joseph Hoare liked that she smelled heavily of garlic), she wrote about fiftysomething white men for a couple of years. Then she started as a fashion reporter at *The Globe and Mail*. After her two children (Max and Simone) were born, she became the editor of *Toronto Life Fashion* magazine. She now lives in a wacky industrial loft in Toronto, pulling her life together after a tornado of a divorce. She is working at *The Globe* again, writing columns, editing, and covering fashion.

MONIKA DEOL is a broadcaster who spent nine years in Toronto hosting and producing for Citytv and MuchMusic, including the show *Electric Circus*. In 1996, she moved to Vancouver, where she now lives with her husband and four children between the ages two and ten. She is an avid community volunteer. She's gone back to work twice since having children, as a newscaster for Citytv and BC-CTV. Both times she ultimately decided to return to her role as stay-at-home mom.

DEBLEKHA GUIN lives with her daughter, Ella Anjali (born August 5, 2004), on an eclectic but sparsely populated southern British Columbia gulf island, Galiano. She currently spends a lot of time leaning on her supportive circle of friends and adjusting to the new reality of being a single working mom. When she's not with Ella, she's usually managing projects for the Access to Media Education Society (AMES), a non-profit she founded ten years ago to help "marginalized" communities use video-based storytelling as a tool for education, advocacy, and outreach.

MARINA JIMÉNEZ has been a journalist for sixteen years. She has a master's degree from the University of London and has worked for CBC Television, *The Vancouver Sun*, *The Edmonton Journal*, the *National Post*, and *The Globe and Mail*. She has reported from around the world, covering everything from the war in Iraq to recent elections in Haiti and Mexico. She has won numerous awards, including a 2003 National Newspaper Award for her coverage of the immigration and refugee beat for *The Globe and Mail* and two 2001 National Magazine Gold Awards for a story in *Saturday Night* magazine on the Chinese boat people who washed up on the shores of British Columbia in 1999. Before becoming a journalist, Marina taught English in Tokyo and did a short stint as a hostess at Ginza's Club Olive, where she sang karaoke songs and served whisky to "salarymen." She lives in Toronto with her husband, the journalist John Geiger, and their son, Alvaro.

ALISON KELLY has spent the past twenty years making her living as a writer, actor, and acting teacher. She has co-written four plays: *The Stay Fresh Special, Wince, Mom's the Word*, and *Mom's the Word 2: Unhinged*. She is currently working on two books for young audiences. As an actor, Alison has performed as far afield as Australia. She is a graduate of Vancouver's acclaimed Studio 58, where she is currently an instructor. Alison lives with her two teenage children and her husband in North Vancouver.

ESTÉE KLAR-WOLFOND is the mother of a young autistic son named Adam. She is a freelance writer and art curator. In 2005, she curated *Beyond Words: The Drawings of Jonathan Lerman* to raise awareness about autism. Due to its overwhelming success, Estée decided to start the Autism Acceptance Project to empower parents and autistic people. Estée is writing a book about her family journey with autism. She also has a weblog titled "The Joy of Autism."

CHANTAL KREVIAZUK was born in Winnipeg and moved to Toronto at age twenty, when she released her first album. She now commutes between Toronto and Los Angeles with her husband and fellow musician, Raine Maida, and their two sons, Rowan and Lucca. When she's in Toronto, she spends a lot of time shuttling between her home studio and her house, juggling the demands of parenthood with a rich career as a singer and songwriter. Her latest album is *Ghost Stories*. Among the many songs she has written are "All I Can Do" inspired by her role as mother and about her children and "Asylum," about her nanny, a war refugee from the Democratic Republic of Congo. When she's not working on her own music, she writes songs for other artists, including Avril Lavigne and Gwen Stefani. She also works for Warchild Canada and the Canadian Mental Health Association.

JOY KOGAWA is the author of the novel *Obasan*, published in 1981. She is a Member of the Order of Canada and the Order of British

Columbia. An opera for children has been made based on her children's book, *Naomi's Road*. She has won dozens of literary and community awards, and in 2006, her family home in Vancouver was saved from demolition at the eleventh hour and will be established as a writers' retreat. Joy currently splits her time between Toronto and Vancouver. This is the first time she has written with her daughter.

DEIDRE KOGAWA-CANUTE graduated from the University of Toronto in 1981 with a bachelor of arts. She worked in the marketing and public relations fields until she had her first child, after which she stayed home full-time. As a stay-at-home mom, she taught piano from her home studio in Hawaii. She and her two children, Matthew and Anne, moved to Canada in 2005. Her husband currently resides in Honolulu while working in the golf industry and comes home as often as he is able to. After twenty-three years away, Deidre is glad to return to her Canadian roots, but the islands still beckon. They return to Hawaii whenever the children's school schedule allows. She currently lives in Surrey, B.C.

JEN LAWRENCE is an MBA and former banker who left the world of corporate finance and power suits for the world of sippy cups and Goldfish crackers. She is the creator of "T.O. Mama," a popular online urban survival guide and chat group for Toronto parents. Her thoughts about mothering, feminism, infertility, depression, urban living, retail therapy, and celebrity gossip can be found on her blog, MUBAR (Mothered Up Beyond All Recognition). Her writing has appeared on "Literary Mama" and "The Philosophical Mother." She lives in Toronto with her husband, daughter, son, and a very overweight beagle. She is working on her first novel (isn't everyone?).

MARY LYNK was born in Halifax to a Scottish father and a Lebanese mother. At nineteen, she moved to Paris, cleaned the house of a corporate executive, and went to the Sorbonne. At twenty-one, after finishing a political science degree at Dalhousie

University, she ended up in India, where she worked in an orphan-age. Her journalism career started at *The Sunday Express* in Newfoundland. She spent five years as a producer at CBC Radio's *Morningside* with Peter Gzowski in Toronto, then went to work as a producer for Pamela Wallin's TV talk show. She now lives back on the East Coast, where she is an award-winning documentary and TV producer, although her life is much humbler than it once was. Ensconced in a house by the sea, she is madly in love with the artist Alexander Graham and is mother to her dream come true, Laila.

RACHEL MATÉ lives and works in Vancouver with her extremely patient husband, Sam, and her two beautiful daughters, Maayan and Edden. She was born and raised in Vancouver, leaving briefly to attend Reed College in Portland, Oregon. She came home to go to law school at the University of British Columbia, clerked at the British Columbia Court of Appeal, and is currently a staff lawyer for the British Columbia Teachers' Federation. Rachel has spent most of her legal career pregnant or on maternity leave. When asked at her last job interview whether she had any experience in conflict resolution, she wondered whether sandbox disputes counted. This is her first attempt at a non-legal piece of writing, and she had to resist the urge not to include citations.

CHANDRA MAYOR is the author of a novel, *Cherry* (conundrum press 2004), which won the Carol Shields award, and *August Witch: Poems* (Cyclops Press 2002), which won the Eileen McTavish Sykes Award. She is also the recipient of the John Hirsch award for most promising writer. She is the poetry co-editor for *Prairie Fire Magazine* and was the 2006–07 writer-in-residence at the Winnipeg Public Library. Chandra lives with her daughter, Julika Emilynn (born in 1994), in Winnipeg.

AMI MCKAY started her writing career as a freelance writer for CBC Radio. Her radio documentaries have aired on public radio programs throughout Canada, the United States, and around the world. Her first novel, *The Birth House*, was published in 2006 by Knopf Canada. She writes, cooks, cleans, cuddles, and lives with her husband and two sons in an old farmhouse on the Bay of Fundy in Nova Scotia—all without the aid of a watch.

CARRIE-ANNE MOSS is a Canadian actress who achieved worldwide fame following her appearances in *The Matrix* film trilogy. She was born and grew up in Vancouver and started her career as a model. She has appeared in many popular films including *Chocolat*, *Memento*, and *Suspect Zero*. If wearing sunglasses, she is sometimes confused with Trinity, the latex-clad hacker she portrays in the *Matrix* films. But generally, when not filming, she keeps a low profile and stays close to home with her husband, fellow actor Steven Roy, and their two sons. She is an avid practitioner of yoga and attachment parenting, and unlike every other celebrity, she hires nannies only when she's working, and sometimes not even then. She lives in Los Angeles.

SUSAN OLDING was born in Toronto. She studied philosophy, law, and education and taught secondary school for several years before she finally worked up the courage to do what she wanted—write. Her prose and poetry have since appeared in literary journals throughout Canada and the United States and have won numerous prizes and awards. She is a stepparent to three, now adult, children and mother to a daughter adopted from China. She lives with her family in Kingston, Ontario.

SHEREE-LEE OLSON is the editor of *The Globe and Mail*'s weekly Style section. She has published fiction and poetry in numerous Canadian literary magazines and is working on her first novel, set on the Great Lakes. She lives in Toronto with her husband, two sons, and two metrosexual cats.

KATRINA ONSTAD's first novel, *How Happy to Be*, was released in 2006. She writes for CBC Arts Online and is an internationally published arts journalist with three National Magazine Award nominations. She lives in Toronto with her partner, Julian, and their two children, Judah and Mia.

ELIZABETH RENZETTI has been a magazine editor and, at *The Globe and Mail*, a reporter, columnist, and editor of the arts section. She currently works for *The Globe and Mail* in London, England, where she lives with her husband, Doug Saunders, their children, Griff and Maud, and a cat named Perdu who keeps getting lost. During the birth of their first child in Los Angeles in 2001, Elizabeth's husband read her stories of shark attacks to keep her spirits buoyed. Four years later, their second child was nearly born in the front seat of an Escort on the streets of London.

HARMONY RICE is a Pottawattomi/Ukrainian/Cayuga/Seneca girl from Wasauksing First Nation, an island in Georgian Bay, Ontario. A real island girl, Harmony makes art and writes words with her daughter, Nadia Bay, at home, while publishing *Spirit Magazine* in an effort to add some balance to the Canadian magazine industry. Published from Wasauksing, *Spirit Magazine* is an identity-based art magazine focusing on indigenous resistance to globalization. Harmony aspires to perfect her Japanese rope bondage skills and her knack for South African beekeeping and then publish her first novel, titled *God's Cool Timing*.

RACHEL ROSE is a poet and writer. She lives in Vancouver with her two children, Benjamin (born in 1999) and Gabriele (born in 2003), her partner, Isabelle, and a dog and a bird, in a little blue house with a picket fence. She has worked recently as a biographer in a Jewish home for the aged, gathering life stories for residents, caregivers, and family members. She lectures on writing and healing at Simon Fraser University, University of British Columbia, and various writers' festivals throughout the United States. Rachel's first book, *Giving My Body to Science* (McGill/Queen's University Press) was a finalist for the Gerald Lampert Award, the Pat Lowther Award, and the Grand Prix du Livre de Montreal, and won the Quebec Writers' Federation A. M. Klein Award. Her second book, *Notes on Arrival and Departure*, was published by McClelland & Stewart in spring 2005.

DENISE RYAN is an award-winning fiction writer, journalist, and editor. Now based in Vancouver, she was born in San Francisco to a U.S. Marine Corps officer and an emergency room nurse. A graduate of the University of British Columbia, she co-founded the award-winning weekend newspaper section *Mix* and has served as books editor, features editor, and reporter at *The Vancouver Sun*. Her fiction has been shortlisted for the Journey Prize and was included in the 2006 *Toronto Life* summer fiction issue. She is currently working on her first novel for Thomas Allen Publishers. She has a six-year-old son whose relentless questions about God, cold fusion, and the theory of relativity bring on regular anxiety attacks and occasional bouts of lucidity.

CRISANTA SAMPANG worked as a maid in Singapore from 1984 to 1988. She started her writing career there penning short pieces about her experiences as a maid for the *Straits Times*. In 1988, she moved to Vancouver, where she worked as a domestic and later as a counselor, helping other nannies sort through their immigration and employment problems. After taking some evening courses, Crisanta started working in TV and film, winning an award for a documentary on extreme mountain biking. She published her first book, *Maid in Singapore*, in 2005. She now works as Canadian news correspondent for *The Manila Times* and is developing a feature film. She lives in Vancouver with her partner, Daniel Wood. Her dream of bringing her children to Canada remains on hold.

CAROL SHABEN lives in Vancouver with her husband, Riyad, her son, Max, and a tankful of low-maintenance fish. She has been a journalist, writer, and communications specialist for nineteen years, including stints as a writer/broadcaster with CBC Radio and as a reporter in Jerusalem. In 1993, she started her own international trade and intercultural communications business with which she has worked locally, nationally, and internationally. In 2005, the same year Max started Grade 1, she started an MFA in creative writing at the University of British Columbia. She now prefers sweatpants to suits and her basement office to any uptown address. She is currently working on her first book.

JOANNA STREETLY was born in Trinidad in 1968. After attending boarding school in England as a teenager, she studied outdoor education at Capilano College in Vancouver. She moved to Tofino in 1989 and has lived and worked on the water ever since: in kayaks, canoes, rowboats, motorboats, and floathouses. Her books, *Silent Inlet* (fiction, Oolichan Books, 2005) and *Paddling through Time* (nonfiction, Raincoast, 2000) were written entirely at her floathouse in Clayoquot Sound. She lives part-time on her floathouse and parttime in Tofino with her partner, Marcel Thériault, an Acadian, French-speaking scuba diver and captain from New Brunswick, and their daughter, Toby, who was born on August 18, 2004.

DOROTHY WOODEND is a freelance writer and film critic. Her work has been featured in *The Globe and Mail*, *The Tyee*, *Cinema Scope*, *Chatelaine*, *Elle Canada*, *Rabble*, *The Vancouver Sun*, the *National Post*, *Saturday Night* and *Vancouver Review*. Internationally, she has written for *Eat Magazine* (Japan), *Slow Food* (Italy), *Firecracker* (U.K.), and *Alternet* (U.S.). She lives in Vancouver with her son and her husband.

JAMIE ZEPPA set off for Bhutan in 1989 to teach English. She had a two-year contract, ninety kilograms of luggage, and no idea what she was doing. Luckily, she was rescued by her eight-year-old students, who taught her how to climb a mudslide in flip-flops, sharpen pencils with a razor blade, and remove leeches with salt. She fell in love, first with Bhutan and its people and then with a young Bhutanese man. Their son, Pema Dorji, was born in 1992, and they lived in Bhutan's capital until Jamie and her husband split up in 1997. Jamie and Pema now live in Canada but visit Bhutan as often as they can. In the summer of 2006, Jamie re-experienced separation anxiety when thirteen-year-old Pema flew off to Bangkok by himself to go travelling with his father. Jamie is the author of the memoir, *Beyond the Sky and the Earth: A Journey into Bhutan*. She teaches English at Seneca College in Toronto.

FOR MORE PERSONAL STORIES ABOUT MOTHERHOOD

MotherTongue is a new magazine devoted to the personal stories of mothers around the world. A monthly magazine for the smart, savvy, thinking mother, it offers an antidote to the commercial, advice-driven magazines currently on the market. *MotherTongue* will focus instead on exploring the personal, deeply personal, stories of mothers from North America, Europe, Asia, South America, and beyond. It is a place for mothers everywhere to come for conversation, to talk about issues of real relevance to their day-to-day lives, and to compare the differences and similarities of the motherhood experience across geographical, cultural, and socio-economic lines.

Provocative, funny, and honest, the magazine will feature letters, essays, fiction, and poetry about the issues faced by mothers today, whether it's negotiating bedtime rituals with your husband, managing the transition to single mother, or adjusting to a new identity or ambition.

If you're interested in receiving a free online subscription, please email the editor at corih@telus.net. We look forward to hearing from you.